PERSONS AND LIFE AFTER DEATH

LIBRARY OF PHILOSOPHY AND RELIGION

General Editor: John Hick, H. G. Wood Professor of Theology
University of Birmingham

This new series of books will explore contemporary religious understandings of man and the universe. The books will be contributions to various aspects of the continuing dialogues between religion and philosophy, between scepticism and faith, and between the different religions and ideologies. The authors will represent a correspondingly wide range of viewpoints. Some of the books in the series will be written for the general educated public and others for a more specialised philosophical or theological readership.

Already published

William H. Austin	THE RELEVANCE OF NATURAL SCIENCE TO THEOLOGY
Paul Badham	CHRISTIAN BELIEFS ABOUT LIFE AFTER DEATH
Ramchandra Gandhi	THE AVAILABILITY OF RELIGIOUS IDEAS
Hugo A. Meynell	AN INTRODUCTION TO THE PHILOSOPHY OF BERNARD LONERGAN
Dennis Nineham	THE USE AND ABUSE OF THE BIBLE
Bernard M. G. Reardon	HEGEL'S PHILOSOPHY OF RELIGION
John J. Shepherd	EXPERIENCE, INFERENCE AND GOD
Robert Young	FREEDOM, RESPONSIBILITY AND GOD
Patrick Sherry	RELIGION, TRUTH AND LANGUAGE-GAMES
J. C. A. Gaskin	HUME'S PHILOSOPHY OF RELIGION

Further titles in preparation

PERSONS AND LIFE
AFTER DEATH

Hywel D. Lewis

Essays by Hywel D. Lewis
and some of his critics

First published 1978 by
THE MACMILLAN PRESS LTD
London and Basingstoke
Associated companies in Delhi
Dublin Hong Kong Johannesburg Lagos
Melbourne New York Singapore Tokyo

Printed in Hong Kong by
SHANGHAI PRINTING PRESS LIMITED

British Library Cataloguing in Publication Data

Lewis, Hywel David
  Persons and life after death — (Library of
  philosophy and religion.)
  1. Future life – Addresses, essays, lectures
  I. Title   II. Series
  129'.08   BL535

ISBN 0 333 23496 0

Contents

Preface   vii

1 Realism and Metaphysics   1

2 Ultimates and a Way of Looking   17

3 Religion and the Paranormal   35

4 Life After Death. A Discussion   49
   Anthony Quinton, Hywel D. Lewis, Bernard Williams

5 Survival   75
   I *Hywel D. Lewis*
   II *Antony Flew*

6 Immortality and Dualism   110
   I *Sydney Shoemaker*
   II *Hywel D. Lewis*

7 The Belief in Life After Death   148

8 The Person of Christ   161

   Index of Names   189

   Index of Subjects   191

Preface

This book contains papers which I gave on various occasions on themes related to my earlier book, also in a Macmillan series, *The Self and Immortality*. It can be regarded as a sequel to that book and *The Elusive Mind*. Some of the papers were prepared for talks and symposia in which I was asked to participate, and it would have been pointless to include them without the contributions of the other speakers. I therefore sought and obtained the consent of the authors concerned, and the appropriate editors and publishers, to include their papers along with my own. I am grateful for this kindness. The presentation of some sharply contrasted views will, I hope, be appreciated by those who read this book.

The first paper was prepared for the meeting of the International Society for Metaphysics at Varna, Bulgaria, in 1973 and subsequently published in *Idealistic Studies*, Vol. 4, No. 3, in September 1974. The theme of this is extended in my contribution to the Oxford International Symposium organised by the late Professor Gilbert Ryle with the assistance of Dr P. W. Kent and published in the volume of the proceedings edited by Professor Ryle under the title *Contemporary Aspects of Philosophy*, Oriel Press. There follows my own contribution to the volume *Philosophy and Psychical Research*, edited by Professor Shivesh C. Thakur and published by Allen and Unwin in 1976. We then have the discussion between Professor Bernard Williams and myself, with Mr Anthony Quinton in the Chair, on B.B.C. Radio 3 soon after the publication of *The Self and Immortality*. Part of this was published in *The Listener* on 9 August 1975. We have then two symposia, one on the subject of 'Survival', con-

ducted by Professor Antony Flew and myself at the Joint
Session of the Mind Association and the Aristotelian Society at
Canterbury in 1975 and published in the *Proceedings of the
Aristotelian Society, Supplementary Volume XLIX*, the other a dis-
cussion of 'Immortality and Dualism' between Professor Sydney
Shoemaker and myself at the Conference on Reason and
Religion arranged at Lancaster by the Royal Institute of
Philosophy and included in the volume of conference papers
edited by Mr Stuart Brown and published, under the title
Reason and Religion, by the Cornell University Press in 1977.
This leads to my Drew Memorial Lecture on Immortality, 'the
Belief in Life after Death', delivered in London in 1973 and
published in the volume of essays in honour of Professor Peter
Bertocci edited by Professors John Howie and Thomas O.
Buford with the title *Contemporary Studies in Philosophical Idealism*,
Claud Stark and Co. 1975. I am deeply grateful to all con-
cerned for their help and the permission to include these papers
in the present volume.

The concluding essay is an amplification of an address given
in Welsh at the General Assembly Meeting of the Presbyterian
Church of Wales in 1972 and originally printed in Welsh in
Y Traethodydd, September 1976. It was intended for a more
general audience than the other papers and the mode of presentation is inevitably a little different. But I was anxious to
include the address in this volume for various reasons. At the
close of the Drew Lecture I indicate that the main positive
reasons for our expectation of a future life must be religious
ones, and the distinctively Christian hope of life after death is
bound up essentially with the central theme of the Christian
faith about the role of Jesus as the medium of the ultimate
sanctified relationship we may all expect to have with God. If
there is substance in this claim, which seems to me central to the
New Testament and the main course of Christian experience,
it would be odd, to say the least, to suppose that the fellowship
established by this peculiar outpouring of a 'love so amazing, so
divine' could be thought to be anything other than abiding. The
view has been advanced by some leading theologians and
Churchmen today that eternal life consists wholly of some
quality of our present existence or of some place we may have
in God's memory of us. The attractiveness of the latter view, to

balanced and reflective leaders of religion, seems to me to be one of the most extraordinary indications of the poverty of religious sensitivity and understanding today. An Unmoved Mover may find satisfaction in contemplation of his own perfection. Will this, or the enrichment of his own memories, meet the case of the God whom we meet in Jesus 'in the form of a servant' 'obedient unto death'? We may not all understand 'the price that was paid' in the same way, but it is hard to think of it, in any proper Christian context, as anything other than a price that was paid *'for me'*, and we need not sentimentalise that to make it significant.

The reluctance of many of our contemporaries to recognise this comes about, I suspect, from an excessive eagerness to concede the claims of fashionable views today about the essentially corporeal nature of persons. Yet, oddly, the theologians who take this course continue, so it seems at least, to think of God as an essentially spiritual being.

A further consideration that weighed with me was the necessity for those who do have some form of religious commitment not to keep it in some isolated compartment of their thought. Precious it may be, but, if it is worth adhering to, it must be capable of appropriate presentation in the context of our other thoughts; and as the traditional Christian claims about 'the Person of Jesus' present accentuated difficulty for those, like myself, who stress the finality of the distinctiveness of persons, it seemed proper to present, at least in outline, the way I myself approach these questions and view the distinctively Christian claims which seem indispensable for any peculiarly Christian hope of eternal life.

The proofs of this book were read for me by my friend Dr Julius Lipner of the University of Cambridge, and the index was made by my gifted former student at King's College, London, Mr Timothy Bond. I am deeply grateful to them both.

June 1977   HYWEL D. LEWIS

1 Realism and Metaphysics

Not so long ago I attended a conference of philosophers and politicians. I was introduced to one rather opinionated politician as one of the philosophers. He promptly asked me, 'What sort of philosopher?' I turned the edge of this by replying rather tartly in turn, 'Quite a good one, it is generally thought'. This may seem a little naughty, but there are some uses for prevarication, and few of us care to attach a too explicit label to ourselves. When we do so we often find ourselves keeping the wrong company. There are still some isms around, but we have weeded out most of them from our syllabuses. There is more important and rewarding work to do than fighting pitched philosophical battles between closely regimented troops.

It is for this reason that I am not too happy about the title of this paper. There is as much to be said for describing me as an idealist as there is for placing me among the friends of realism. I did indeed agree to be one of the editorial advisers for an excellent new journal called *Idealistic Studies*, and I did not need a great deal of persuasion. It is most regrettable, in my opinion, that the great idealist movement of the late nineteenth century suffered so complete an eclipse in the middle of this century. It had insights we can ill afford to neglect, and many of them have slowly forced their way back in much less satisfactory forms in a peculiarly embarrassing meeting of extremes. The considerable renewal of interest in Hegel, after a period of almost contemptuous disregard, is a sign of a welcome new appreciation of idealist philosophy, and Bradley was never battered out of his place by hasty iconoclasm. It was never a disgrace to admit to learning something from him. His logic, as well as his more

© *Idealistic Studies* 1974

overtly metaphysical works, contains a fund of wisdom we peculiarly need in our present dilemmas and it is presented in delightful style. I never tire of urging my students to read the chapters on the Association of Ideas in Bradley's *Logic* (Book II, Part II, Chapter 1).

My own closest point of affinity with idealism lies in my strong partiality for a Berkeleian approach to the problems of perception. This could also perhaps be described in some quarters as phenomenalism, and I have always been impressed by the sturdy persistence of A. J. Ayer in defending phenomenalism against arguments taken rather uncritically to be quite conclusive. Where I would join issue with him myself is at the point where phenomenalism tends to merge into neutral monism. I hold very firmly that experienc*ing* is quite distinct from the experienc*ed* and that the self or subject is in no way part of the world around us. This also brings me close to much that idealists have maintained.

On the other hand, idealism has often found it hard to do justice to the presented or 'given' element in experience, and some, notably T. H. Green ('the father of English idealism'), tended to reduce all experience to a 'system of unalterable relations'. Common sense seems quite opposed to that. Likewise, I stand in sharp opposition to absolute idealism on the question of the distinctiveness of persons. The view that individual persons are just centres of unification in one 'whole of being', and that the distinctiveness vanishes the more we fulfil ourselves and become identified with 'the whole', has seemed to me altogether unacceptable. Related to this are familiar difficulties of absolute idealism in respect to freedom and evil in all its forms. It was thoughts of this kind that drove some notable thinkers, such as C. A. Campbell and A. C. Ewing, nurtured as they were in a strong idealist tradition, to break the bonds of the more rationalist form of absolute idealism in favour of some kind of suprarationalist metaphysics which owed much to Bradley. This can be seen magnificently in a remarkable, but much neglected, book by C. A. Campbell, called *Scepticism and Construction*.[1] This book is a mine of wisdom and splendid writing, and it would be very great satisfaction to me to be able to revive interest in it. In his posthumous book, just published,[2] A. C. Ewing breaks fairly sharply with traditional idealism on the questions of personal identity and freedom and, to some extent, on the question of suffering. The break is much sharper than in Ewing's earlier writings,[3] and it seems to me an essential corrective to post-Hegelian idealism.

For these reasons I would be loath to describe myself as an idealist. In many respects I find myself more at home with the philosophy of common sense and I have learned as much from G. E. Moore as from my other mentors. The positivist reaction against the facile construction of obscure metaphysical entities will no doubt have the warm support of many who do not hold with outright positivism. If 'Clarity is not Enough', we can certainly not get too much of it, and there are few things more uncongenial to the philosophical temper of mind than the exploitation of obscure verbiage, a besetting sin of many lesser lights of today as in the nineteenth century or the Athens of Socrates. It is in this vein that I find myself taking comfort in what is sometimes known as a realist approach to philosophy.

I must now, however, make it clear that there are some forms of realism which I do not set out to defend. The term often stands for the view that is sharply contrasted with nominalism as a theory of universals. Perhaps no one can altogether skirt round the problem of universals or avoid confrontation with it, intractable though it seems to be. But I certainly hold no brief for the view that universals subsist in some 'realm' of their own like Platonic forms or admit of being reified in some fashion. We certainly do not 'manufacture' universal properties or mathematical and logical truths, even when we speak of alternative logics. We discover what is somehow there and are under the strict discipline of it. The fashionable relativities of today and the evasive devices which support them make no appeal to me. But it goes quite against the grain of my philosophical mentality to hypostatise values and universals, and few things have led men into a more dangerous morass than the tendency to do so.

It will be evident also that I am little attracted to a view of the physical world which makes it altogether independent of being perceived. However disposed we may be to suppose that the world of nature is somehow over against us and existed long before we came on the scene, I find the idea of some totally independent physical reality almost quite incomprehensible. Perspectival distortion is always with us, and what a physical entity could be that is not eventually comprehended in terms of what is actually presented to us I find impossible to conceive. Nor do I see what explanatory function it could serve. It is perhaps worth recalling that G. E. Moore, after insisting most emphatically, in an almost Johnsonian vein, that the railway carriage runs on wheels which have a completely independent existence of their own, asserted equally firmly a few passages later that, for all we know, these wheels could be just points. This takes us far indeed from the common sense insistence on the reality of the material world.

Perhaps the best approach to our subject, for the purpose of these meetings, is to refer to the course of the realist and common sense strain in recent British philosophy. This is associated largely for scholars abroad with the name of G. E. Moore, but it owes quite as much, for its original impetus and the course it has taken, to the influence of a less eminent figure whose influence has nonetheless been very pervasive, namely, Cook Wilson. I do not know how well scholars abroad know the work of Cook Wilson and his place in British philosophy. He taught at Oxford from 1874 to 1915 but published little during his lifetime. He was, in many respects, the most influential thinker at Oxford in his day, and the work of some of his disciples, notably H. A. Prichard and W. D. Ross, will certainly be widely known. It is perhaps less well-known how much they owe to Cook Wilson. The writings of Cook Wilson himself were assembled and published posthumously under the editorship of A. S. L. Farquharson and with the title *Statement and Inference*. There is distinguished work in the two volumes of this book, but most of it is on logical questions. Only some of the papers give a proper indication of the realist epistemology which took its subsequent impressive course under the influence of Cook Wilson's disciples at Oxford and elsewhere.

The main claim which Cook Wilson made, if I may put the matter very tersely for the purpose of this paper, was that there were certain things we know without need of justification beyond the knowledge itself. The word intuition is sometimes used here, although it is in many respects a misleading term. The terms 'knowledge for certain' were abjured on the grounds that knowledge involves being certain. There are then, it was claimed, some things which we know ('for certain' the layman may add) without being able or needing to adduce 'further reason'. We know, and there can be no question about it; this is our starting point, not the end of inquiry, a view which has of course a long ancestry going back in some fairly obvious ways to Aristotle, though not to be attributed to him without qualification.

Among the things which Cook Wilson would claim to be known beyond reasonable dispute in this way is the reality of the external world, the existence of other finite persons and the existence of God. In the work of his two most eminent followers, Prichard and Ross, the certainty of immediate insight was invoked especially in respect to certain ethical principles, and intuitionism thus became for a while the dominant strain in English ethical theories.

The application of these views to religion found a remarkable expression in one of the most celebrated of Cook Wilson's own papers, entitled, 'Rational Grounds for Belief in God' (*Statement and Inference*, Vol. II). This paper was described by the late John Baillie as 'one of the most important theological documents of our time',[4] and Baillie made its central theme the basis of his own work in most of his own major works, including his Gifford Lectures, *The Sense of the Presence of God*. The main contention is that rational grounds for belief in God are not required, and that the traditional arguments fail, for what we have is an immediate certainty which requires no vindication beyond itself. No one can fail to know that there is a God.

But what, in the light of this comfortable doctrine, do we say to the atheist? There seems to be an increasing host of unbelievers. Are they all insincere? By no means. They are just subject to a delusion whereby they honestly deny 'at the top of their minds' what they also sincerely believe at the bottom of their hearts. I have examined these strained apologetics elsewhere[5] and drawn attention to the excesses to which Baillie in particular is driven in seeking to prove that all of us are not only theists at heart but also Christian believers. In the case of Baillie and Cook Wilson there is a marked attenuation of the content of belief at the point where it becomes peculiarly implausible to maintain the universality of orthodox Christian belief. Religious experience tends to become just the awareness of moral obligation.

There is indeed one respect in which there is an element of immediacy in our knowledge of God, the sense of the finite character of the world involving some transcendent source mysteriously beyond it. But this is not easy to characterise and it

waxes and wanes in the course of our lost consciousness. It needs
to be elicited in peculiar ways and is easily lost in sustained preoccupation with our daily round. Many persons seem to be quite
without it. It requires a special sort of sophistication to deal with
it philosophically and, on the other hand, certain sorts of
sophistication are inimical to it. Beyond the sense of the transcendent itself, experience of divine reality is far from simple or
immediate. It is involved in many ways with the variations and
complexities of our present existence. There is no once for all
grasp of static formulas about God and his ways. Understanding
must be renewed and stated anew in the varieties of public and
private experience, and there is no infallible short way or any
means of avoiding effortful thought.

The position in respect of perception is interesting in the same
way, indeed peculiarly so in the light of much recent treatment of
the subject. According to Cook Wilson there can be no doubt
about our knowledge of the external world. We certainly know
that it exists, just as there can be no doubt of the existence of
persons other than ourselves. One of the ablest contemporary
successors of Cook Wilson put the position unmistakably in the
course of a symposium on the subject at a meeting of the
Aristotelian Society. I refer to R. I. Aaron's paper, 'The Casual
Argument for Physical Objects', *Proceedings of the Aristotelian
Society*, Supp. Vol. XIX.

Here Aaron holds firmly that there can be no doubt that the
pencil I hold in my hand exists. I may be wrong in everything
else I hold about it, about its colour, length, weight, etc. But it
would at the same time be absurd to deny that the pencil is real.
This view, I must confess, I find very baffling. There is certainly
something veridical about my having this particular experience
now, it is one kind of experience and not another. But to describe
it properly is another matter, and to go from my present experience to certain assurance that some distinct physical reality
exists is a considerable leap for which the warrant is far from
clear. If I should be mistaken about all the properties of the
pencil, of what exactly am I assured when I affirm that it must
at least exist? Of what was G. E. Moore assured when he held
up his two hands?

What is very strange, however, is that, in spite of the obvious
difficulties of this appeal to immediate certainty and common

sense, this strain in recent philosophy has been so persistent. The subtleties of various treatments of the problems of perception are brushed aside by simple recourse to what we say or by crushing insistence that no one at a horse race supposes that he is seeing various patches of colour fleeting past – he is 'seeing horses' and no one supposes that he sits on a sense datum – he sits on a chair. This short way with the dissenter, and indeed with all inquiry, has had an extraordinary vogue among English-speaking philosophers to the very great impoverishment of hard and subtle philosophical thinking which is only gradually making its way back.

At this point it will be an advantage to look briefly at one of the most impressive presentations of the tradition we associate in Britain with Cook Wilson, namely, a book published by the Oxford Press recently for R. I. Aaron, whom I mentioned a moment ago. It is called *Knowing and the Function of Reason*. I much commend the book as a ripe and cautious statement of a down-to-earth position which British thinkers find very attractive. It is all the more significant because it makes no crude appeal to ordinary language.

Aaron has always been drawn to empiricism, and is himself one of the best authorities on Locke. But he is not an uncompromising empiricist, and at times his views are reminiscent of Kant. But he relies less on some *a priori* feature of experience than on the quality of experience itself; and what is distinctive, for our purpose, in this appeal to experience is the insistence that there are certain things which we undoubtedly *know*. This is our firm foundation. I *know* now that I am sitting at my study table, that I have a pencil in my hand, that the rain has stopped and the sun is shining, that my wife's name is Megan, that Heath is the Prime Minister and that Kant was a famous philosopher, that Plato lived many centuries before Christ. All this I say I *know*, not I 'believe' or 'am firmly convinced'. I know these things and that is what knowledge is like. But have we not felt convinced in these ways in the past and found ourselves in fact to have been mistaken? Mr. Heath may have suffered a collapse and be no longer Prime Minister. My memory may have begun to fail and I may be getting confused about familiar matters. I may be subject to optical illusions or the victim of a clever practical joker. That is highly unlikely when I can get up and move around and put my doubts to the test in various ways. Nonetheless we do make mistakes and have on occasion been proved wrong about things which seemed very certain at the time. Just when are we entitled to say that we know?

Some would reply with Plato and others that we know when we have a firm belief and 'a good reason' for having it. But this is the start, not the end of investigation. What is 'a good reason'? Aaron himself takes a different and bolder course. He admits that we are fallible, but will not for that reason rest content with a high degree of probability about matters of fact. We must insist that we do *know* certain things. We are not presuming or taking for granted or taking the odds against being mistaken to be so slight that we can wholly disregard them and have what is sometimes oddly called 'moral certainty' – we *know*. In Aaron's own example, I know that there is a bird singing outside my window now. It is absurd to say anything else, I hear it. But have we not been mistaken even about things like this? There are people who can imitate bird songs. If in fact I heard only an imitation, could it be said that I knew that I heard a bird singing?

Aaron makes no attempt to burke this difficulty. His book is indeed a sustained attempt to deal with it. His main ploy is to distinguish between 'primal' knowledge and 'absolute' knowledge. The former is however genuine knowledge, not just provisional certainty. It is not relative, or knowledge 'for me'. Here are the author's own words:

> It is customary to speak of infallible knowledge as 'absolute' and this might suggest that fallible knowledge should be termed 'relative'. But this latter term will not do, since it might imply that the second sort of certainty is only relatively certain, and this would be misleading since it is completely certain. It would be misleading too to call it *prima facie* certain knowledge, for this would suggest that it was not in truth certain but only appeared to be certain. Some more neutral adjective is required and I suggest that we call the fallible certain knowledge *primal* knowledge and the infallible absolute knowledge.[6]

Aaron inclines to doubt that absolute knowledge is within our reach at all, even in matters like basic logical principles such as the law of contradition. Every system, he maintains, must be consistent, but its application to the world around us is another matter; there are, after all, 'alternative logics'. I myself would take a somewhat less accommodating line at this point. There has been much loose play with the implication of 'alternative logics'. But Aaron himself does not belittle consistency. What he holds is that it arises out of the way our experience conditions the way we must think. And this brings us to what he says about 'primal' knowledge.

'Primal' knowledge, we are told, in the first place is personal and private. No one can be certain for me or instead of me. Secondly, it is final, the matter is settled for me at the time. 'We can be sure at the present moment that the statement is true, but later we may come to doubt this, and may even become sure that it is false,thus settling the issue once again, but in another way'.[7] When the issue is 'settled' for us there is more than subjective certainty. We are under a 'constraint' through our consciousness of the world around us. This is clearly a vital consideration. Many things are 'settled', or seem so, at the time for the madman or the fanatic. There seem to have been people who were quite certain that they were Napoleon or that the end of the world was due in a few hours. We are very certain of things in dreams, to the extent of being quite terrified in nightmares. Aaron refers rather cautiously to this latter example and does not say much beyond the observation that we are in fact subject to the 'constraint' of the world around us in dreams we have at the point of awakening. At other times, and in the case of the madman, we are not presumably subject to the constraint of the world, and there is no problem. But what, after all, is the alleged constraint when it is operative and how do we recognise it? What makes it so final? What is the discipline or impact of the external world which converts strong probability into knowledge? On these questions we hear much too little and we are left at the same time in the embarrassing situation of having to say that we knew at one time something which we subsequently came to *know* to be false. This seems to be a position in which we cannot really rest, however acute the dilemmas which drive us to it.

In pursuance of the same theme Aaron refers to further 'illustrative cases'. They include our consciousness of our own existence and that of other people. Now I have argued in various places that we have a certain knowledge of our own existence in the very fact of being ourselves. We do not just infer the existence of a self or know it obliquely. But this is awareness of one's own existence as a mind or mental being. I am aware also of having a body, I see it, I feel it, I am sensitive in and through it. But this is all the same a different sort of certainty. I have this certainty at the time in dreams respecting the body I have in my dream and not my real body stretched out in bed. The problem of mind and body is a hard one, and I have taken a bolder course over it in the dualism I have defended in my books than many would like. But for Aaron and many others there is no problem, at least initially. There are consequential '*metaphysical*' problems, but they proceed upon the initial certainty we have about our own embodied existence. I am a being which has experiences, but I also, with equal certainty, 'take myself to be a physical object in space'.[8] What, one wonders, is the implication of saying this for any expectation we may have of life after death? My own reaction here is that, while there is a certain obviousness about our being embodied and that, for many purposes, we just identify ourselves with our bodies ('I am lighting my pipe', 'he is smiling', 'he is sweating', etc.), the facts of our embodied existence, including somatic sensations and the body-image, etc., are starting points for reflecting, not the data of initial certainties, and that dualism is at least one plausible answer. To foreclose the argument at a certain level and invoke primal certainties respecting it, even if we are prepared to open it again at another level as a metaphysical question, is, in my opinion, a prime remedy for confusion at all levels. What sort of metaphysical question can we ask about mind and body if we set out with the initial assurance that one is 'a physical object in space'? The scope allowed for metaphysics to alter our thinking radically is very restricted here, and is that how we want to think of metaphysics, some after-play which leaves the main issues where they were? On the other hand, metaphysics is not to be a law to itself or relegated to a world apart. That would be an equally grave mistake, and there are plentiful sad examples of it.

We are all in the same strait regarding our knowledge of *other* persons. We have, it is alleged, 'perceptive assurance' also of their existence as embodied beings. 'If the question is posed, "How am

I sure of the existence of my friend sitting opposite me?'', the answer is plain, that I see him.' But this is surely a short way. All that I properly *see* is my friend's body. I gather without difficulty as a rule also what he is thinking and feeling and how the world goes for him. But I do not strictly see his thoughts, however close and easy our intercourse may be. On occasion there may be grievous misunderstandings, tragic writing is full of them. I may even be wrong about the actual body, as happens when taken in at the waxworks. Or suppose various persons were thought to occupy a body in turn (could it even be simultaneously?) – *Eve White and Eve Black*. Of whose existence am I certain in these cases when 'I see' my friend?

Likewise when we turn to a somewhat different problem, that of causation. We do not perceive causal linkages as such, as every young student of Hume is made to understand. But we believe there is such a relation. We could make little sense of anything without cause and effect. In some way we are all looking for causes all the time and mystified when we cannot find them. Something, we say, must have brought this or that about. But what then is the causal link? Hume's answer will not do, and there seems to be more involved than a Kantian *a priori* condition of the kind of experience we actually have. Do we not sometimes speak of an 'efficient cause'? Aaron's answer is to have recourse again to actual experience, in particular our own experience as agents. We are conscious of our own efforts making a difference, as when we press hard to force a door open, and we can 'interpolate' this awareness of effortful agency into our understanding of causal agency in the external world. In this way causation is no longer an ultimate 'mystery not to be comprehended by human minds'.[9] It becomes intelligible to us. This leaves me unconvinced, as did the attempt of G. F. Stout in *Mind and Matter* many years ago to extend our own consciousness of effort to the external world. I find nothing here beyond a fanciful reading into events in the physical world of a feature peculiar to conscious activity. In my view no ultimately adequate account of causality and the principle of induction is possible independently of our invocation of a transcendent ground of all reality whose mode of operation is bound to remain mysterious to us. We discover causal relations in experience but the confidence we have that these are not fortuitous but somehow necessitated cannot be found in the course of our experience itself. Even in our own most obviously effortful striving to produce outward changes (as in my pushing the door), I have no real understanding of why the physical changes occur beyond more detailed understanding of the physical changes themselves. My success in opening the door remains as baffling to me in the last resort as the flame consuming the candle.

The upshot of this also is that we cannot divorce metaphysical considerations from our normal examination of philosophical problems as they present themselves in our experience of ourselves and the world around us. If, as I am convinced, there is a metaphysical side to the problem of causality, this is not something to be deferred for consideration in due course by those who add to their normal philosophical preoccupations a further optional taste for some distinct metaphysical reflection. Metaphysics lies at the heart of all philosophy, and this is what is exhibited in a peculiarly instructive way in the inadequacy of the 'short ways' of many forms of common sense philosophy. It just does not work to take one's stand on day-to-day certainties, whether or not confirmed in ordinary language, and then seek consolation against questions and paradoxes that remain by lip service to some further philosophical luxury in which those who so desire may indulge. The vital problems are there in what our experience is like, in perception or awareness of one another. There is no burking these if we are to philosophise to any purpose at all.

Perhaps we should go further and insist that there is no strict demarcation to be made between metaphysics and the normal course of philosophical thinking, just as we should be very wary of sharp demarcations between different branches of philosophy, ethics, theory of knowledge, etc. We have heard much of late of various forms of meta activities – metaethics, for example, and even meta-metaethics. But when the overtures are ended we find ourselves just doing what philosophers have always been doing in respect to ethical questions, but with the confusing complication of supposing that something – not often spelled out – has already been satisfactorily examined and settled in proper philosophical terms, thereby leaving a significant area of proper philosophical concern not investigated in effective relation to the rest. The unfortunate effects of these bifurcations of philosophical activity are only too sadly evident in the recent history of the subject.

It might be thought then that the proper course should be to ban the term 'meta' altogether, and I must admit that this is a proposal which has much to commend it, along with a ban on the proliferation of isms. However, I do not think we can go quite that far. Plato is an excellent guide here as in so much else. There is a distinctive activity which he called Dialectic. This is not a circumscri ed activity with rules and conditions peculiar to itself, but rather the culmination of continuous philosophical activity, the 'coping stone' according to Plato, in which various investigations, as they arise from different aspects of experiences, are considered in closer relation to one another to give us a more unified conspectus. In the case of Plato this would involve peculiar further insight into a transcendent Good, but there is no suggestion that this nullifies our earlier undertakings or converts them into preliminaries which are subsequently dispensable, as in some forms at least of Buddhism. Philosophy remains one enterprise, and nothing in the final course of it should encourage us to be lax or abandon the full rigour of its discipline at any stage.

There is a twofold moral for us here. One is the point with which I have been largely concerned, namely, that we must not foreclose our answers to problems which directly force themselves upon us by what we find our existence to be like. There is no unassailable initial platform on which to stand. This does not mean that there is nothing which the philosopher can take to be established on its own account – far from it! My main concern could well be taken to be that we take proper account of what the world and our experience force upon us. We are not just to spin a web out of our own philosophical bellies. Nor are we left without any resting-place. The world is the kind of world it is, and there are insights which validate themselves without needing or allowing of further justification. There are things we just see to be the case, and to make this evident, in opposition to attempts to manufacture the world and its conditions for ourselves, is the very considerable achievement of the Cook Wilson line in British philosophy. The importance of this in ethics elevates this movement, in the work of Prichard, Ross, Broad, and others, to a place of lasting importance in the history of thought. We may not care for the word 'intuition', and we certainly cannot settle easily what is its exact place in ethics or mathematics. But that there must be insights of this kind is hard to dispute, and a great deal of philosophical skill and wisdom turns on being able to recognise them. Wittgenstein was given to insisting that a wise philosopher must know when to stop, and in this, at least, I heartily concur with him. The drawback is that many stop in the wrong places, or too soon. Even if, as seems to me inevitable, we have to admit intuition or immediate insight somewhere, there are still questions to be asked about this, that of conflicting intuitions, for example, so helpfully treated by A. C. Ewing in his *Reason and Intuition*. But the world, I repeat, is there, however endlessly varied, and there is a stage where argument is pointless. The philosopher will disregard this at his peril. But he must also be persistently vigilant to ensure that the light of his peculiar sort of reflection continues to play over all aspects of experience, and he must not burke the impact of the world upon him. In the last resort, the world is the master, and we must philosophise about what we find to be the case.

A closely related moral is that, while we must take nothing for granted until we are sure that philosophy has done its proper work with it, we must not proceed on our course through a series of rarefied ethereal concepts prescribing their own relatedness and culminating in systems into which we then try to force the world of nature and our experience. Much ingenuity can be spent on this kind of a priorism; and one has often to admire it. But it is the bane of sound philosophy, and it is no less insidious when sustained, as it often has been, by learned allusiveness and preciousness to maintain the facade. The rationalists have badly led us astray here, including in some respects (but some only) the two thinkers I especially admire, Plato and Descartes. The *a priori* offers no more a royal road to truth than the dogmatisms of common sense. There just is no 'short way', and of this at least Plato never tired of telling us. Few things are more frustrating to eager philosophical minds than to be pulled away from the truly philosophically perplexing aspect of things to pursue the course of seemingly self-determining abstractions – the famous 'bloodless ballet'. It is the latter, together with the exploitation of obscure terminology, that brought metaphysics, and with it almost our whole philosophical enterprise, into such bad repute earlier this century and set up the plea for analysis and clarity.

Neither of these is enough. There is synthesis also, a picture of what things are generally like, in ethics or perception, for example. But the synthesis is not preordained, it is sustained by *looking* at what we find to be the case.

I have not said much about ethics. But ethics does provide a prime example of the inhibiting and distorting character of bad metaphysics. Systems of thought have been completed, often with a splendid architectonic of their own, which preclude entirely some of the conditions which, initially at least and inescapably for some of us, make accountability and moral achievement possible. The example of Spinoza comes obviously to mind. From his fertile imagination we can draw a great deal that creative metaphysics requires – the idea of 'infinite attributes' in its application to the idea of different kinds of space, for example. But the possibility of a genuinely open choice is excluded independently of any reflection on what we find actual situations to be like or the implications of moral distinctions.

That we may draw together, in a unified conspectus, what presents itself to us philosophically in different respects, is a legitimate and noble aspiration. It is perhaps what we should describe as metaphysics *par excellence*, and what warrants the prefix 'meta'. But there are few more dangerous enterprises and few that have had more distressing results. Philosophy is always difficult and tricky, and this is why so many great philosophers have been so concerned to warn away those who had not certainly shown their flair for it. Plato never tires of warning us against the charlatans and shams attracted by the reputation and superficial glitter of the subject, the pseudo-philosophers of the pseudo-problems and the short ways. Nowhere is this warning more necessary than in the ambitious synthesis of metaphysics, where the open sesame of some new key concept or fashionable turn of phrase is thought to open all doors by its own magic. I do not rule out creative metaphysics, but we must approach it by the 'steep and rugged ascent' of the cave and we must always be careful lest our last stage be the worst.

This is why some of our down-to-earth philosophers of today, finding themselves restless and hankering after some kind of metaphysics, announce their programme as that of 'revisionary metaphysics'. But while this reflects a most estimable caution, it tends to overreach itself, like 'vaulting ambition', and fall into the toils of the very methodological metaphysics which our bolder empiricists set out to cure. A revision of language or of general concepts is not what we should be seeking, but a conspectus on what things look like when they are considered philosophically, and for this we need more than formal procedures and skills, we need to know how to look; even if our tasks were simply that of improving the 'maps', we would still need to explore the country; and happily some of those who write about revisionary metaphysics have sometimes been more enterprising than their announced programme allows and provided intriguing speculations which are only marred by the wrong sort of caution.

Caution there must be, but not lack of enterprise, and we must not be held back by formal preconceived notions of what we are to do. Only we must never neglect, whether in dealing with ethics or perception or the elusiveness of our own identity, that we start with what, in sustained reflection, we find to be the case. To that extent I am an unrepentant realist and welcome the insistence on the 'impact of the world' and the discipline of experience. But there must be no inhibiting or prejudging of the philosophical enterprise itself. The appropriate freedom of the exercise itself must not be curtailed, and we may, if we are bold enough, soar with Plato but remain true to the here and now of the world around us in the subtle analyses of G. E. Moore, than whom the wise metaphysician will not easily find a better tutor today.

NOTES

1. Cf. also his *In Defence of Free Will* and his *Selfhood and Godhood*.
2. *Value and Reality*.
3. He defends an outright indeterminist view, for example.
4. *Our Knowledge of God*, p. 50.
5. *Philosophy of Religion*, Chapter XII.
6. Op. cit., p. 60.
7. Op. cit., p. 56.
8. Op. cit., p. 68.
9. Op. cit., p. 228.

2 Ultimates and a Way of Looking in Philosophy

By 'ultimates', for the purpose of this paper, I do not understand in the first instance, some one supreme being or some alleged final source of all other conditioned existence – the infinite, the absolute, the transcendent, the unconditioned, God, or whatever term or description be thought appropriate. Not that I consider these notions unimportant for philosophy, or want to exclude them from what I want to maintain here about ultimates. They would in fact provide one excellent example of what I have in mind and provide a variation on my main theme which is significant and instructive in some special ways. But what I am concerned to put forward holds irrespective of whether one is disposed to consider seriously the idea of some supreme existent or reality along the lines indicated, and I am anxious not to confuse the present issue or give a wrong impression of what I am mainly concerned to advance at the moment.

For the same reason I must also make it clear that I am not concerned with the idea of some basic philosophical principle which we need to recognise before we can make proper progress with other questions, or some key idea which will unlock all the other mysteries, evolution, relativity, a self-representative series, etc. Indeed I am very little attracted to clues of this kind in philosophy and suspect that many have been badly led astray by them. I do indeed believe that philosophers, like all others, have to respect one basic principle, namely the principle of non-contradiction and would defend this, in the proper place, against suggestions that it may be conventional or limited in its application. But while I hold that we must respect this principle I would make no further claim for it or suggest that other philosophical ideas may somehow be deduced out of it.

The place of the 'Form of the Good' in Plato's philosophy, provides an interesting half-way house which may be worth noting here. On the one hand, 'the Good' is an ultimate which is not established by argument but by a glimpse or noesis. Nothing is known in the vision of 'the Good' which can be communicated in any other way. The vision is all, but it is only within the reach of suitably equipped and accomplished philosophers. It does, however, once achieved, provide a means of exhaustively understanding both the inherent necessity of the other forms and their essential interdependence. It is the prime source of philosophical wisdom. At the same time, little in the conduct of Plato's general treatment of various philosophical questions is directly affected by the notion of 'the Good'. *Ex hypothesi* it could not be, for the discussion is not addressed solely to the few who have come to the ultimate attainment. Most of the time Plato continues as the rest of us might. In the account of 'the Good' as something which is apprehended peculiarly for itself, and in the insistence on a peculiar philosophical flair for doing this, Plato is taking the course I especially wish to commend. That the 'glimpse' has implications for further questions is also important. But I do not subscribe at all to the notion of one supreme insight, however fine and distinctive, from which the proper understanding of all other issues is made manifest. The major philosophical questions must be taken on their merit, whatever the ramifications there may also be between them. Nor am I thinking, along the lines of Plato, of a quite exclusively philosophical insight. What the philosopher apprehends in the cases of what I here call ultimates is what is usually evident to all in the common course of experience. What is peculiar to the philosopher is his appreciation of the distinctiveness of the awareness involved and the way to treat it intellectually without lapsing into misleading aberrations.

But having paid our respects in these terms to Plato, let us now return from this historical excursus to our proper task. What I particularly want to claim is that, in a number of central philosophical contexts, there is a point to be reached where further explicit consideration ends and we can do no more than note the way things are and declare them to be so. This does not, as should be obvious, concern ordinary matters of fact which we may note and record for our usual purposes from day to day.

But it is on the other hand not just a way of talking about the world or of the way things are in general, it is in the first place an appreciation of the way things are, of what we ourselves and the world around us are like and, in that way, of what we may also say or affirm.

The main point is that, in all philosophical discussion, we reach a stage where further analysis and argument is at an end, not because of our own failings and limitations, but from the nature of the case and unavoidably. Argument may indeed end because of the stubbornness or the seeming inanity of one's opponent or some blind spot or bias to which even the most reflective may be prone in subtle ways. 'There is no point in trying to argue with him', we may say, or more politely, 'We must agree to differ'. It is not our aptitudes or temperament that prescribe the sort of finality or terminus with which I am now concerned, but the nature of the philosophical enterprise itself. A point is reached where we see, or seem to see, the way things are and can only declare this, though much will indeed turn on the care and precision with which the declaration is made – perhaps that is where peculiar philosophical skill is most evident, and this in turn helps us to appreciate the persistent preoccupation of philosophers with words and their equally evident fear of words. Words are our tools but they seem to be never quite right or appropriate for us. We seem to hit on the right words but then in no time it seems to be all wrong.

One embarrassment in the view of philosophy which I am seeking to outline is that the last thing a philosopher would wish to be accused of is an unwillingness to go on arguing his case. It is by discussion and argument that he exists, they are his life blood. Our patience may easily run out with certain kinds of discussion, but to give up discussion and argument is to give up our practice. We must continue on the 'long and circuitous route' and not seek an easy resting-place or 'a short way'. Dogmatism and unreason are what we most wish to avoid, and when the philosopher meets them in others he is understandably affronted and dismayed. That much intellectual activity of a sort, in politics and theology for example, is just an elaborate ringing of changes on initial dogmatisms is a solemn enough warning of which, one would hope, philosophers stood in little need. But dogmatism and the closed mind take their course sometimes in very subtle ways and no one can be wholly unmindful of the hold they may have on us, the sceptically-minded as much as the rest. No philosopher likes to be accused of unreason or of 'knowing all the answers' or of giving up the discipline of hard and continuous thinking and of listening properly to what others have to say. It becomes him more ill than any to have recourse to subterfuge, prevarication or similar ways of scoring an easy victory, and for that reason he will not take it lightly to be thought to lack openness and flexibility of mind and just to 'dig his heels in' and take his stance in serene assurance that he is right. To be troubled becomes him better, a certain sort of doubt is part of his attitude of mind and he knows well how hard it is to find any adequate resting-place at all in his subject.

This has in turn a tendency to induce its opposite, namely the almost total refusal to commit oneself, either by not putting pen to paper, except perhaps for wholly negative criticism, or by inventing curious philosophical moves which involve no subscription to any positive content, an evasion which seems to keep us genuinely engaged with our problems while remaining sublimely superior to the seeming futilities of others. Some play the safe game by rigid adherence to a fairly simple policy like strict empiricism. But while caution is estimable, indeed indispensable, where it is so easy to *say* the misleading thing even when on the right course, we must not give up the philosophical task of indicating how things in general seem to us to be, about ourselves and the world; and this will involve commitment, for the time at least, to some positive views. My present contention is that we must not be deterred, by the fear of dogmatism or, like J. S. Mill, of being 'found out', when we come to the point where we can only affirm how things seem to be without adducing further considerations or arguments.

The danger is, I must repeat, that this requirement be invoked before it is inevitable or proper from the nature of the case, either out of intellectual indolence (and we must remember how very demanding and trying genuinely close philosophical reflection is bound to be) or from fear of refutation. I would not impute either of these motives, at least in any overt form, to so tireless a philosophical thinker as Norman Malcolm, but I have elsewhere[1] noted how he makes things easier for himself by resorting at an inappropriate point to Wittgenstein's celebrated and very proper insistence 'that it is an important thing in philosophy to know when to stop'. Malcolm will not have it at all that dreaming is some kind of waking state, an immediate vivid impression the moment we awake. But he will not have it either that the dream is anything that goes on, while we sleep, though there is no doubt that 'people really do have dreams'. We tell the dream but the dream is not the telling. Just what is it then? Here Malcolm tells us we have 'to stop', and I have insisted, with perhaps some impatience, that he is not entitled to stop there. The question just cries out for an answer, and Malcolm seems to be 'stopping' because, it seems to him, no further move is possible to him (he is in a complete impasse) when there certainly ought to be. He retreats into silence when it is not reasonable to do so.

Malcolm is in no way alone in this. For while it is important (that is the main theme of this paper) to know that we must stop and when to stop, it is only too fatally easy to stop at the wrong place or where it is convenient. This has happened in some celebrated ways. Let me note some examples.

One of the pioneers and architects of recent realism, especially in its English variety, is Cook Wilson. How much he is read today is hard to tell, though he seems always mentioned with respect. I think it would not be hard to show that his genius has presided far more than is realised over the course of philosophy at Oxford during this century, even though the strict allusions to him may not be very extensive. He held[2] that there were certain things we undoubtedly know without further reason. These include the existence of the external world, the self, other minds, causality, God – a formidable list which leaves little scope for the sceptic. How far this is meant to extend to particular items is not always clear, but some of Cook Wilson's closest followers certainly meant it in that way. I have discussed the views of one of them, R. I. Aaron, elsewhere.[3] Aaron is forced to the peculiar position of maintaining that while in all matters of fact we are fallible I can affirm now that I *know* that a bird is singing outside my window, though I may have later to affirm that it was an imitation and that I did not know this. The course that Cook Wilson himself took was to say that, in all the contexts in question, there could be 'philosophic doubt' – I know that there is a 'table before me', as Berkeley has it, but thought about illusions and perspectival distortions etc., cause me to doubt this in some rather special way which leaves the original certainty quite unaffected. It is not easy, however, to see just what this amounts to. Berkeley was as certain as any that there was a 'table before' him. His normal reaction would not be in the least affected. But he was all the same denying something substantial in his famous immaterialism. External things would not for him have any geniune reality when not perceived. This is certainly at odds with a widespread impression, and while we may or may not incline to Berkeley's view or some variation on it, the questions raised in this context, from ancient times to Berkeley and later, cannot be settled out of hand by invoking an initial or basic certainty not to be affected by further philosophical thought. It may be that there has to be some form of realism in our view of the external world, and I imagine that there would be few today who would go with some post-Hegelian idealists in dissolving the world into a 'system of relations', We encounter the world of nature, we do not make it, it is in some sense there. But before we take our stance on this or any rival claim we have to do a great deal of hard philosophical thinking to discover what sort of stance we are forced to take. Cook Wilson and most of his followers are stopping too soon, to the serious detriment of philosophical thought.

A similar comment is invited by much in the course of the twin form of realism about the external world, namely the philosophy of common sense as practised by G. E. Moore and those he inspired. No one would now agree that it will do to hold up our hands and declare that here are two physical things. Indeed few have shown a more subtle grasp of the complexities of the problems of perception than Moore, as readers of his *Some Main Problems of Philosophy* will be well aware. In one place he suggests that the external object may be just a point, a far cry from the impression generally conveyed by the famous British Academy Lecture, 'Proof of an External World'[4]. The main point here again is that we must be careful where to stop and not indulge ourselves with the comfort of a resting-place, or seem to do so, before we have earned it by exhausting all the appropriate philosophical considerations in the first place.

Of course we all know after a fashion that there is an external world and we have every confidence in much that we believe about the 'furniture' of it and what happens to it. But this is the beginning not the end of philosophical reflection, and the ghost of Berkeley (and many perplexed thinkers before him) is not to be laid by just invoking this day-to-day assurance. To retreat on that is a prime example of stopping at the wrong place.

Nor is it possible, as some have tried, to avoid being involved in any issue of commitment by simply considering how the verb 'to know' is most commonly or advantageously used. It may well be that, for most purposes, the proper course for me to take is to say that I *know* that my elbows are resting on this table and, indeed, a host of things not so immediately plain, that a boy is mowing my lawn away from the window, that King's College is in the Strand etc., extending to much that I know about the past. It would be misleading to say 'I believe' in these cases. If I said that, as evidence in court, I would be thought to prevaricate, and the advocate could well ask me sharply to say did I or did I not *know* that the boy I had engaged and whom I glimpsed from time to time was cutting my lawn this morning. It would be pedantic to start to qualify, and yet, in all these matters, there is an element of fallibility. We have, with reason, been certain and proved wrong. Shall we then decide to say that we *know* only when there can be no possibility, not even the most remote, of error? My point is that nothing of real philosophical importance hinges on this. Linguistic conventions depend, or should depend, on convenience, but the situation which the philosopher seeks to understand remains unaffected.

We have in short to say something, or take some stance, in the study of perception – or give up philosophical study of it altogether. The world around us is not made in our thought, it is in some sense 'there', we have to take it as it is and come to terms with it, disagreeable and pleasant features alike, we 'encounter' things and they make their 'impact'. This is the strength of the realist case and common sense philosophy, though whether the best way to deal with this is to say that something is 'given' is a moot point. My present insistence is that it is not enough to invoke the obvious reality, in some form, of external objects and our practical certainties. This is the start, not the stopping place, and I would not care here, in this peculiarly tricky subject, to say where I think we must stop – though I think I shall not find Berkeley very far from my elbow when I do so. Common sense realism has certainly stopped too soon in the past.

The same goes, though a good deal more obviously, for the appeal to ordinary language and the paradigm case. It may be a useful way of bringing out something that is lacking in the sense-datum theory to say that we do not see patches of colour flash past at the races, we are watching horses. But to say that, *and no more*, is just to give up. There are problems, very exciting ones too, connected with perspectival distortion, the working of our physical organs, nerves, brains etc., which are evident to the most elementary student, and we cannot just sweep these away, to say nothing of reverie and dreams, by noting that what we see are chairs, horses, people and not patches of colour or sensations. Likewise, the free-will problem is not settled by noting that we would clearly say that we are free, in some sense, most of the time. I am free now in the sense that I am not in prison, I write these words of my own accord since no one is guiding my hand, or again in a different sense because I have no aversion to writing in this way or some like psychological hindrance, or yet again because there is no law against it. To disentangle these various uses closely is a proper task for philosophy, and there has been much careful work in this vein of late. It is also important to consider what sort of freedom is involved in our accountability, by no means an easy task and certainly one not to be settled entirely on the basis of linguistic practice. But here again I would maintain that a point must be reached, in respect for example to the implications of moral accountability and of our exercise of the appropriate freedom, where we must have to affirm how the matter seems to us.

Likewise, elsewhere in ethics, Professor Toulmin, on one occasion, poured great scorn on the alleged 'inner eye' by which W. D. Ross claimed to come to know things in ethics, only to close his paper with the insistence that the important thing in ethics is to appreciate that we know some things without further reason. There may, or there may not be, ethical intuitions. But *ex hypothesi* this is not a matter to be itself settled by argument. We must reflect on how we do come to say that certain things are wrong or right or good. That, however, is in no way a simple matter of sitting in one's chair and noting whether flashes of intuition happen to us from time to time, like twitches of pain. To suppose this is the unworthy travesty to which much fine work in ethics has been exposed. The kind of thinking that goes to settling these matters is very special, and before we reach the point of saying, with or against the intuitionist, that this is how it now seems to us, a great many subtle considerations, including what we might say in this or that circumstance, are relevant. There are also alleged fallible intuitions, and when we have gone through all the appropriate motions we may find that a term like 'intuition' has misleading associations and is best replaced by another – 'insight', 'judgement'[5] etc. But none of this precludes there being some point where, not from philosophical weariness or desperation, but from what the situation philosophically calls for, we have to exercise some final judgement and stay with it as long as things seem so to us.

I myself strongly favour the view that, at some point in ethics, intuition must be invoked. But I also think that, once this was clearly appreciated by outstanding thinkers earlier this century,[6] notably G. E. Moore, there was a lapse into the besetting philosophical sin of making this notion do more work than it should. Intuitions were apt to proliferate, to the serious discredit of the concept. This seems to me to be a further case of philosophers stopping too soon or too conveniently at the wrong place. That is how I would judge the controversy, very much alive at the moment in a very different garb, between intuitionists like Ross and utilitarians like Moore or Pickard Cambridge. In both cases some kind of ultimate was invoked and it is of interest that Moore, while surrendering under attack the attempt to establish non-natural properties by arguments about the 'naturalistic fallacy' etc., still clung to the notion of a distinctive insight into a non-natural quality of goodness. The dispute was as to where this insight came about, for Moore in the assessment of worth and, perhaps, in the general duty of maximising good, for Ross in this and the apprehension of other *prima facie* duties, like truth-telling and keeping promises, which had also to go into the final reckoning.

There is no easy solution to this problem. On the one hand it seems odd to suppose that we ought to do something which will not produce most good on the whole for those affected, on the other we have compunction about disregarding promises made to the dying man etc., and we feel there is something in the view that 'a promise is a promise' etc. I believe that it is not impossible to bring the latter under the utilitarian principle if we think hard enough about subtle aspects of the cases where the strain is felt; and if I am right in this and in inclining more to Moore's 'agathistic utilitarianism', then it would seem that the intuitionists (of the Ross variety) and their 'consequentialist'[7] descendants now, are just stopping too soon when they should go on thinking still harder to locate the precise point where a special insight or intuition is to be exercised. The distinctiveness of ethics which we find it impossible to avoid, however hard we try (and the more tough-minded as much as any), seems to make an insight of that sort inevitable somewhere. The point is, just where?

Let me now refer to problems about persons. First a word about 'other minds'. Cook Wilson regarded immediate and certain knowledge of other persons as a prime example of the sort of basic certainties he had in mind. In one respect he is clearly right. No one seriously doubts that we have knowledge of other persons, the solipsist is a figure of fun and does not even take himself seriously – as was underlined in Bertrand Russell's oft-repeated pleasantry about the solipsist who was surprised that her view was not shared by more people. But this tells us nothing about the mode of this awareness. One sees, in a way, the point of Cook Wilson's famous jibe about not wanting 'inferred friends'. We want our friends to be close and intimate and our companionship simple and easy. But when all has been said in this vein – and that would be a theme in itself – the fact remains that we do not know other minds as we do our own, we must have some basis for what we believe about one another. Usually, and in close relationships, this involves mainly observation of one another's bodies. But it is the body that I strictly observe, and on that basis I learn, easily and spontaneously as a rule, about thoughts, feelings, sensations and so on. I do not strictly observe another's pain, I find the indication of it in what I see or hear.

I have stressed this a good deal elsewhere, it is a point on which philosophical opinion could be a good deal firmer. Strawson[8] may speak to his heart's content about watching someone 'coiling a rope', and Aaron,[9] reflecting the initial persistent Oxford realism a little more explicitly, may say very boldly that I know my friend is there because I *see* him. But all that I strictly observe is bodily appearance and behaviour. I do not properly *see* the thoughts and intentions, though in many cases I have no doubt or hesitation whatever about them. I know that the fisherman passes the rope through his hands as he does to coil it, but I know this, without consciously pausing to infer it, as the obvious explanation of the movements of his hands and the posture of his body and his situation. It is the thoughts and intention that I learn about, but, very obviously it seems to me, in a mediated way.

It is worth noting here a curious procedure of many philosophers today who, impressed by the fact that there never is any real doubt about the existence of other minds, however liable to error we may be in particular cases, feel that this requires them to give at least a partially physicalist account of the nature of persons. They feel that the inferential element brings in a degree of uncertainty. It would leave at least a remote possibility that solipsism is true. How this can be eased by falling back on a requirement of bodily continuity is not as plain as might be thought. For there again some sort of uncertainty may creep in. But without looking at this in more detail (I have again noted it more fully elsewhere[10]), we may list this also as a case, and in some ways a peculiarly significant one since not so overtly realist, of taking a common sense or day-to-day conviction as a final insight or closure point, however desperate, from the writer's general view, the course it prescribes, rather than persist with further reflection.

These considerations seem to be underlined by the fact that, however happy we may feel in one another's company and serene in our mutual understanding, we may also be badly in error and completely misunderstand what our friends and others are about. The further we go from actual bodily presence, the greater seems to be the likelihood of error. If this were not so, historical problems would be greatly simplified. Cook Wilson himself, and the strictest of his followers, could hardly have believed that what I know about Julius Caesar and the philosophical thoughts of Plato came about through immediate contact with their minds (there would be no 'Socratic problem' if things happened that way). I know what I do know here from books and related evidence, and the position in principle seems no different in less remote contacts and when people are physically present. There is physical mediation by which I know what is not physical.

Followers of Martin Buber sometimes yoke themselves

somewhat uneasily with common sense and tough-minded realists on this issue. Elsewhere[11] I have expressed my regard for Buber and indicated fairly closely what are some of the important things which his treatment of the 'I–Thou' relation reflects. It is a great pity that those who invoke his views and find them suggestive do not think more closely about their true import. But one thing seems to me certain, namely that there is not a direct contentless relation with persons (man or God) which is quite distinct from knowledge about them and need not involve it. Indeed I doubt whether the idea of such a relation is meaningful. The facile invocation of it, as an easy way of evading tough philosophical problems, is one of the most conspicuous theological counterparts to the 'short way' with difficult questions in various forms of common sense realism in recent philosophy. One hopes its day is over.

These matters are in no way affected if we find that the evidence for telepathy and related phenomena is strong or conclusive. Whatever happens in telepathy I do not think it even conceivable that it should involve the same knowledge of other minds as we have of our own. Often a vision of certain events significantly correlated with their so happening is involved, and the mediation here is evident enough – we do not strictly see the shipwreck or hear the cry as those on the spot do. But even if visions or voices of this kind are not involved there must be some other way in which the absence of the normal physical mediation and evidence is met. I have myself, in my book *The Self and Immortality*,[12] discussed the possibility that communication between totally disembodied creatures might take a quasi-telepathic form through some intrusions into the course of our own thoughts of ingredients we might have reason, by their substance or the mode or occasion of their happening, to ascribe to some outside influence we might learn in due course to recognise. But the mediation in its own way is equally evident here. To deny this is to stop, in our philosophical reflections, at the one point where it is most inappropriate to do so.

I believe, in short, that the search for an ultimate, in the way I now use this term, in our knowledge of other persons, is a most wasteful and delusive pursuit of a philosophical will o' the wisp. For a reason to be stressed more in a moment, I think it inherently impossible to know the mind of another, man or God, in the same way as one basically knows one's own thoughts or sensations expressly in having them. But this brings me to the contrasted case of our knowledge of ourselves which is the main context in which I wish to highlight and stress the central theme of this paper.

For what has to be said of self-knowledge is radically different from what has to be said about knowledge of others. There is indeed a great deal we may know about ourselves from evidence or observation, our own and that of others. I discover where I was and what I did this time last year by looking in my diary. My friends, and presumably a psychiatrist if required, could tell me much about the sort of chap I am. But there is a more basic form of self-knowledge, namely that by which I know that my particular thoughts and other mental states, and thereby my traits of character, are mine. Two distinct points need to be sorted out here, and both of them provide prime examples of what I understand by ultimates in this paper.

The first concerns the nature of experience itself. This is sometimes said to be neutral, as between a corporealist and non-corporealist account. Everyone agrees that we do perceive, argue, resolve etc., but this, it is said, proves nothing. Thus Professor Flew, in admitting[13] that my understanding my wife's call that lunch is ready is decisive in my going downstairs, urges that this leaves the corporealist view unaffected, and Roger Squires[14] firmly denies Robert Kirk's claim that sentience depends on private access. I know of no argument that will settle this question, any more than the debate with more old-fashioned materialists, if the latter are consistent enough. On the other hand, nothing seems plainer to me than that seeing, hearing, pondering, resolving etc., while they have behavioural and dispositional aspects, are essentially non-extended, non-physical on-goings. The simplest stock example is having pain. However 'physical', the pain itself is just not a state of my body, but what I feel. But if I am asked to adduce a reason for this I am at a loss, and I marvel that anyone should request a reason for what seems to me so evident in itself. The appeal to our consciousness of pain, or any other experience, seems quite conclusive here, but if it is denied and arguments requested to show why the pain we admittedly do have, and our thoughts about it, must be thought altogether different from physical processes, then one is put out of court before the only possible plea can be made. The thoughts that I put on paper now cannot themselves be located though much that concerns and conditions them can. If this is not plain in itself I do not know what is, and I could hardly fail to do my case the gravest injustice if I took up the challenge to adduce further arguments for what I maintain. What could they be that would not give the case away, and yet it seems so manifestly clear a case.

The same goes for the claim that will be more widely contended, namely that the processes in question, sensing, perceiving, arguing etc., are 'owned' or 'belong' in some way. The precise term does not matter, and one is not quite happy with any, but I do know quite clearly what I mean when I say that I, and not someone else, am having these thoughts and sensations now. This has nothing directly to do with our separate bodies, or the different contexts in which these thoughts might be had in different cases. Quite irrespective of any distinctness of this kind, there is what I am almost tempted to call the brute fact that *I* am having these thoughts. That is an ultimate of which no further account appears possible.

Take again the stock and fairly simple example of pain. I know, in my own case both that there is pain and that I am having it. In the case of others, a reason is in order. I may hear a scream and conclude that someone is in pain, and wonder who. I do none of this in my own case. I may indeed wonder whether I or someone else has been wounded – whose blood is flowing, whose crushed foot is that. But if I have not been too numbed to feel the pain then I know that there is pain, with no possibility of pretence or delusion, and that *I* have this pain. I know both things in one and the same experience, and both are beyond doubt. But knowing that the pain is mine is more than knowing that there is the pain. I know that beyond doubt in having the pain.

Not many, at the moment, would deny that it would be absurd for anyone to look for reasons to help him decide whether he or another was in pain, or whether he was in pain at all. What could he do? Trust his own report, look at his bleeding limb, listen to his own screams? Quite obviously all that is absurd. I just know that I have this pain, whether or not I can describe it properly or know the true cause of it. But many who would not oppose me on this seem curiously reluctant to accept the implications or the proper force of it. This is how Professor Zemach is able to declare that Strawson, 'in spite of his rejection of the Cartesian ego, is basically a Cartesian'.[15] Zemach himself seeks the answer, ingeniously enough, in 'an assembly of this experience with other things'.[16] But is not this quite plainly the wrong tack from the start, whatever may be said about the alleged 'assembly' or its importance. It is not a case of Zemach, or any other, not being quite clever enough, not developing his own line to the best effect. He is from the start attempting the impossible. I know from the start that my awareness of myself is not that sort of thing. Similarly Shoemaker, admitting, indeed stressing, that there are no criteria of self-identity etc., goes to great lengths to avoid the proper import of this.[17]

The view is not, incidentally, as Zemach suggests, that we know '*a priori*' that 'my experiences are mine', though that may not be out of place in the case of Strawson. Or, if I do know *a priori* it is because I know in the first place, in having any experience, that I am having it and what this means. The problem is of course to say what it means, and this, I suspect, is why many are reluctant to own to a Cartesian view. They fear a philosophical dead-end, or of naïvely (perhaps for suspect vested interests, moral or religious, not appropriate in a tough-minded age) affirming something for which they can make no further case. It is at least expected that something should be said about the self so invoked.

Professor Antony Flew brings this sharply to a head in the closing pages of his reply to my own paper at the Joint Meeting of the Mind and Aristotelian Societies.[18] He writes:

> But though the Lewis investigation is properly philosophical, it is still about how we might know, and when we might be entitled to claim to know. Yet the primary question here is precisely what we should know if we knew that this incorporeal substance at time two was the same as that incorporeal substance at time one.

and again:

> In part my difficulty arises because those who argue on this assumption never seem to make any but the most perfunctory attempt to show that it is true. One of my hopes of the coming discussion is that someone will indicate the lines in which they think this might be shown.

Professor Flew's hope was not fulfilled, at least not by me. But I warmly applaud, and did at the time, the unambiguous and sharp way in which he points up the central issue. What he says, with typical incisiveness, is what many say and feel about a Cartesian-style dualism, and perhaps this will become also a 'Flew's Challenge'. It does indeed seem awkward to have to say, in response to questions like his, there just is nothing we can say. Is not this just burking the issue? We clearly should be able to say something. Otherwise, as Professor Bernard Williams put it to me in the B.B.C. debate about the same time[19] – I seem to be 'running out of steam'. That is of course infuriating, as, in a way, it is quite true. There is nothing more of any substance to be said. But this is not, whatever one's limitations, because of philosophical ineptitude. From the nature of the case no answer can be given.

The force of the temptation to provide an answer is almost overwhelming, especially as much ingenuity can be provided in trying to do so. But ingenuity is not philosophical wisdom, and if we have reached an ultimate the proper course is to admit it. That does not mean that the ingenious explanations have no point, they may illuminate something by the way and also help us to appreciate better just what the appropriate reticence really involves; and there is indeed a great deal around the edges of the subject that can, and should be, said. We can stress the awkwardness of seeking the right terms, allow for the dangers of terms like 'ego' 'substance', even 'subject', go over the moves which preclude us from saying too much while still saying something enormously important and distinctive, note the level at which a person *can* be described and identified – by himself as well as others – in terms of his appearance or his psychological traits, or his history, what he is like and what has been the course of his life etc. All this is appropriate and important, and even when we come to the crunch over the question, 'But what is it for this appearance and these likes and aptitudes etc., to be mine?', we can indulge in the skilful handling of pointers or 'slantwise' considerations ('assembling of reminders', some would have it) by which we come to appreciate better what it is that we ultimately claim just to 'see'. We shall understand better, for example, that what is being invoked is not something occult, or something which only a few can come to know in special conditions (like appreciating poetry or music or having some transcendental vision). We shall likewise learn how misleading it is to think of the self or person as just a presupposition, in a Kantian or any other style, much less a remote 'thing in itself'. A person is what someone is and knows himself to be.

There is, in short, no mystery-mongering. Nor is there an arbitrary or a dogmatic taking up a stance, much less a lapse into a non-philosophical brute acceptance. There is all the subtlety in the world involved, *of its own kind*. Indeed, this is just where the finer philosophical skills are displayed, and where the old insights have to be presented anew without the misleading accretions acquired in repeated and too familiar statements. The perils of the wrong sort of confidence are only too evident in the bewilderment of critics, indeed the parodies and travesties to which sound philosophy is so easily exposed, and which puts the premium in debate on the skilful teaser. Plato must have suffered a great deal in this way, not at the hands of just stupid and undiscerning philistines, though there were some around as always, but from truly philosophical minds who had not the peculiar philosophical persistence and high merit to stay with the philosophical task of 'turning the eye of the mind to the light' and going on looking in the appropriate philosophical way, aware all the time of the insidious charm of words and how fatal it is to be too wholly under their spell. What is right when you say it becomes almost immediately misleading.

The caution in all this is of first importance, and it has been as brilliantly displayed in fine philosophical work in the East as much as in the West. Time will not allow me now to illustrate this in the way I had hoped. The affinities between the more overt scepticisms of the East and of the West can be crudely presented in a way that takes away the true significance of both. But subject to a very necessary warning against cheap exploitation and listing of superficial resemblances, I would like to emphasise how much philosophical wisdom may be deepened by attending, in an informed and reflective way, to those aspects of Oriental thought and religion, where caution is struggling with explicit utterance in a profoundly philosophical way of looking at the world and ourselves. To highlight the ultimates in philosophy is in no way to encourage philosophical stupefaction and staleness. If we seem to know all the answers we give the wrong impression. The 'right way of looking' like the vision of God, if the comparison may be

made without impiety, has to be recovered, reconveyed, reculti-
vated and constantly cleansed of the accretions it generates itself.
It is also, in itself and in other ramifications, supremely rewarding, and the vistas it opens out, the new philosophical
destinations to be reached, can only be glimpsed by those who
foresake the easy triumphs for the strains of maintaining a
peculiar way of looking at provokingly elusive things which can
only shine, like the Good Will, by their own light.

NOTES

1. *The Elusive Mind*, p. 140.

2. See especially 'The Existence of God', *Statement and Inference*, Vol. II.
For more detail see Chapter 12 of my *Philosophy of Religion*.

3. Page 7 above.

4. G. E. Moore, *Philosophical Papers*, pp. 127–50.

5. In his contribution to *Contemporary British Philosophy*, Series 4, (Ed.
H. D. Lewis) Professor R. M. Hare comes round to the invocation of what he
calls 'judgement'. See p. 116 op. cit.

6. They had of course been anticipated in essentials by others, like Richard
Price.

7. 'Consequentialism' is a fairly new term. The theory is opposed to
utilitarianism, but insists all the same that we must look to the consequences.
If this means that we must consider what our action will bring about it is too
general to be significant. It excludes absolute prohibition, but what else? Its
advocates have not yet made it sufficiently clear how their view differs from
Ross's doctrine of *prima facie* duties. For an informative discussion see 'It
makes no difference whether or not I do it', Jonathan Glover and M. Scott
Taggart, *Proceedings of the Aristotelian Society*, Supp. Vol. XLIX.

8. *Individuals*, p. 111.

9. Cf. p. 11 above.

10. In the discussion of A. J. Ayer's views in my *The Elusive Mind*, pp. 251–9.

11. *The Elusive Mind*, Chapter XIII.

12. Chapter 9.

13. *Proceedings of the Aristotelian Society*, Supp. Vol. XLIX, p. 242.

14. *Proceedings of the Aristotelian Society*, Supp. Vol. XLVIII, pp. 162–3.

15. 'Strawson's Transcendental Deduction', *Philosophical Quarterly*, p. 123.

16. Op. cit., p. 125.

17. As I have tried to show in *The Elusive Mind*, Chapter X, Cf. also
Chapter VI.

18. *Proceedings of the Aristotelian Society*, Supp. Vol. XIIX, pp. 244–5.

19. *Listener*, 3 July 1975. See Chapter 3.

3 Religion and the Paranormal

There can be little doubt that, if some of the alleged findings of parapsychology could be established, they would have very great importance for religion. I hope to give some indication of this in due course. But first a word of warning. We must try to view these alleged discoveries in the proper perspective and avoid exaggeration and distortion. It has often happened that, when new discoveries are made, they are taken to provide a major clue to all remaining problems, the one key for which we have been waiting. A major fault of some philosophical systems, Hegelian idealism, for instance, or some features of linguistic analysis, has been to present themselves in this way. Process philosophy has lately been casting itself for the same role. In the late nineteenth century, evolution was supposed to be the open sesame, and we had 'evolutionary ethics', 'evolutionary social theory', and even 'evolutionary metaphysics'. Some turn to the teachings of Teilhard de Chardin in the same way. But it is extremely unlikely, in my opinion, that we shall find any marvellous once-for-all clue of this kind. Problems do ramify and they may be more interrelated than some have supposed, but they have also to be tackled on their merits. We must continue with 'the long and circuitous route' and resist the delusions of the short way.

One point at which this warning is very much needed, in respect to parapsychology, is where the findings of psychical research are invoked to counter materialistic theories or break down some other form of the alleged dependence of mind on body which rules out the possibility of some life after death. Many have rejoiced in the prospect of settling the issue of materialism and related doctrines once for all in this way. The day has dawned

© Allen & Unwin Ltd 1976

when we need not be troubled by these awkward doctrines any more – their spell is finally broken. But this is very false comfort. Materialism seems to me about as implausible a view as any we could adopt, and I marvel that ingenious thinkers still persist in it. I also believe that there are fatal objections to various forms of the 'identity thesis'. But this must be shown on its own account: if materialism is false, it must be shown to be so as a general account of behaviour and consciousness. If we fail to do this we cannot turn, as a last desperate resort, to psychical research. For, if a materialistic account of consciousness in general is plausible, it will not be very hard to extend this to the peculiar experiences and situations presented in psychical research. We must take the case for the non-material character of consciousness on its merits; it must stand or fall quite irrespective of any particular finding of either recent psychology or physics. The appeal must be, for us as for men in times past, to what we find consciousness, in its varied forms, actually to be. We have no advantage here over Greek philosophers or any others. Experience itself must be shown not to be neutral here. If that will not do, nothing will. We must win the major battle and not allow our forces to be deployed wholly in a skirmish on the edges of the field and without proper support.

This being said, I must add, however, that those whose anxiety over corporealist views of personality stems mainly from the threat to expectations of afterlife, may well find considerable reasons for continuing to have those expectations in the findings of psychical research properly assessed. It will be unwise to proceed as if the issue rested solely on such evidence. If the corporealist views are sound, no amount of evidence will help. For, on that assumption, there could be nothing which could survive the dissolution of our corporeal existence. Some seek to retrieve the position here by extending their notion of our corporeal being, for example, to include an astral body. But, in addition to many other difficulties in this notion, there must surely be little point or comfort in the expectation that, when the body of which we are normally aware is reduced to ashes, an astral body, and that *alone*, will survive. Invoking the astral body will only help if it is allowed that a great deal more is involved. The idea of an astral body could indeed have significance if it were shown that strict continuity of our present materia existence is essential for any thought of our continuity as persona beings. But it is also well to point out that the arguments for some kind of identity or other corporealist thesis rest on ways in which the body, as we normally apprehend it (affording a 'point of view' in perception etc., and causally affecting our mental processes) is vital, or thought to be vital, for an adequate under-standing of persons and their experience. The astral body hardly comes into the picture here, and it is hard to see what function it could be thought to serve which could not be ensured equally well by some other body, an entirely new one which we might acquire or have conferred upon us. Indeed, much of the alleged evidence for the astral body could support equally well the idea of some different body or materialisation which comes about in special conditions. But even if there should be outright physical evidence for a properly physical astral body, or some like extension of our corporeal existence, this would seem to have little interest for us except as a means of sustaining more than an astral body in itself. To the extent that the astral body is a feature of our normal physical body or in some way continuous with it, the question must also be asked how plausible it is to suppose that the one can survive what seems to be such a total dissolution of the other. I will not pursue this further now, as I am convinced that those who entertain ideas of an astral body have not yet done their philosophical homework upon it. I return therefore to the main point that, with or without the idea of an astral body, such evidence as we invoke must relate explicitly to what we find ourselves, as experiencing beings, to be.

The substance of the evidence alleged to be relevant here, must consist largely, it seems to me, of ways we may be thought to acquire information which could not easily be explained except on the basis of its being communicated to us by persons who were once alive in this world but are now dead. The form which this might take, and the stringency of the tests we should apply, have been considered in more detail by me in my book *The Self and Immortality*. It is in terms of communications most plausibly attributed to 'departed' persons, rather than on eventualities of a more strictly or exclusively physical sort, that the most serious claims for psychical evidence for survival have usually been advanced. If some material component of me, and that alone, were shown to survive, it would not interest me more than some assurance that my bones were indestructible. To prove that conscious or intelligent creatures survive I need some evidence of their existence as conscious or intelligent creatures.

To examine the evidence we have in these ways for some kind of afterlife is too ambitious a task to be undertaken here, and it falls outside my scope. But it is not without significance that clear-sighted thinkers and investigators like H. H. Price have found the evidence in some cases sufficiently strong to warrant a firm indication of some kind of life after death. My own verdict, from a much more limited experience of the subject, would go the same way. If this is a reasonable view of the present state of these studies, then the implications of it are very great indeed.

Admittedly these findings of psychical research will not give the religious person all that he wants, or anything like it. The most that seems to be established is that some persons live on for some time after the destruction of the present body, though with a presumption, one might well suppose, that, after surviving so radical a change, the soul is not easily destroyed. Nothing is established about life eternal, and there is little indication of the quality of the 'life beyond'. Much that seems to 'come through', in mediumistic and other evidence, is remarkably trivial, although there is significant indication of a concern the dead continue to have for the living. But Professor Price has effectively pointed out that the appearance of nonsense or triviality in many of the supposed communications may be due mainly to complexities and imperfections in the mode of its transmission at present. It may not even be possible to convey to us, in the particular conditions of the present life, any distinctive richness of a radically different mode of being. But even if all this is granted, and if there proved to be nothing peculiarly exciting or inspiring in reports of a life beyond (and that is certainly too gloomy a view of the available evidence), the mere fact that there was distinct indication of there continuing to be life for us after we are dead – this would be quite momentous in itself.

That the evidence at present does not cause much of a stir is mainly due to the fact that, as in more popular accounts of hauntings and curious visitations, the reports are deemed to be too ambiguous and uncertain to be taken very seriously. They are thought to be stuff for the credulous and the uncritically pious. But if the evidence proved to be such that sensible people would have to accept it, or accept the substantial consensus of competent opinion, as we do in astronomy or medicine for example, then I find it hard to believe that this would not cause the greatest excitement, and indeed lead to radical changes of outlook.

This does not imply that the thought of a future existence is invariably agreeable. As many, including Broad and Price, have pointed out, it has its sombre and daunting side. Indeed, on some religious views, the fear of death is greatly inflamed by intimations of terrible punishments to be incurred when we come 'to face our Maker', unending torment as some Christians have thought in their curious commendation of the doctrine of a God of infinite love. Quite apart from aberrations of this kind, there are many ways in which the thought of another life, especially one whose quality will be much affected by what we have made of ourselves in this one, is daunting. Indeed any radical change makes us nervous and can be extremely disconcerting. The outright pessimism of C. D. Broad may be idiosyncratic, but he is not alone in hoping that we do not have to live beyond our present span. The prospect that opens before us can certainly be daunting. It has an unmistakably sombre side.

At the same time I am firmly convinced that the great majority of men would find unbelievable comfort in an assurance which they could firmly accept that their existence is not finally ended at death. The dauntingness of the change, and the strangeness of anticipations of life in some quite different mode, are not the root causes of the fear of death, but rather the thought of our total extinction. To pass out into the black night of total oblivion is a fate which is peculiarly dreaded, to the extent that the prospect makes a real impact even with the further thought that we shall have no cognisance of it. The latter thought affords little mitigation of dread, and rightly so in my view. One's experience must be peculiarly jaded for us to take consolation in the thought that there is nothing beyond it. If, on the other hand, life has been found enjoyable and rewarding, if much has been achieved, the thought of further attainment and new experience and of fulfilment and enrichment not possible now, and of relief and compensation for many present ills, must surely be profoundly exciting and comforting. There should be nothing craven or cowardly in the thought of a life beyond.

I shall not pursue this further here. My view, for what it is worth, is that expectation of a future existence is a natural and proper one in itself and that the great majority would rejoice in any assurance of it. Indeed, if such assurance were unmistakable, that would not merely bring comfort to many, most of all at the death of their friends, but also open out new prospects and perspectives, sombre and exciting alike, that could radically alter our conspectus on a great many other matters and give us a more restrained and balanced view of our present fortunes. It would not give us all that various religions claim that we need, but it would give most of us a very new outlook and prospects which would substantially transform our attitudes and expectations from day to day. Life would not be the fleeting transitory thing which it seems to be for many. *Carpe diem* is not on any view a sound motto, and humanists know it well, they do not just eat and drink and be merry. But it does not follow that there may not be profound frustration for many at the limited and transitory character of present achievement.

The scriptures tell us of those who will not 'be persuaded though one rose from the dead'. This may be so as far as the profounder insights and transformations required by religion are concerned. But if anyone were unmistakably so to return, I can conceive of nothing that would hit the headlines more. And rightly. Far more would be involved than idle curiosity. The event might bring about a radical shift of interest, it would shake many to the foundations, and could perhaps work a major move forward in human affairs. Explorations of space might be nothing to it.

All power then to psychical research. It is not a panacea for all evils. Its potential is limited. But within its limits it could well have results, not merely of immense excitement in themselves, but far-reaching and profoundly beneficial for human society. Religious folk do ill therefore to look askance at, as very many do, or to fight shy of psychical research. They do well to insist that it is no substitute for religion, and that it does not come within its scope to meet the peculiar needs to which religion is addressed. It could well be that all, however fine and remarkable, could eventually defeat itself without religion. But there is no reason why psychical research should aspire to the place of religion, and it rarely seeks to do so. Religious people should not therefore look on parapsychology as a rival, or a dangerous pedlar of inadequate religious wares. They should view it, as many enlightened religious people do, as an ally capable of great achievements in a common cause and peculiarly helpful in a confused and sceptical age like our own. Indeed, nothing which markedly extends the range of human achievement and understanding is alien to religion.

As has been pointed out, however, the claims of religion itself are addressed to much deeper needs than those which can be met by psychical research, however novel and profound. The sort of phenomena of which we read in psychical research are those of clairvoyance, telekinesis, precognition, having dreams or apparitions which turn out to be of special significance, out-of-the-body experiences, etc. There is no inherent reason why any of these should not be understood in secular terms or admitted by a humanist. Even intimations of communications from the dead would not in themselves give assurance of more than an extraordinary extension of our own finite existence. This does not mean that we query the peculiarity of psychic phenomena as such or offer an account of them so attenuated that they are not paranormal at all. Nor does it seem plausible to me to account for paranormal phenomena exhaustively in terms of material conditions, as some would do. I believe such an explanation of any experience is in any case inadequate. All the same, we do not seem to have, in any of the alleged occurrences, more than remarkable extensions of the sort of powers we exercise normally.

Take causation at a distance. If I could lift the spoon at the far end of the table by just willing to do so, instead of walking round and picking it up in the usual way, this would be no more remarkable in the last resort than the control I normally exercise over my own body. It is just brute fact that I can change the state of my body in certain ways, and thereby bring about other changes. Explanation of how this happens is in terms of regularities in what we find in fact to be the case. If causal laws were different, or if we were endowed with different powers, these would be just further finite facts, and if they led out in some way to religion they would do so only in the same way in principle as any other fact of our experience. If we lived in a world of magic, as we might think of it now, there would be no more cause for wonder than there is already at the way we find things now.

The case is not substantially different, it seems to me, in respect of clairvoyance or precognition. If it is proved that some people do have such powers, this may seem very bewildering in relation to normal expectations, and it may baffle explanation. But this would be only in the sense that such powers do not fall within the course of what we normally anticipate. Would precognition be any more remarkable in the last resort than the fact that we normally see things when our eyes are open? We can explain the latter in terms of affectations of our eyes and in consequence our brains. But why should this extraordinary thing come about that we have this sort of experience when the brain is in a certain state? To this we can ultimately give no answer. If our powers were different, that might be very important in various ways, but they would still be exercises of finite powers.

In an earlier discussion of this subject, I drew a distinction between states which are paranormal in respect of causal antecedents or the way they come about, and those which are in themselves inherently different from what we experience in the normal course of things. Lifting a spoon with a nod of my head would be very remarkable in the first way, in itself it would be the trivial thing it normally is. If I had considerable extension of such powers, this might have momentous consequences, but only by way of my being able to accomplish things I cannot undertake now, as someone who has learned to swim might rescue a person who would otherwise be left to drown. Acquiring a sixth sense would be a very different matter. I can form no idea what it would be like any more than someone totally blind from birth could have any proper idea of what colours are like. There may therefore be certain ecstatic experiences to which no proper analogy may be found in present experience, and of which no explicit account can be given to those who have not had such experience themselves. No one can deny that people do have such experiences, unless they claim that something inherently impossible happens, like seeing a square circle. There is no inherent reason why all experience should be the kind of thing we find it now, and if some people claim to have been lifted 'to the seventh heaven' or had some other experience of which they can give the rest of us no proper indication but only speak of it 'slant-wise', in terms of its conditions or accompaniments or in some very general terms from normal description ('wonderful', 'dazzling', 'horrible' etc.), then we certainly cannot rule this out in the sense of denying that they have had such an experience. They may have, but on the other hand we cannot accept this on their say-so. They may be lying, they may be deluded and not be having quite as odd an experience as seems to them. But the main point now is that, even if people do have experiences which are paranormal, in the present more intrinsic sense, this again does not in itself give us more than an extension of experiences which finite beings enjoy. We would have a parallel if most of us had been blind or deaf and some began to see and hear.

The mere fact of being paranormal does not, therefore, in either of the senses distinguished, provide anything of a properly religious significance. Everything will depend, as in normal experience, on the kind of paranormal experience it is. But this conclusion depends in turn, in some measure at least, on how the term 'religion' is understood. If everything which falls outside the normal course of our experience is thought to be religious, then paranormal experiences are obviously religious. In that case magic of any kind would be religious, and we might even find some persons apt to regard exceptional feats of science as religious – walking in space for example. There is no royal way of settling disputes about the meaning of a term like 'religion'. It is certainly used in a variety of ways and the list of possible definitions is a notoriously long one. But I should argue, however, as I have done at length in my book *Our Experience of God*, that the sustained and serious use of this term involves a reference to some ultimate existence in relation to which the fleeting and limited events of our finite experience find a more complete or abiding significance than they can ever have of themselves.

This may not require the sort of transcendent ultimate being, distinct from all other conditioned reality, which is prominent in most theistic religions. The case will be met, for some, in a monistic mysticism which accords a different role to seemingly finite things. But I should be prepared to argue that there must be a reference to some ultimate existence if the sort of aspirations we normally associate with religion are to be met. Postulation of beings vastly better endowed than we are and without our more obvious limitations, would not, I think, suffice although some would find it odd to withhold the term 'religion' in such cases. My own view is that the aspirations men have in worship, prayer, meditation and all religious living direct us eventually to a transcendent being to which we stand in a special relation. What significance has the paranormal in that sort of context? It should be evident that, if the word 'religion' is understood along the lines indicated, then the paranormal has no explicit religious significance as such. It provides only further finite phenomena, and it is important that this should be stressed if the proper aims and conditions of a religious concern are not to be distorted, and energies directed misleadingly to wrong religious channels. At the same time, intimations of paranormal experience have had a prominent place in various forms of religion down the ages. This is due partly to peripheral affinities, and to false and superstitious beliefs and misunderstanding. But this is by no means entirely the case. We have to hold the importance of the paranormal in religion in the right perspective, but that is not to deny its substantial importance, in itself and historically.

Some of this may be discerned in the initial or basic insight by which we become aware of some supreme or ultimate reality on which all else finally depends. Such a transcendent reality is essentially mysterious and, in essentials, incomprehensible to us. We know only that it has to *be* as the ground of all limited and imperfect existence. But from the nature of the case the apprehension of such an ultimate unconditional being has no proper parallel in ordinary modes of reasoning or in other finite insights. It requires a very special insight which is itself evoked by enlivened apprehension of the essentially incomplete and conditioned character of everything else, including all that we encounter day by day. Such insight is aided and stimulated by those features of our experience which stir us out of the normal round and complacent acceptance of things as they are. Privations, untoward events, and disruptive experience, enrichment of experience beyond what we normally enjoy, these and like occurrences help to elicit the sense of a reality mysterious, not in the limited existence which baffles and amazes at the finite level but which is not inherently beyond comprehension, but in the sense of wholly imcomprehensible being; and among the evocative and disturbing modes of experience and occasions which have this character there must surely be accorded a high place to any paranormal experiences which can hardly fail to disturb the unquestioning acceptance of things as they are, and point to a reality which does not fit at any level into the categories of normal accountability. This must be a major reason for the prominence accorded to seemingly preternatural features of existence in traditional religion.

Religion rarely stays, however, at the level of an intuition or insight into the peculiar necessity of transcendent being. In oblique and mediated ways the 'beyond' which eludes our proper understanding in itself may be reflected in the limited world of our own experience in various ways which religious life and the study of religion disclose to us. Proper account of these intimations of God in present experience and history is a considerable topic in itself. But it should not be hard to see that considerable scope may be found for paranormal awareness to ally itself with these intimations and disclosures of God, and be brought into their service. It could well be, for example, that the glory of God is reflected in some distinctively enriching way in modes of existence and awareness surpassing those available to us now, but of which we may have occasional glimpses. As the expression of religious insights understandably takes markedly figurative forms, the peculiar mode of experience encountered in some paranormal states could provide new and stimulating symbolism for the enrichment and communication of religious discernment, and there seems little doubt that this is in fact extensively suggested in prophetic utterances and kindred expressions of religious awareness at diverse times and places. Affinities with art, both from the side of religion and the paranormal itself, will likewise be very extensive in this particular context.

A further feature of these phenomena which we need to heed very carefully is the possibility of distortion and perversion, and therefore the perversion of religion itself. We may allow the preternatural to impose itself unduly upon us and mar the balanced judgement of our present existence and its aims which we need to cultivate and maintain. Religion itself is peculiarly open to perversion as the persistent warning against various forms of idolatry makes very plain. Religious practice has its dangers as well as its comfort and enhancement of being; in particular, in becoming aware of the demanding, disturbing character of the impact of the transcendent upon us, we tend to evade it by diverting its rigour and splendour to related features of the media by which it is conveyed to us, thus, as I have put it elsewhere, encapsulating the divine in the limited media, including our own religious roles and practices. Such perversion could in turn be aggravated and extended by its involvement in such preternatural factors as religion can most readily draw into its service, most of all if the latter are themselves abused or cultivated in ways at odds with the requirements of a rounded existence, whether in the furtherance of private aims or of our commitment to one another.

At this point we have, therefore, a highly significant clue to much that is suspect in the history of seemingly paranormal powers and their association with religion. In unholy alliance, religion and the paranormal can be peculiarly and extensively harmful, and it is a gravely irresponsible matter to play with either. We may, or we may not, invoke actual evil agencies other than ourselves with which we may traffic or by which we may be influenced or corrupted, and there is certainly nothing inherently improbable in such possibility, but in one way or another, in overt demonology or less explicitly, we may find the preternatural in religion a source not of enhancement and illumination, but of peculiarly ugly and harmful perversion. *Tantum potuit religio suadere malorum.* Rarely is this more evident than in the present context. The remedy is not to forswear all concern with the preternatural but to achieve proper understanding of it and its place in a properly guided religious awareness. Though all our highest attainments admit of perversion, that is no reason for resisting them; we should merely exercise greater care in the direction of them to their proper courses.

A further topic to which these investigations relate is that of miracles. It is again notoriously difficult to indicate all that a miracle involves, but it is hard to use the term 'miracle' in a meaningful way without presupposing some radical break in the course of events as they happen in terms of the regularities we establish on the basis of experience or observation. But such a break could include much besides miracles – genuinely open choice, for example, and paranormal events. To constitute a miracle, there must be not only the rupture in the normal causal sequence, but some association of this with a supreme or transcendent reality on which the finite order itself depends. How this is established is a further issue in itself. But it follows, if my main submission is right, that the paranormal as such is not expressly miraculous. On the other hand, it would not be surprising if elevated and highly charged religious states were to stimulate various paranormal powers which might otherwise be dormant. In that case the study of miracles and of paranormal powers might be found to throw much light on one another.

Closely related to this are the problems of the peculiar claims made by persons in various ecstatic states. These are also notoriously hard to assess, especially as the accounts that are offered of them are in highly figurative language. Some claims, as intimated earlier, may be dismissed at once if taken at their face value, for they seem to be inherently impossible. But the study of other paranormal phenomena, including those which may be deliberately induced by various physical stimulants or exercises, could help us to understand better what in fact is being claimed in ecstatic or visionary experiences. Study of the latter in turn could help us in psychical research. The important point here, as in the case we considered at more length at the start, namely evidence for survival after death, is that the properly religious issue, however conceived, should not be straightway equated with that of the preternatural as such. In practice the blend may be very close, but that gives us all the more reason for heeding the appropriate distinctions. Religion has to do, in most forms at least, with some reality altogether beyond finite conditions, and the considerations centrally relevant to it have little to do expressly with paranormal phenomena. Religious life proceeds for many people without thought of preternatural events, other than some relation mediated in present experience with a transcendent reality, involving, for most theistic religions at least, a continuation of our personal existence. Evaluational considerations will have a central part in this and thoughts of preternatural events, including miracles if they happen, will be peripheral and subordinate to more distinctively religious concerns. At the same time, if these warnings are properly heeded, the religious person disregards the evidence for paranormal phenomena at his peril. He throws aside a peculiarly valuable aid in directing attention from the more mundane course of events, or the mundane view of them, to suggestive and stimulating aspects of experience which may be closely involved with properly religious insight, and may help to arouse and enrich it. Properly conducted, the study of alleged paranormal events could prove to be of inestimable value in the due appreciation of religious claims in a largely secular age. That could be exceptionally fruitful when religion is considered in close association with the study of art and literature. I would thus like to close my present discussion with a passage in which I summed up my own understanding of the subject in my fuller treatment of it elsewhere:

The accounts we have of some supernormal occurrences suggest very strikingly that they may have an exceptional suitability for the purpose of enlivening religious awareness and providing a focus for it. It appears from some reports of paranormal states artificially induced, and thus subject to more deliberate and designed inspection, that they involve a very sharp impact on the mind of real objects in one's vicinity or of hallucinatory ones. This has interesting affinities with art and religion and if these should be confirmed and seen to affect imaginative power in general, it would give us reason to expect exceptional states of consciousness to have a function, not unlike that of art and in combination with it, of focusing and sustaining and extending our religious life as a whole. But if this should be the case, we come back again to the integration of individual occurrences, however extraordinary, with our total religious impressions as they disclose to us the character of God and of His dealings with us which are much more vital for our relationship with God than any incidental feature of the setting in which they appear.

4   Life after Death

A discussion between: Anthony Quinton (chairman), Fellow of New College, President Elect of Trinity College, Oxford; H. D. Lewis and Bernard Williams, Knightbridge Professor of Philosophy, University of Cambridge.

Quinton: In the past, although there was disagreement as to whether or not people actually did survive the death and dissolution of their bodies, it was not doubted that the personal survival of death was a conceivable possibility, that, whether it was true or false, it was an intelligible hypothesis. But in recent times many philosophers have denied this hitherto unquestioned assumption. They have argued that the mental life of human beings is in various ways essentially, and not just as a matter of earthly, and perhaps temporary, fact, bound up with their bodies. H. D. Lewis, professor of the history and philosophy of religion at King's College in the university of London, is going to argue the case for the possibility of survival against the conviction, that is now widespread among philosophers, that it is inconceivable. After he has spoken Bernard Williams, who is Knightbridge professor of philosophy at Cambridge University, and who is a leading exponent of the view that persons must be embodied, will question him. I will take part in the discussion from a position which is, I think, suitably intermediate between Lewis's positive belief in survival and Williams's denial of its conceivability.

Lewis: I recently read a tribute to a very fine lady who died last Spring. At the close of it the author said that this lady had

Radio Three © British Broadcasting Corporation 1975

now 'received the commendation of the Master himself'. Does this mean anything to us today except as a nice literary way of ending a tribute? The Master here is a man who lived very long ago in substantially the same conditions as ourselves (except for modern amenities), who ate and drank and got tired and slept, who enjoyed the world of nature and the company of friends, and who died a cruel death. Christians claim that they are in genuine fellowship with this man now and that after we die we are in a peculiarly intimate relationship with him and with others we have 'lost awhile'. And not only Christians. The claim that we live again after we have died is central to most religions. On a view that is very widely held we have many such lives. How many believe this today, or look for anything beyond the present life? That is not easy to answer, least of all if we think of a firm expectation and not some vague adherence to some traditional orthodoxy. Is there any sense in such an expectation?

It must be said at once that, if the view that prevails today among philosophers, especially in English-speaking countries, and is even endorsed by many theologians – if this view is sound, then that settles the matter for us; there can be no afterlife. The case for it is not just difficult, it cannot get off the ground.

I refer here to the corporealist view of persons, including what is usually known as the 'identity-thesis'. The most uncompromising form of this is materialism, of which there are gifted and vigorous proponents still. Unlike the 'old-fashioned' materialist, such as the behaviourist J. B. Watson, who held that our thoughts were literally movements in our vocal cords, unlike this the materialist today is more subtle and claims to have a proper place for intentions and purposes, and to distinguish properly 'between men and puppets', persons and clocks. But he can only do this in terms of complexities and patterns of physical behaviour, hypothetical statements and dispositions. He can, that is, allow no distinct mental process. Argument with such thinkers is most frustrating, for they expect us to counter their cases, if at all, by arguments which do not involve appeal to one's own awareness of having thoughts and sensations in the very process of having them; but the way we know that we have a pain, to take a simple example, and what pain is like, is just in having it. And so at all levels. It is not a case of looking in, in introspection, at what goes on. We know what our thoughts and sensations are like in having them, though of course there are further things to be said.

Now the 'identity thesis' allows for the existence, in some form of distinct mental processes but claims that they are nonetheless bound up with the body or identical with it in the last analysis. Two things may be involved here. One is the obvious causal dependence of mind on body in the conditions we know. The other is the more logical indispensability of the body, making possible a point of view in perception or a possible account or way of accounting for our continuous identity. I have discussed both these points in my recent book, *The Self and Immortality*. Indeed, I stressed the importance of the body in many ways in a chapter of that book. But I also insist that the course of our thoughts is not wholly determined by the body, it moves in terms of what it is in itself as well, and I hold, of which more in a moment, that we can be conceived to exist without at least the present body.

For the moment the main point I make is that, if any version of these fashionable views is sound, the idea of afterlife is out. For no one surely denies that there will be a complete end of my present body when I die. We may think romantically at times of the dead sleeping 'beneath that yew tree's shade' but we all know well that there are no people asleep in the cemetery, only corpses; and most of us nowadays will in any case be cremated; if we drown we shall be consumed by yet other creatures. Some will reply 'Ah, but it is not the resuscitation of corpses that we have in mind, but the resurrection of the body'. But in what sense the body? If a new body somewhat like this one, then that is a different view, and I shall come to it. But if I am identical with my present physical body, then the end of that body is the end of me.

To this some religious thinkers reply that 'with God all things are possible'. All right, but are we then seriously to think that God reassembles the dissipated elements of our bodies, or the basic constituents, atoms or electrons or whatever they may be, from the four winds or wherever, collects them to create literally the same body again? What conceivable purpose could this serve? What of any value could turn upon it? Surely, if we think of some further embodied existence, it must be with a new body, however like this one, If you persist in saying it must be this one, I must ask 'At what stage, of this body, when one's body changes so much?'

Now one further recourse that some have here is to the notion of an astral body. But there is much obscurity here. Such evidence as may be adduced for an astral body would seem to support just as well some other paranormal possibility. Nor is the evidence for it well sifted. We get by normally without much thought of an astral body, and the arguments which try to show that the body is essential for the concept of a person pass it by. Whether I have, quite unknown to me, such a body or not, that is not what I wonder about if I ask whether I shall survive or not. If, as is alleged, this astral body is a genuinely physical one, detectable by 'an instrument', as it has been put, it is strange that it is so little in evidence.

What possibilities, then, remain? One is reincarnation. We may live again on this earth, or its like. This is not, in my view, inconceivable, provided we can maintain the view of identity in a non-corporeal way which I have supported in my writings. But whether there is a good case for it otherwise is another matter. The general arguments, for example in terms of retribution or reward, seem to me very thin, and they are rarely exposed to critical scrutiny. The citation of evidence, the famous twenty cases of reincarnation investigated in a recent book, has many loopholes. In my last book, I indicated the sort of situation for which the idea of reincarnation might be the most plausible explanation. But it is hard to think of any case which would begin to have, that is any actual case, which would begin to have, the firmness and precision required.

There remain two major possibilities. One is that we shall live again, not in physical space, but in some other embodied form, or with a different sort of body. The model for this, as a rule, is the sort of body we have in a dream. We do, of course, retain our physical bodies when we dream. We do not 'leave' them. My body, curled up in a chair or in bed, continues to function, and to condition my experience causally. If I have a fever the state of my body will give me delirious dreams, indigestion gives me a nightmare. In some physical states while still asleep I may not perhaps be dreaming at all. Even so, I am not, as a rule at least, aware of my physical body when I dream. But I do have some kind of body, I 'see' things from a point of view and do things like playing tennis, walking in the fields, talking to friends, or running from a burning house in a nightmare. It may be said that I do not really see anything in a dream, because there is nothing there, no house is actually on fire. But my experience is so like seeing that I do not know any different at the time. The tree I climb is just like a real tree – it is not mental pretending. There are coloured shapes, sounds (though no one else hears them), quasi-sounds if you like but the experience is the same, somatic sensations, pain, sense of stress of things weighing on one or being crushed. I can likewise see parts of my dream body, just like looking at my arms and legs now.

The odd thing is that this dream body and the things in the scene around me do not behave like things in the real world, they change or disappear in a very random way, though we sometimes have very coherent dreams. They leave no effect on the physical world to which we return, and this is why we say they are not real. A real fire would have left my house in ruins. But they are real enough in their way, and so are the mental images I conjure up in a reverie; there are real coloured shapes before me at the time. And the suggestion is that another world might be like the world of images and dreams we have now except that there are stricter rules and consistencies determining the way things happen. If my body were whisked away while I dream and I nonetheless continued to have a coherent dream experience, this could be an excellent model of one sort of after life we may envisage.

Now hard problems arise of course when we think of communication with others. But there are problems about this in any case. Our awareness of other beings is mediated; even in telepathy we do not know the minds of others as they know them themselves. Why could not the same conditions hold in essentials in the image-world as in the physical world? Could there be communication also with the living? I do not see why not, provided the dead, in their world, and ourselves in ours, found that some of the things we do had repercussions, though not of course in line with physical laws, in one another's worlds. How could we know these things, with such a 'gulf fixed' between? In line, I suggest, with the way we might communicate with beings in outer space in terms of certain sights or sounds which look like

a code we learn to decipher and put to the test. In my book I
have worked out more closely how this might go.

The same principles apply in essentials, but obviously in ways
we find harder to anticipate, if we think of the remaining
alternative, namely that we should live again with no body at all.
It is hard for us to form any conception of what this would be like.
But we may approach it if we think of ourselves so deeply
absorbed in some intellectual activity that we become almost
oblivious of our bodies and our surroundings and suppose that
our bodies were then whisked away and we continued with our
train of thought. If this continued we would have what I have
elsewhere called 'a world of thoughts alone'. How would we ever
then in those conditions get across to other persons? Telepathy, I
think, affords some clue here. But there may be general ways in
which we might find some things seemingly imposed on our own
thoughts, not just normal disruptions of our concentration, and if
this followed a pattern, with appropriate changes according to
our own responses, we might find this the basis of what would
become in due course an easy and spontaneous way of communicating. It would indeed seem to us now that such an
existence would be an anaemic and colourless one. But intellectual exchange is not always unexciting, and there might
be many compensations and new modes and media of existence,
rich and rewarding and intimate beyond anything we can
comprehend now. We only know mind and matter. What other
dimensions might there not be? As Spinoza brilliantly implied,
we should not close the door on this.

But what then of our own identity in either of the states
described? My view, very sharply, is that everyone is aware of
the being that he is in just being himself. He may, in loss of
memory, forget his name, his home and much besides. But he
still knows that he is himself. Personal identity is ultimate, and
our awareness of it. But how do I know that I am the same from
one state to the next – and one world to another? Partly on the
basis of continuities of circumstance and awareness, but more
firmly and expressly through memory, in the stricter sense of my
remembering particular things myself, like coming into this
studio. I recall not only the coming in, but the total situation
including the same awareness of myself at the time as I have now.
This is not bound to happen in afterlife, that is we may live again

without memory of this life, as on some notions of reincarnation. For further reasons, connected with the kind of hope and reason we have for a further life, I think that unlikely.

A word before I close on the sort of reasons we may have for supposing, not that it is conceivable that we shall live again, but that we shall in fact do so. General philosophical arguments will not help much here, even though some of the most notable thinkers have tried it. The evidence of psychical research could be more important. It will not give the religious person all that he wants, but, if successful, it could make a radical and startling difference to our outlook. Religious persons are unwise to neglect or despise it. But the basic reason is religious, faith if you like, but not *blind* faith, a view of ourselves and the universe in which rational considerations are closely blended with sensitivity to the available religious evidence.

Quinton: Well I think a good point where we might start from, and I think probably the thing we should begin with, is that of the negative considerations that count against the idea of survival. I think what you referred to as the 'corporealist' view of persons in fact could be seen to embrace a number of different lines of attack on the idea that human personality can survive death. So I think it would be a good idea if I just disentangled three of these, because I think they're of different degrees of strength or radicalness in the undermining they claim to carry out on the view that personality can survive the death of the body. I think the one you perhaps spoke most about, what's sometimes called central state materialism, brings the least pressure to bear. This is the view that as a matter of fact, every state of mind is at the same time a state of the brain, that, as it were, the state of the mind and the state of the brain are two aspects of one and the same occurrence. But it does hold that this is as it were a matter of fact. It's a law of nature that, let us say, when states of the brain in a living organism reach a certain degree of complexity, they become at that level states of mind, one feature of which perhaps is that they are in some sense announcing themselves to the possessor of that brain in such a way that he's conscious of, and if suitably linguistically equipped, can report that this is going on in him. And the thing about this view is that all it says is that as a matter of fact all the mentality in the world we know of is associated with brains and it proceeds to exploit and develop this fact. But that of course doesn't say that the existence of mental states without brains is impossible. It just says that wherever there are mental states, there are in a very thorough and systematic way, brains.

So that's merely a dispute about how nature contingently happens to be. A more radical view, I think is what perhaps had better be called philosophical behaviourism. I'm thinking of the view put forward in Ryle's *Concept of Mind* where a mental state is said to be essentially a disposition of a living organism of a certain kind to behave in certain ways. And the thing about this is that there is no sense in ascribing a mental state to an individual organism unless that organism really is an organism capable of displaying the behaviour. It does not have to be displaying the behaviour when it is in a mental state, but for it to be in that mental state is to be disposed so to do in the way that a rubber ball lying on a shelf is disposed to bounce if dropped and so therefore is still elastic, even if not actually bouncing. Now this brings a more powerful challenge to the doctrine of the survival of death, because what of course it implies is that it is strictly inconceivable that there should be totally disembodied existence of persons. But it always seems to me that the Rylean doctrine is compatible with reincarnation. It doesn't require that a given mind, a given connected sequence of mental states, because a mind is at least that – and it may be more – that a given mind has to be affixed to one body, if that mind can be identified in terms of the memories it has at later stages of what it thought and felt at earlier stages, and again in terms of a, shall we say, continuously developing set of character traits, if a mind can be identified in that way, that particular pattern of character traits and memories could be exhibited, in principle, by another body. So although it does not acknowledge the conceivability of totally disembodied existence, it does at least allow for reincarnation. But there is, I think, a third view, and I think this is one that Williams would want to hold, which is that the concept of the body is indispensable for the work of identifying a person at a given time as being the very same person as some person who existed at a previous time, that it is a condition of doing this kind of thing effectively; and of course it's what we do whenever we recognise somebody, or use a proper name to refer to somebody, a proper name that's been used to refer previously. But this is only going to be possible in the light of the continuity, the identity, of the body that person has. And in that case of course, there is a body that is as it were proprietary to each person, and no one person could be possessed of two different bodies at different times. So, taking as you do I think the strongest counter-view to Lewis's, Williams, I'll ask you to say something on that.

Williams: Well I think that is a very important distinction that you have introduced there. Certainly the point I would want to press against what Lewis has said is this point about identity. Now as you have very properly distinguished, Quinton, I think we must emphasise that this isn't a question about behaviourism. I do indeed think, that as a matter of historical fact, philosophical behaviourism has tended to be more an answer to a set of questions about how we know that other people have mental states. It's an issue in the theory of knowledge perhaps rather than an issue in what persons are, which I think is what we are here fundamentally concerned with in what Lewis has said. Now I do not want to deny at all that there is as it were such a thing as the inner life – a mental life, concerning which each of us in his own case knows quite a lot. I don't want to deny that for a moment. I think there are a lot of philosophical issues about what the status of that truth is, but I do not want to deny it. But of course, and this I think is a very important point to stress, the fact that there is such a thing as the inner life does not mean that the inner life could go on if there was no bodily person to possess this inner life, and I would want to say that there must be a bodily person to have such an inner life. Now out of several reasons, I think that there are two separate points that I would want to distinguish, which I think are both implicit in what Lewis has said. And I think it is quite important that they are different from one another. The first point is that if I have supposedly a number of different persons existing at the same time – let us suppose that there are three persons rather than four persons existing at a given time – the suggestion could be made, and it seems to me a very plausible one, that the only way of telling them apart, the only comprehensible basis for distinguishing between them is that there are three rather than four separate bodies, exisiting at the same time. And indeed this of course is not necessarily a materialist or antireligious opinion. It was held by St Thomas Aquinas and was regarded by him as

the ground of the doctrine of the resurrection of the body, that if
there was going to be an immortality, it had to be an immortality
which took the form of a bodily resurrection for this very
reason, the, as philosophers sometimes put it, individuation of
persons at the same time. But of course, the fact that any given
person at a given time has to have one and just one body, does not
strictly imply that the same person over time has to have the same
body. Because it might be that at any given time I would have
some body or other to exist as a person, but nevertheless, it might
be thought I could swop one body for another, as in certain
doctrines of reincarnation, as I think you, Quinton, said in your
opening remarks. Now I want to hold the view, not just like St
Thomas, that at any given time you have got to have some body
or other, but that to be the same person, you have got to have the
same body. And I take it that the requirement that in order to be
the same person you have got to have the same body, over time,
does rule out immortality effectively; and certainly I gathered
from what Lewis said that he would not be disposed to disagree
with this.

Lewis: No, I would not.

Williams: Now why should we say this? Well I just want to
emphasise an exceedingly simple point, which is this: that
everybody who has any conception, however hazy, of either a
future life, resurrection, immortality, and so on, or just, come to
that, a conception of his own future, thinks that he has got a
clear idea about the difference between something in the future
happening to him, and something in the future happening to
somebody else. And unless you have that idea, it seems to me you
haven't got any control over the idea of a personal immortality.
Now, if we have got an idea of the difference between something
happening to me and something happening to somebody else, it
seems to me we must also have an idea of the difference between
something happening to me, and something happening to
somebody else who is just like me. Now, take any of the set of
mental properties which Lewis has emphasised, such as, it might
be, a disposition to remember certain events, or to have certain
characteristic dreams, it seems to me quite clearly that the
following scenario is possible – that I should die, and that some
mad scientist, whoever he might be, should rig up somebody else
to have just the same sort of experiences as I used to have, the

same sorts of dreams as I might have had; and I want to say that that would not be me. That would be somebody who had mental properties very like me. And the trouble is, to put it, if I can, in a sort of metaphysical nutshell, the trouble about mental properties, including memories, dispositions to have dreams, whatever you like, is that they are properties. That is, lots of different things can in principle have the same ones. Therefore they cannot possibly secure the difference in it being me who has these future experiences and not somebody who is just like me. And since any belief in immortality is based on the idea that there really is an enormous difference between me having certain experiences in the future after death, or whatever it is, and somebody just like me having those experiences, it seems to me to follow that there must be some basis for distinguishing those two. Mental properties of whatever kind, memory, dispositions dreams or whatever they are, being properties, cannot secure that. And the only thing that could secure it is the identity of the body.

Therefore, to summarise my view, we all believe, if we are at all interested in immortality or any such similar expectation, in the difference between it being me and somebody else. That is the difference between identity and similarity. The only thing that can ground the difference in identity and similarity is the body, therefore I have no future without my body. Therefore there is no such thing as immortality.

Quinton: Lewis, what do you say to that?

Lewis: May I refer first to the three distinctions which Quinton drew? Because, it seems to me they could be a little misleading in one way. Williams's position is really closer to my position than the ones you distinguished earlier, especially the central state theory, because there you do have to identify the mental processes somehow with the state of the brain or some bodily state. You spoke of the brain state becoming a mental state, and so forth, and of association of one with its other, but the brain is indispensable there. You cannot have the mental processes without there being the physical processes. And that, it seems to me, makes it peculiarly difficult to suppose that we could survive the dissolution of the physical states. Similarly when we speak of a kind of Rylean doctrine and of one's surviving in the sense that the same dispositions continue or the same frames of mind, the same skills and so forth. That is very far removed from any sense in which you might really want to say that I have survived and the sense in which one would be interested in whether I survive at all. But Williams does really recognise processes, or an inner life as he called it, which are not reducible even to dispositions, much less to just physical states. And so the crux of the problem really is whether these mental processes can be thought to have an identity, or whether I can *be* as a person having these mental goings on, and can be identified at all, without reference to a body. Now, one thing I would like Williams to consider here is, what about the case of a dream in which I am quite conscious of who I am? It's all happening to me. I am doing certain things, but I am not in the dream conscious of this present body. It is causally effective, admittedly, but that is a contingent relation-ship. But I can quite well recognise myself and have various things happening to me, without at least this particular body – and I identify myself through the dream body. What is wrong with that sort of identification? Could we start with that?

Williams: Yes. I think that that helps me to explain my position, because I think that the question you have just raised is a different question, if I may say so. It is, it seems to me, a question which relates to the issue of how I *know* who I am, whether for instance, in regard to a dream, I have a sense of who I am or not. Now as a matter of fact, one thing about dreams is this, that one of the delusions or illusions one can have in a dream is that one is somebody else, that one is different from the person one actually is. But that is not the main point. The questions you have just raised are questions about how I know who I am. But that's not the point I'm making. The main point is that when you think about what is promised you – some-body comes along and says 'I promise you immortality' – then it seems to me I have to conceive in the abstract, what it is I've been promised and ask 'is what he's promised me enough to make it me?' Now the mere fact that there will be a person alive in the year 3000 who believes he is me, is not a sufficient condition of my being alive or immortal then. For instance, there is a very well-known case, you will remember – well there are various cases – of persons who have been persuaded that they were other people in the past. They have acquired delusive memories. They have had dreams of various kinds and so on. Well-known cases have been cited in the literature of this subject, for example that George IV towards the end of his life, as I seem to recall, was convinced that he fought at the Battle of Waterloo, which was a totally delusive memory on his part. Now to be told that somebody will exist who believes that he did all and only the things that I have done, is certainly no reassurance at all. So I do not think it is a question about how we know who we are. The question is what conditions have to be satisfied for somebody actually to be me.

Lewis: Yes, these are really two different questions. I agree that the question of whether you can be yourself, after your present body has been destroyed, depends on how we understand what it is for you to be yourself now.

Williams: Surely.

Lewis: And on this I take a different view from you. The question *how we know* is a different question.

Williams: Quite.

Lewis: And that question depends upon memory, among other things – the more obvious way of *knowing* that I am the same person is that I might remember what I have done and so forth.

Williams: Of course.

Lewis: And there would, I agree be other difficulties about that.

Williams: And knowing who you are usually means, I mean in ordinary parlance, being able to answer questions about your origins, your past experiences and things like that.

Quinton: It is knowing who you were.

Williams: Yes.

Lewis: Well at a certain level it means that. If somebody asks me 'Do you know who you are?' I would say 'Yes, I'm Lewis. I live in such and such a place. I'm fond of certain things' and so forth. That is one way of identifying me but all this happens to a particular person all the same and the basic question is how do we understand that and how do we identify ourselves at that level? Because these things, my experiences, where I live, the sort of chap I am, could happen to other people and be true of them. And what I say here of course – and this is a point where we really differ – is that there is something immediate and ultimate about the way in which I know that I am this being now whatever my experiences.

Williams: Well of course there is a general rule in philosophy that whenever the phrase 'immediate and ultimate' comes up, one reaches for one's analytical gun. I mean it probably means that you have just run out of steam in explaining what one is trying to say. There is of course a certain something called the sense of identity, but I would want to distinguish two things here. We say we have a certain sense of who we are now, and this seems to me an enormous complex psychological function of one's emotions, one's memories, one's dispositions to have certain memories and, very important, a sense of one's body. I think that if some terrible thing happened to you suddenly and you increased by three hundred pounds in weight, you would in a certain way lose a sense of yourself for a short time. But there is an absolutely abstract sense of the self, which a man could have even if he totally lost his memory. The trouble about that is that it seems to be just equivalent to being a conscious being, and it serves to distinguish nobody from anybody. That is, it is true of absolutely every conscious being, that each X has a sense of being X. But if I am just told that a man is going to be alive in a hundred years' time who has the property that he knows who he is, that does not get me anywhere near to supposing that he has a reason for thinking he is me.

Lewis: Ah, but you said *a* conscious being. But it wouldn't be that. It would be *this* conscious being.

Williams: Yes, but what is the ground for saying it is this conscious being? You see I have described to you a being who exists in the future.

Lewis: Yes.

Williams: And I say, look I am going to tell you some things about this being. Some of his memories partly resemble your experiences, some of his dreams are rather like your experiences. He does not have the same body as you. He has got a perfectly new body and what is more, let us just add for good measure, there are two other people like him at the same time. And they are all you. Now suppose I say that that is absolutely unintelligible. I mean, no ground has been offered for saying they are you.

Quinton: Can I just break in for a moment here before we lose track of something. You, Williams, wanted to distinguish very firmly between the questions of *knowing* one is the same being and *being* the same person. And you said the whole matter of whether the assurance of survival is a real assurance hangs on the second of these, of being the same person. Well now let us consider the, shall we say, unreflective philosophy of those Egyptian leading political figures and rich Californians who had or have themselves embalmed. They clearly were Williamsites if I may so describe them.

Williams: Yes. Surely.

Quinton: As far as they were concerned they wished to be magically brought to life again, or in the Californian case, presumably unfrozen.

Williams: Scientifically brought to life again. Yes.

Quinton: But of course if somebody says, well I am perfectly prepared for a thousand dollars to freeze you and store you for a modest rental geared to the cost of living and unfreeze you – unfortunately we have not got all the bugs out of this yet – you will, when woken, of course continue to exist, but you will be unable to recover any memories of your life now. (You may hear in my voice distant echoes of Leibniz here.) That is, what is the value of the assurance of continuation when it doesn't involve any recollections of your existing life? In other words it becomes a rather hollow assurance of identity of body alone.

Williams: Can I make two points about this. The first is that I regard the question of the value of my survival and the fact of my survival as two different questions. In fact I have the general view that what I regard as the case, namely that survival is impossible, is in fact exceedingly fortunate, because it seems to me that the value of survival under most conditions, and especially those advanced by Lewis, would be very low. But that's a different issue from what we are presently discussing. It is certainly possible for me to envisage its being me, but my having lost my memories. One reason I have for saying this is that we have good reason to try and avoid it. That is, suppose that I am told that there are two courses of action. One of them will lead to my death – I will stop. The other will lead to my vegetating in some fort of dementia condition, no memories, no sense of myself etc. I shall be just sitting there. Now it seems to me I have, and I think that everybody agrees with me about this, and certainly many persons who would support euthanasia would agree, that we all have reason to avoid the second. Now our reason for avoiding the second, namely a state in which we are living in a dementia, memoryless condition, is not just the reason for not wanting another memoryless person in the world. Their reason is connected with the idea that they would not want it to be *them* who are living in the world without a memory. Now that just seems to me to show that we can separate the questions. Will it be me? And will I remember? That is, will I know it's me?

Quinton: Well, I think that is susceptible of other explanations, we are after all familar with plenty of cases of recovery of lost memory – we are not familar with any, shall we say well or very well, authenticated cases of revival from properly certified death, followed by a month or two during which processes of decay go on. I am trying to screw this down pretty tight; in the simple proposition of ordinary psychophysiology, when you are dead you're dead. But when you have lost your memory, like other things, collar studs and what have you, you may not have lost it for good. And you may recover it but be still in a pretty elaborately damaged or debilitated condition. I mean that for many people, in this contingency as in others, there are fates worse than death. And the continuation, coming round, as it were, in a gravely debilitated condition, might be one you would wish to avoid.

Williams: Yes. Well that may be an explanation of course.

Lewis: He might wish to avoid it but he would be the same person in it, and this is the main point.

Williams: We seem to agree about this.

Lewis: Well, you say a person might lose weight or gain a tremendous lot of weight and change in certain ways and at a certain point not feel that this was himself. In a certain sense, this is so. But generally he will say 'this terrible thing has happened to *me*'. *Basically* everyone knows that he is the person he is. And when you say that one runs out of steam when one says this sort of thing, that is not really the case. Even Wittgenstein had to say that a philosopher must know when to stop. There are certain things we do know immediately and we cannot argue further about them. And one of the obvious ones for me is my own awareness of the kind of experiences I am having and that I am having them, and this I is not something you can further describe or analyse; and what you are challenging me to do, and trying to force me to do, is to give a description of this something which I cannot describe and which will survive though not in my view without other characteristics, experiences, emotions, feelings, doing things, and so forth.

Williams: No, I am sorry, that is not right. I think there is a slight misunderstanding here. I am not asking you to answer quite that question about describing this 'I'. Let me repeat my question. I think you will agree with me that there is a difference between being held out the expectation that I shall live in the next century, and being held out the expectation that there will be somebody who will live in the next century who is in various ways like me. Now, if I ask you what is the difference between those two expectations? If you tell me that the fact about this person who is going to live in the next century is that he has the following belief, namely, I am I, then you have not distinguished him from anybody else. Because everybody has the belief that he is he. So you have just picked out a feature of what it is to be conscious, not anything which picks out anybody from anybody else.

Lewis: It picks it out for the individual himself.

Quinton: The thing is, it only relates to what he is at the moment. I mean I am the present I.

Lewis: That's right.

Williams: Well, consider the man who is hit over the head. Maybe the police find him wandering around and they ask, 'who are you?' And he says 'I'm sorry I don't know'. And then being mildly philosophical, he says 'well of course I know I'm me, but I don't know who I was'. And the whole point is about the connection between what makes anyone now and somebody in the future.

Lewis: Well, there are two things. First there is what makes him himself at the time and this is I think more than there being a conscious being. At the core of all our awareness there is the awareness of all this happening to oneself. And there is the further different question, how would I know that the being I am now, having these experiences, is the same as the one who came in half an hour ago, and who did other things? This is a further separate question. And this does involve memory and things of that sort, although I think it can be coped with without any reference to the body.

Quinton: But it is surely that further question that is strictly relevant to the point at issue, isn't it?

Williams: Yes. That's right.

Lewis: Not altogether.

Quinton: Because Williams's question is how are we ever to be sure that some person exists, or how is it ever to be the case that some person existing in the future is the same person as a person existing now.

Williams: What I want to know is what are we promised, you see? It's not how will that man know whether he is me. Because we have already agreed that it is possible to be me and have lost my memory and so on.

Lewis: Yes.

Williams: The point then is not how will he know he is me. My point is, how do you explain the difference between two predictions, one of which is that I shall survive and the other that I will not survive but that somebody else will. Now one way I can sharpen the question is this. Take your sense of identity, I mean this sense of being oneself.

Lewis: Yes.

Williams: This very intimate unanalysable sensation. Now that is a psychological state. It is a certain kind of psychological disposition, well – state or disposition. Right?

Lewis: It is something quite unique and it is not just an ordinary disposition.

Williams: Well now yousay it is quite unique. Quite unique.

Lewis: This is what is difficult to describe you see, because, there is nothing more to be said about it except that everyone just has this awareness of themself.

Williams: But the point is this: it is perfectly possible to have something about which nothing can be said, that is very difficult to analyse; but there could be two of it. That is I could have two things each with an unanalysable quality, as when Moore said you recall, that it is very difficult to capture the essence of yellow – it does not mean I can not have two yellow things. Now if there is an unanalysable sense of being why could it not be predicted that in the year three thousand or two thousand, there will be two people who will have just that sense?

Lewis: Because by the very nature of it, it is something unsplitable, undiversifiable, in that way. It is an immediate sense of something ultimate and final, which is the core of the person as he is.

Quinton: What is clear here is that you are both wanting to put forward different things as the real, individuating factor if I may coin a bit of jargon for the purpose.

Lewis: Yes.

Quinton: And to one extent I think the advantage is on Williams's side because his individuating factor is one we are pretty familar with, that is to say, the human body, the human body for whose continuity through time there exist fairly firm criteria. You Lewis are, to that extent, at a disadvantage because your individuating factor, although it is something about which you feel strongly, you have to admit you find it difficult to express it in an explicit, definite way. So that a coarse person like myself is inclined to say, 'yes of course, you're saying something which is too true. I am I. Just the blank, reiterative, tautological, statement'. On the other hand, I think he is in a way, at a bit of a disadvantage just because of the clarity of your example because it doesn't seem to me that there is any necessary objection to duplication of bodies, for example by amoebic splitting or something of the sort, that puts them in an utterly different case from the splitting of what I'll call personality complexes, all those things you say could be possessed by two different people in the future.

Williams: Well of course there is such a thing as amoebic splitting, and though it is a very large argument about what one wants to say about the case of a body that's split into two, I would say that it was on a quite different footing from the other. I would want to say that if a body split into two then neither of the resultant bodies is the one you started with. I think there are philosophical arguments for saying that. I would say that that would destroy identity. But the thing about that is that splitting is as it were a concrete feature of the history of a body, connected with the whole idea of tracing a body through time, whereas reduplication of these non-material, non-corporeal entities, would have no such in principle detectable or establishable history. It would not be part of the history of any of them. You could just multiply them indefinitely. And I would add another point which seems to me on my side in the contrast that you have made here, namely that it is not just that we are more familiar with bodies as identifiable items, concrete items of our world, which we build identity on, but that the unanalysable, inexplicable sense of being oneself, to which Lewis has referred, also, in one sense, falls into a category of things which we are already familar with. We are familar with mental states; and one thing that is a feature of our way of looking at the world is that we know already that these states are in the class of properties, attributes, the sorts of things that more than one thing can have. So that from the beginning, this other item is as it were doomed to head towards the class of the inexplicable.

Lewis: Oh, no.

Quinton: Actually, I think one could resist that by saying that the characteristic of real personal memories, direct recollections of things you have done, tend, shall I say, essentially to involve the mention of unique things. Such as breaking a particular vase. There are a lot of other things that are just as, so to speak, straight-forwardly spatio-temporally individual as the body, and the memories will contain not just the breaking of a vase of a certain description, but (why not?) breaking a particular vase?

Williams: Right. But then there seem to me two points about that. One is that here you are going back to the appeal to memories, which was not Lewis's strongest point, because he offered us a future in terms of dreams, in terms of intellectual activities, not based on memories. And secondly, insofar as you have appealed to memories, you have appealed to memories where it is a question of being in bodily relations to things. Because what brings me into relation with this vase is being the person, the bodily person who dropped the vase. Now suppose my history was entirely of these rather boring dreams, or these intellectual ruminations to which Lewis referred, even the memories would not be anchored in the concreteness of objects, physical objects in the way that you refer.

Lewis: But there are really two things you must distinguish. The question of what it means to say I shall be the other person if I live again, and on this I stand on this notion of the self as something ultimate and distinctive. But if the further question is asked, 'how would I know in some future state that I am the same self and person as I am now?', there I invoke memory. And you have attacked this notion on the ground that the memory would need to be checked and so forth and that this would involve reference to body; this I also dispute, because it appears to me that there are cases where we expressly, directly, remember and that doesn't need to be checked. And this of course would make it possible for one not only to be the same person in another existence, but also to remember something about the present existence, without even the continuity of a physical brain.

Quinton: I think probably we have gone as far as it is profitable to do on the negative side of things. We've seen what Williams's principal objection is, that for any person existing in the future to be the same person, just to be, not to be known to be, but to be the same person as you, there has to be bodily continuity. Lewis says no, there is this somehow ineluctable sense of the identity of the self. We find that difficult to grasp but I think that is a point where we can stop here.

Williams: That is right. I agree.

Quinton: I think probably the profitable thing to do now would be to look at the positive things Lewis puts forward as sketching what kind of existence could be enjoyed, if that is the word, by a disembodied being.

Williams: Can I make a remark about that or a couple of remarks about it, rather quickly? I think that we have probably all got to agree that there is a certain temperamental element about this. It is perhaps partly a question about what one savours about one's present life as to exactly how far you eagerly look forward to the prospect of immortality, described in various terms. But I must confess that for myself, I found Lewis's very, admittedly, tentative sketches of what direction we might look, somewhat unappealing. It seemed to me that it had two aspects, and I'll make one point about each. One suggestion was that it might be a bit like dreaming, that is like continuous dreaming. This seemed to me to have the odd feature, leaving aside the other metaphysical difficulties we have talked about, that it makes the whole of future life into a kind of delusion. It is very like perceiving, he said, but it obviously is not perceiving, in just the way that dreaming is not perceiving and it seems to me that one thing I do not want to do is to spend the rest of eternity in a delusive simulacrum of perceptual activity. That just seems to me a rather lowering prospect. Why should a future of error be of interest to me? The alternative was the slightly higher-minded alternative, that it might consist of purely intellectual activity, which of course many philosophers have seen as the ideal future. I can see why *they* might be particularly interested in it; others might be less so. The question I would like to ask about that does tie up with our previous metaphysical discussion, namely, the more pure and impersonal the intellectual activity becomes, the less important does it seem to me that it

should be me. If, for example, we are going to have the intellectual love of God, or something, conducted in the future, might it
not as well be conducted by Spinoza or Plato or the world soul or
itself or something as by me? I am afraid I associate my life
rather concretely with my tastes, some of them are of a rather
bodily character, those I love and so on, rather than this somewhat etiolated system of delusions, which you seem to be offering?

Lewis: Ah, well, I do not think that the image world or the
dream world need be regarded properly as a world of delusion,
because in the course of it you would be having varied, colourful,
possibly quite exciting and interesting related exeriences, and
you would also presumably be in contact with other people, and
having richer inter-relationships with other people on the basis
of this richer fellowship.

Quinton: Can I just ask this: would it be that it would be just
seeming to you that you were having these relations...?

Lewis: No, no, I think there would be every good reason for
believing that you were really communicating with other
people on the same basis as we do now.

Quinton: Well, you might have reason for it, but whether you
were actually doing so is the question, but still – leave that for the
moment. If the alternative is that the dream is only a rough
analogy, not an actual description, of this future state, then it
seems that the natural thing for the person in it to do would be to
take himself to be in another world, as it were to have been
conveyed. I mean another world like this world. On your first
description of it, it would be a world with physically embodied
beings and so forth.

Lewis: Yes. Well things like physically embodied beings, not
subject to the normal physical laws, and this might require a
great deal of analysis. But there would be certain things happening which could be very exciting and rich and rewarding,
including some media for communication with other people at
this level. Now I am not completely committed to this. I am not
completely sold either on the more intellectual version of a
possible survival. But I do not think that this tends in the least
towards the direction that Williams was suggesting, namely
something entirely abstract. I would be having these exciting
thoughts, mathematical thoughts, logical thoughts, whatever
they might be, and I might be communicating on the basis of

them with other people. And I could come to love, and admire, or perhaps hate, these other people in this way. It could be the medium for a rich relationship, and of course we are speculating here about a great deal which is bound to remain obscure to us and making the best guess we can. There may be all sorts of other things that would help out here, and it does not have to be either anaemic or abstract or remote, and of course I would invoke at all points my sense of one's own finality and distinctness; and this is I think the very core of the enrichment of our love of one another and so forth, all this could happen at this intellectual level as well.

Quinton: Could I just ask one question. In your discussion in the later stages of your talk, about these hypothetical possibilities of survival, in both the versions of it, the more or less dreamlike one and the more intellectual one, in both of them, you laid a certain amount of stress on how communication would be possible in this state of affairs.

Lewis: Yes.

Quinton: And I can think of two reasons for doing that. One a more or less emotional one, that a world of dreams might seem, or of dreamlike images might become, a very lonely place, and that one might find it so; the other one, the intellectual hypothesis, might become such a disembodied affair, like conducting your personal relations with computers, who would make rational answers, depending on the sophistication of their circuitry, to the questions you put them. But there is another and I think more fundamental reason. I do not know whether you would agree that this was working in you – that if you are not in communication with other persons, you are unlikely to preserve a sense of yourself. And if you have not ever had communication with other persons you will never acquire a sense of yourself.

Lewis: Well, I think one would preserve a sense of oneself, but it would be an appalling state if I began to realise that everything around me was a delusion. I would require, to sustain any kind of sanity or to prevent such a condition from being intolerable, to be assured that it really was contact with genuine other people.

Quinton: Yes. That puts one in mind of something else – this form of, I do not know whether it is psychological experiment or torture, or one leading to the other, these experiments in sensory deprivation. Now consider your final conjecture about how the afterlife might be in terms of mere telepathic intellectual communication. You said something like – thoughts seeming to be impressed on you from outside as a result of which you would assign them to some external source and somehow – I am not quite clear – communicate with them, with a kind of *umph* think something and get a response to it. Well, this looks awfully like an experiment in sensory deprivation. That is that all that's left is the thinking.

Lewis: Ah well, yes, it could be that. And it might involve this difficulty, though possibly there are some ways of overcoming it, or some compensatory factors, I do not know. But this is why I say I am not wedded to either of these views. It could be one or the other, or still something different again for all we know.

Williams: Could I make a quick comment on this? I think it is important to remember here that immortality has always been offered to us, or at least, if not always, in good part, by the religions as a hope. And for it to be a hope it seems to me that it has got to offer something which is of significance or value to oneself and to some extent at least to oneself as one now is. At the very least, one's got to be able to conceive of oneself as being a person to whom this will be of value. Now the trouble is, it seems to me, and this is a very broad remark, as you'll understand, that the scenarios for immortality tend to fall into two kinds. One of these is really rather like present life, and therefore it is inexplicable why I should want to go on like that for eternity. This seems to me true of all versions of spiritualism to which Lewis referred, where the. . . .

Quinton: the 'cigars are wonderful' type of thing. . .

Williams: Yes, exactly. I mean the drab offerings of the continuation of lower-middle-class Brighton life to eternity is really of such an insufferable character that the thought that I can not take an escape road by suicide is very depressing indeed. But the alternative is something vastly more, as it were, more refined than that, less literal, less materialistic than nineteenth-century spiritualism paradoxically was. And then the problem is the one of the identity of interest. I mean, suppose that the prospects of Heaven or the future life are those of intellectual contemplation and I am a jolly, good hearted fun-loving sensual character from the seaside, these prospects appear to me to command very little hold on one's loyalty.

Lewis: But ordinary people are capable, not necessarily of rising to tremendous intellectual heights, but of having a subtle refined appreciation of the things that count most in life. What troubles us about it all is that it is so limited and so restricted and fleeting and transitory, and the expectation is, and what makes people interested and concerned, is that they would want to expand their experience, to develop, not all necessarily along the same lines – some of us more intellectual, some less so, but having personal relationships at the very core of it, and there is endless scope for development, for enrichment, for colour, for excitement, in all this; and of course it is not for us to try to anticipate or set what limits there might be to developments in these ways.

Williams: You do not think that the significance of our personal relations is rather grounded in the actual contour of this life?

Lewis: Oh, no.

Williams: For instance in the notion of getting older.

Lewis: Oh no, not at all.

Williams: ... and eventually dying?

Lewis: No, not at all.

Williams: Well, that's a profound difference between us.

Lewis: Personal relations depend on what you really find yourself to be and what your circumstances and relationships with other people are like, these are capable of considerable extension and enrichment and of course if we invoke religious things and bring God into it, there is a whole other dimension of the enrichment of which it is capable which we haven't really touched upon.

Quinton: Yes the trouble is that so many of the emotions that are most fulfiling in life seem to have, if you like, an irrational element, I mean the love of a unique person who is in fact perhaps in the eye of an unprejudiced observer not terribly different from a lot of other people but to you it is something absolutely special and in this final conjecture of yours, there really is no place for that. All these rationalities as it were converge into something like Aristotle's God in purely intellectual communion with itself.

Lewis: Oh no, ...

Quinton: We have lost the plurality and richness of actual personal life in it.

Lewis: Oh no, no, no. The plurality is there and all the diversity as well which is what you regard as important in the plurality. I think there is more than that. But why could there not be all sorts of types, even if you think in this more rarified intellectual sort of way? People will be doing it in all sorts of different conditions and circumstances, with all kinds of possibilities of diversification. I do not think that it is bound to be drab if it goes beyond what we nowadys recognise as the most obvious ways of identification.

Quinton: Well, I think perhaps we had better leave it there. And thank Professor Williams and Professor Lewis for this discussion.

5 Survival

I HYWEL D. LEWIS

There is one point on which, it seems to me, my fellow symposiast, Professor Flew, and myself ought to find it easy to agree. It is this: if the corporeal view of the nature of persons, or some other variation on the fashionable identity thesis about mind and body (if there is one that is not properly labelled corporeal) were to be accepted, then there would be no point in raising the question of the possibility of our survival of death. Professor Flew himself refers, in one place,[1] to the universal fact of death, as 'an enormous initial obstacle'. I do not think that it is, in itself, as enormous as all that. It is what sets the problem. But if we hold some form of what is often labelled to-day as the corporealist theory of persons, then the fact of death itself puts an end to further debate. We do not deny that we do in fact die, however hard it may be to make this a 'real' and not a 'notional' belief in our own case, and when we die this seems to be the end, in a very final way, of our present bodies. It is not, on the view that identifies us with our bodies or regards the body as in some way essential for persons, that there is an 'enormous obstacle' to be overcome or that the case for survival becomes more implausible; the case just cannot get off the ground on this assumption, the question is closed at the start.

When we die, whatever the exact clinical definition may be, the body very rapidly ceases to function as the organism we have known and deterioration sets in very quickly, in due course it decomposes, leaving at most a skeleton. For most of us to-day, I imagine, as over the centuries for people in other cultures, there will be a cremation and the body we have now is at once reduced to ashes. It is no longer an identifiable body which could in a proper sense be identified with a person. For pious or sentimental reasons or the like we may label these ashes or the spot where they are placed, if not scattered to the four winds, with the name of the deceased, but no one seriously thinks there is anything other than lifeless dust in the casket, no labelling device we may adopt gives us any sense of survival in which we may be seriously interested. Likewise, when men drown and their bodies are consumed by other creatures in turn consumed by yet others, there seems to be as final an end of the body as could ever be possible. If I am my body I clearly cease to be when I am cremated.

The reason why people have not always appreciated this is that many, in some cultures especially, tend to take a highly romantic and unrealistic view of physical death, encouraged by much in our ritual. The 'rude forefathers' 'sleep' beneath 'the yew tree's shade', the dead are 'laid to rest', they are 'at peace', or they wait, like King Arthur's knights, in their dark retreat until the bell sounds and the hour is come when their country needs them again and they awake. But while our attitudes may in fact be coloured at times by these romantic ideas, no one now seriously supposes that there are people sleeping beneath the tombstones or that the ashes, however preserved, will be stirred to life again. That, in some Christian contexts at least, people have supposed that the graves and the seas will one day yield up their dead again is due largely to the highly unrealistic view men have been apt to take, with one part of their minds perhaps or in some moods, of decomposing bodies.

This may seem so obvious a point as to hardly warrant space in a paper of this kind. But in fact many religious people have taken comfort in the prevalence of various corporealist views of persons for the endorsement or support they think is found in them for what is sometimes thought to be orthodox Christian teaching. Even Professor Ryle, little though he may fancy himself in that role, has been hailed as one who has substantially helped to rescue orthodox religious thinkers from a grave predicament, one in which no less a person that William Temple thought we had been largely placed by the unfortunate influence of Descartes. Even Professor Strawson reminds us, with his tongue a bit in his cheek, one suspects, that 'the orthodox have wisely insisted on the resurrection of the body'. But I do not suppose that he considers his own position to be any substantial strengthening of the 'orthodox' expectation. There would be more to hope for in making the attenuated disembodied existence which Strawson thinks, with doubtful consistency in my view, to be at least conceivable on his notion of persons, a little less attenuated and unattractive. But then it would have to be less firmly related to oneself as 'a former person' in Strawson's sense.

The plain fact is that, however desperately 'orthodox' believers may seek comfort in the widely held corporealist view of persons and related teaching, such views are altogether fatal to most religious claims and certainly, on my understanding, to Christian ones. They are so, indeed, in more ways than one. For Christians have not only expectations of some 'life beyond', they also believe in a personal God. Critics have in fact invoked what they take to be the obviously corporeal nature of persons as a fatal objection to the idea of God as well. Thus Mr Jonathan Barnes, after a brilliant critical analysis of the Ontological Argument, sums up his own position tersely by noting that 'it is becoming increasingly clear that persons are essentially corporeal' and 'if this is so, then if Gods are persons, then Gods are essentially corporeal. Allow this, and it is reasonable to assert as an empirical truth that no Gods exist'.[2] This seems to me unanswerable granted the premiss. But this is another issue. At the moment what I mainly stress is that no form of identity thesis of mind and body, or any corporealist view, can offer the slightest comfort to religious believers. On the contrary they are fatal.

That is no reason why they should be rejected. Notions that are not reconcilable with religious claims, Christian or any other, must be examined on their merits. But we must not suppose, as many seem to do, that the task of the religious thinker is just to effect any kind of bridge or reconciliation. Our concern, whether religious or not, is not with building bridges but with the pursuit of truth. If doctrines incompatible with religion are sound, so much the worse for religion. We must not cry 'Peace' where no peace exists; and that is just the position where corporealist views of person and the belief in life after death are concerned.

It might be thought possible to avoid this conclusion in one of two ways. The first would be to invoke the omnipotence of God. If God is all powerful, is it not then allowable that he could reassemble the scattered elements of our decomposed bodies to constitute again the body we have now? There are some, it appears, who seriously expect this, although others, while stoutly maintaining their belief in the resurrection of the body dissociate themselves with equally firm, if somewhat odd, disdain from the notion of the resuscitation of corpses. My difficulty, or at least one basic one, with the present suggestion is to be altogether precise as to what is expected. What counts as the ultimate ingredients in my body to be reassembled after it has been consumed by worms or fishes consumed by generations of other creatures – or scattered as ashes? The original cells, we may be told. But these are, in any case, changed or lost in the course of my life. What number of them, or at what stage acquired to constitute me is thought proper; and what if they are now essential ingredients of some other organism, perhaps of the kind which may also expect to be reconstituted?

We may also ask, just what would be the point of this reconstitution. Assuming that God, if he is omnipotent could accomplish it, just why would it be thought that he would go to work in that way? What of any significance could be accomplished? Could not God, as omnipotent, equally well have provided a duplicate, a new body, original cells and all, exactly like my present one? I would certainly not know the difference.

If this seems a little light-hearted, let it be noted that no less a person than my distinguished former colleague in London, Professor E. L. Mascall, writing about 'the Real Resurrection',[3] as he puts it, is emphatic 'that Christ has risen in his body'. This body 'is unimaginably transformed, so that it is no longer limited by the restrictions of time and space though he can manifest himself in time and space to meet our needs. He is neither a ghost nor a zombie, but a living and transfigured man'. It is not enough 'to suppose that Jesus did really appear to them (the disciples) as a disembodied spirit, while his body remained and decayed in the grave'. He appeared 'as flesh and blood' though 'transformed flesh and blood'. He would not otherwise be 'totally victorious'.

This is contrasted with the view, firmly rejected, 'that Jesus was indeed alive among them, but only in a spiritual way, his body remaining in its grave'. The latter is the view of 'people who want a purely spiritual religion' and 'whose views about the ultimate nature of matter are derived from the physics and chemistry of the eighteenth and nineteenth centuries rather than from those of the twentieth'.

My main reaction to this is that I just cannot see what of importance, for general religious thought or Christian theology, is involved, in this context, in the insistence on actual flesh and blood and the same body in a strict sense. It would not, in my view, do for Christian theology, to suppose that Jesus was anything other than 'flesh and blood' 'in the days of his flesh', although what matters here also is that he should live and feel and sense things as we do. I would also insist that Christian claims, and central Bibilical themes, require the acceptance of substantial historical truth in the Gospels and the New Testament generally. My reasons for such acceptance and the way I understand and place it in the context of Christian doctrine, is too vast an issue to embark upon here. I certainly do not regard the Gospels as mythology, and I would not be content to say that the disciples just had 'hallucinations' and thereby 'persuaded themselves that he (Jesus) had come to life again'. They encountered him, and, in all likelihood, I should add, in some visible and tangible form, whatever its nature, though that in itself would not suffice to sanction their claims about him. But why, in this context or any other, should much be made to turn on whether his body actually came out of the tomb, as a transfigured body, whether it did or not?

To press this a little further, what is the difference between a body 'transfigured and transformed almost beyond recognition' and a new 'spiritual body'? What sort of continuity is there between the latter and the body that was laid in the grave? What of the latter has to be retained for any purpose that matters? I agree that we should not seek 'a purely spiritual religion' if this means taking a dim view of our bodies and the world around us. We differ much also, as philosophers, in the accounts we give of the nature of the external world and the way we know it. But wherever we stand between the extremes of a Berkeleyan view and some firmly non-phenomenalist or objectivist view of the present physical world, I find it hard to see why anything of worth should be made to turn on whether the particular body we have in the present existence is retained, in any significant sense, in any further existence we may have reason to expect.

Professor Mascall mentions 'the physics of the twentieth century'. He knows a great deal more about this than I do, indeed there are few theologians or philosophers who could claim his competence in that field, but I still find it very hard to know what it could be about recent physics and bio-chemistry which could make it more significant or plausible to suppose that something of the material composition of our present bodies can be retained in another 'glorified' or 'transformed' body when the former have been reduced to ashes. If we think of similarity of appearance or function (in some respects at least) then this gives us a sense of identity or 'the same body' which is quite consistent with the other moulding in the grave and not coming out of it, and this goes for whatever further structural affinity we may have in mind. The most that I can suppose here is that the ultimate bio-physical components of our bodies, whatever the scientists tell us now that they are, are somehow reconstituted as basic ingredients of a new body. If, for other reasons, we hold that this is the only way our continued personal identity could be conceived or established, then that is another issue. But even here I find it hard to understand how the case for bodily identity as a condition of personal identity is affected by anything the bio-physicist may tell us, however important on its own account. Such considerations figure very rarely in the philosophical controversies, and, if they did, some outstanding contributors to the debate would be badly handicapped. Is the philosopher's problem about the material world affected at all by physics?

There seems to me therefore little to be said, even when we invoke the omnipotence of God, for the view that, in some future existence, we must have again the body which has decomposed or been cremated. The best thing to say about that body is that it no longer exists; and if it is inconceivable, or otherwise virtually out of the question, that I should exist without it, then that I no longer exist. The body is no more and *ipso facto* I am not.

We have not however quite done with variations on the present theme, for, quite independently of any special invocation of God, some have ascribed to our bodily existence a feature, of a very special sort, which would make it intelligible that one's particular body should persist even when we fully allow for the processes of decomposition, cremation, etc. This is the alleged 'astral' body, a notion we usually associate with the less reputable and less plausible aspects of psychical research and theory, but which is apparently taken more seriously to-day by established investigators and thinkers, including Professor Flew himself, at least to the extent of regarding the doctrine of the astral body as a much more plausible basis for the belief in after life than any other. The 'insuperable' difficulties of 'the Platonic-Cartesian way', he writes, 'should now lead us to look with a new interest and respect at the way of the astral body'.[4]

There is however some confusion, and I feel that Professor Flew is in some measure guilty of it, about what we should understand by the idea of the alleged astral body. It could be thought to be some kind of non-physical 'dream' or 'image' body, or some quasi-body not in physical space and quite distinct from our present body, which we may have or enter when we discard the body we have now. The latter is, I think, a notion we can take seriously, and I shall return to it. But the astral body, however different from our normal physical body, is supposed to be a body we do have now, presumably all of us; and it is detectable, in principle at least, and under special conditions, in the normal way. A photograph could be taken of it and shown to anyone who cares to look. Accounts of the astral body are a little obscure, and it is never clear to me how it (or its close relative the 'aura' or 'subtle body' of Aurobindo and others) is related to my normal body. One has sometimes the impression that it encases the latter, or at least it takes its form and location from it. Sometimes it appears to be a feature (function?) of our present bodies, and at times it seems to be more like another body, conditioned perhaps by our normal one. But it certainly seems to be detectable in normal ways.

Professor Flew warns the supporters of the notion of an astral body of the danger that they will so qualify it that it become 'in effect not a body' but 'an incorporeal Platonic-Cartesian soul'. But I do not think he has in mind the distinction we need to draw carefully here between a strictly or totally disembodied soul, a soul in what I have elsewhere[5] called 'a world of thoughts alone', and a soul with an image or dream body not in pyhsical space. The main danger is of confusion with the latter. But if the notion of an astral body is worth considering at all in this connexion, as a distinct idea, it must be on the basis of its having physical properties of some sort or being detectable in physical space.

The word 'detectable' may however offer some difficulties here. For it is conceivable that an 'image-body', in H. H. Price's sense, should manifest itself from time to time in the form of apparitions, observed perhaps by more than one person, or even as a poltergeist which would leave physical evidence of its agency. How this might be understood and the source of it ascertained has been considered by me at greater length in the book mentioned earlier.[6] But it would still be odd to say that such agents were in physical space, even though they might materialise in it, and even be active at times. They would not normally be locatable at all, and their transactions with other agents would be in another sort of space. By contrast the astral body is meant to have at least a permanent footing in physical space, related to the location and apprearance, colour as well as shape it would sometimes seem, of our physical body. Sponsors of this notion are not as precise as one would wish, and much more careful analysis will be needed if it is to be examined seriously and with some bias in its favour by philosophers of Professor Flew's standing. But there seems little doubt that it is meant to be, not an occasional manifestation, but a permanent feature of our bodily existence (brutes presumably as well as human beings) or some attachment to it detectable, in special conditions, by physical means, an 'instrument' in Professor Flew's word.

It is not, in my view, worth spending much time over the notion of an astral body or its near relations, except to be sufficiently clear to avoid confusion with ideas for which more may be said – and that is, I think, important. The objections to it are twofold. Firstly, the inadequate character of evidence adduced in support of it. Secondly, that such evidence, when it can claim to be taken seriously, could support equally well alternative and otherwise more plausible hypotheses, such as the occasional materialisation or appearance of a non-physical or image body or other non-corporeal being. There is, to my mind, a substantial body of evidence, in the *Journal of The Society for Psychical Research* and elsewhere, which is taken by reputable investigators (Broad, Price *et al*) to create at least a strong initial presumption of some transaction with the dead or other non-terrestrial beings. It does not seem to be altogether

'ESP ongoings among ordinary corporeal people', in Professor Flew's terms again. But little of this evidence seems to me to point to the notion of an astral body, and it is only taken to support it because the alternatives are not clearly envisaged. If I am wrong the onus of marshalling the evidence effectively lies with its sponsors.

In addition one cannot but note the oddity of our having what might almost be called the encumbrance of an astral body when we have normally no consciousness of it and when it seems to have no function related to our normal transactions in this world. Why, if I may so put it, do we need it now? Will the soul come adrift in some way if it has not this spare bodily harness ready to contain it when we die? Admittedly there is much about our present bodies of which we are normally quite unaware. Apart from the fact that most of us are very ill-informed about our own physiology, it is only at odd times (usually if something goes wrong) that we think about it at all. I breathe all the time but hardly ever stop to think of myself filling my lungs with air. I could do most that I do without knowing that I have lungs at all or, as our ancestors did, without knowing that the blood circulates. We are certainly quite unaware of what the brain specialist could tell us, or, even more, of what the bio-physicist knows about one's body. But I do not question that I have millions of cells in my body etc. In this case, however, I do have reasons, including empirical evidence, for trusting the scientists when they claim evidence which they and suitably equipped people have for what I would otherwise not know at all about my own body. There seems to be nothing approaching this in the claims made for the astral body.

Nor, in spite of what Professor Flew says, is it clear how the case for survival would be helped if the matter were otherwise. The relevance of the idea of the astral body is, presumably, to the view that our personal identity requires bodily continuity. But the continuity ensured here is very tenuous. The astral body has, I suppose, the location of the known physical body. But how much more does it have of the properties of the latter? If very many, we might have again 'the death by a thousand qualifications'. If the astral body is distinct, but still undetected except in very special conditions, will it meet what the corporealist wants? The requirement of bodily continuity is usually made, in reputable philosophy, in respect to a point of view and the confirmation of memories etc. Can the alleged astral body, of which we have normally no consciousness at all, serve the purpose here? Would it do so in a way that could not be met just as well by a new body more appropriate perhaps to my post-mortem state? An unknown appendage appears to have little to do with me as a person; and, if there is a gain in causal continuity, this seems to be on a level with the supposition that the cells in our bodies might be recomposed. The connexion is too tenuous to matter.

These are the sort of considerations which, it would appear, the sponsors of the theory of the astral body must examine. They have not, it seems to me, begun to do so or to consider the relevance of their supposition to genuine problems.

A much more attractive course is to consider whether it may not be possible after all that we should survive notwithstanding (as most of us expect) that we come to the end of our physical existence when we die. If my present body is totally destroyed, what then? This seems to be a more hopeful line of enquiry than seeking to salvage the position in terms of desperate extensions of the corporealist view. There seem to be three main possibilities.

The first is reincarnation. On this view, we return to the present world in another body, not of necessity resembling the present one. This expectation is not widely held in the Western world, although, it would seem, there are thoughtful Christians who endorse it. But it is a central feature of both Hinduism and Buddhism and is entertained to-day as in the past by millions of people. It is part of a major culture, and we may do well to remind ourselves of that.

Even so, I will deal very briefly here with this notion. Much will turn, it is obvious, on the sort of identity we require. If we think solely of the way one person lives on in the lives or memories of others, there is no problem. Everyone can admit that. We may also say, without being misleading, that Guy Fawkes is back again if we find someone behaving like him. But this is metaphor. We would need more than that to say seriously that Guy Fawkes is back. If we think of identity in terms of some continuity of a pattern of experience, or, as some hold, that some divine element distinct from ourselves as we normally know ourselves, is identical in all of us and persists from one life to the next, then these are positions we can understand and consider. But in both cases we seem far removed from what we normally understand by ourselves, it is not a very full-blooded return to this world. I have elsewhere indicated the sense in which we may say more explicitly that a person who has died has come to life in the world again. This requires an 'entity' or 'substantival' view of the self. I have argued that on such a view, there is nothing inconceivable in the supposition that we may have more than one life in this world, even though there may be no remembrance of one in the other. The difficulty is to know that this ever happens. We may put our case on *a priori* grounds, such as that justice requires that we live out our *karma* in this way, or that it is part of our progress to greater enrichment. But we would have to face considerable difficulties, among other things, in showing how the fulfilment of the alleged requirement is guaranteed. The obvious alternative seems to be to appeal to evidence.

The difficulty about the evidence is that it is never precise enough. It usually takes the form of someone seeming to remember things he could not otherwise have known. An initial presumption of pre-existence may be created in this way. But the evidence, and the exclusion of possible alternative accounts of it, needs to be very firm indeed before we begin to have a plausible case. In the book I have mentioned I have sketched what would seem to me to be reasonable evidence for a strong presumption of pre-existence, though without wholly excluding other explanations. But I am not aware of any alleged cases that come near the strictness and precision we would require.

There are of course other problems, especially the much discussed situation where two or more people seem to have the memories of someone who has died. I have said what I think must be said about this in my book. We may say, for example, that the memories, in some cases, must be pseudo- or quasi-ones, or perhaps entertain the possibility that the same consciousness may be involved in more than one body, not so completely out of the question perhaps as we may at first suppose. But, for the purpose of this paper, I must be content to observe that while, on my understanding of persons, the idea of reincarnation is not ruled out on principle, the general case for it and the evidence invoked seem both to fall very far short of what we would consider a reasonably plausible case.

The second possibility is that we should live on, not in the physical world at all, though presumably in time, with a non-physical body, possibly resembling in some respects the present one. The best model for such a body would be H. H. Price's 'image-body' already much discussed by me and others. But we must not be too wedded to the form in which Price himself first mooted this. On such a view it would be conceivable that we should survive without memories of our previous existence or any thought of it, though *ex hypothesi* we would not know anything of a past existence in that case. But it is hard to see what purpose could be served by the bestowal of a further life on us in this way. Perhaps our earlier lives might be brought to consciousness, in part perhaps, at some higher stage. But one's initial expectation would be that in a future existence there would be some consciousness of the present one, and some continuity. The hard questions would be how would we know who we were ourselves, how would we identify others, how would we communicate and how, if we knew that we had lived before, would this be established?

I have said something on all these topics in my book *The Self and Immortality*. I have maintained, for example, that there is a basic sense in which everyone knows who he is independently of any mark or criterion. Each one knows who he is in being himself, but as others, like Professor Shoemaker, have maintained, though with a slightly different intention, no description of the self, in this basic sense, which distinguishes it from others and identifies it, is possible. In this basic sense, a person in some future existence would know himself in exactly the same way as now. But a linkage with a previous existence, as in the past of one's present life, depends mainly on memory which must be considered, for this purpose, to be extensively, though not infallibly, defensible in and for itself. Around the identity so established may be built up further describable features of a person, his likes and dislikes, history, etc., a man's identifiable character about which others may know in substantially the same way as himself. At the core is the way each individual is aware of his own basic identity, and, in ascribing experience to others credits them with the same awareness of their own irreducible distinctness. In essentials, there need be no difference in these matters in a future existence, provided communication is possible, but the latter could be ensured, in principle in the same way as now, through the consistent behaviour of image bodies, or their like, which, though not subject to physical laws, could have laws or consistencies of their own.

How, in more detail, this would operate I cannot unfold further here, and must refer you again to the fuller discussion in my book.[7] But the argument does presuppose a mediated knowledge of other minds whereby we pass, easily and spontaneously, from observation of bodies to apprehension of distinct mental existences. The stock objection that we would need initially some 'inner' awareness of other minds to make this possible has never seemed to me to have force. We credit the bodies of other persons with animation by minds like one's own as the obvious explanation of the way they behave, and if this argument can be sustained in the here and now, there does not seem to be any reason why the situation should not be the same in principle, though no doubt with many other differences unknown to us now, in another existence.

There may of course also be other means of communication, such as the extension of some form of telepathy, if we find reason to accept evidence for the latter now; and, as at present, the operation of such paranormal communication would be rendered easier by the initial communication and identification through our non-physical image bodies.

The question of a linkage, in a future existence, with our present existence, has further difficulties. They would partly be met by dependence on memory, and I see no reason to doubt that, if I became convinced that I was in another existence, and seemed to have clear memories of the present life, I could put considerable credence upon it, as I do now when I wake up and without any checking. Admittedly, there has been other checking in this life, but it does not seem to be just for that reason that we trust our memories. One person's memories might also be checked against those of others, and there seems to be no reason why other linkages might not be established. No one would be in physical space, and there could thus not be normal observation, but this need not rule out certain limited ways in which events in the world of physical space might have repercussions in another sort of world and reduce what would otherwise be total isolation. If any evidence of communication from the dead is acceptable, it might involve such repercussions as part of the explanation, but there could also be invoked some form of paranormal communication across, so to speak, terrestrial boundaries. I see no reason in principle why these things might not be allowed if, as in the case of communication through physical media we obviously must, we allow them 'here below'.

A further possibility might be that, instead of individual image bodies by which communication would be facilitated, we might be effective in a different existence through manipulations we could effect in one another's otherwise private image world, or some such medium. This would be like people in the present world having contact entirely through writing and other signals. In a different medium this might be more complete and satisfying.

The third form of future existence which we may envisage is one that might be labelled 'total disembodied existence' for which I have also elsewhere used the words 'the world of thoughts alone'. Here there would be nothing resembling our present bodies, no image bodies or their like. The problem of communication, for our understanding at least, would be much accentuated in this case, and the spectre of solipsism rears itself higher. But the position does not seem irretrievable, for there might be ways in which we could recognisably modify the course of one another's thoughts, effecting such patterned unexpected changes in them with subsequent response to one's own response etc., that the basis for what might become very full and intimate communion of persons might thus be established. That this seems peculiarly difficult now does not preclude its being easier in some radically different state.

A misgiving which many will have, no doubt, about these speculations is that the existences envisaged are thin and anaemic, or too intellectually rarefied, to compare favourably with the fullness of our present embodied existence. But that may be due to our limited understanding of what may be possible in these ways. Admittedly our bodies are important, not just in incidental causal ways but also through what they more directly make possible, and I have very much stressed that myself. But there does not seem to be any inherent reason why all that matters in present bodily existence, the tenderness of intimate contact, gesture, look, etc., might not be provided equally, and perhaps more, effectively in one of the modes of future existence I have

envisaged – and without many of our present extensive dis-
abilities. Indeed in new media there may be much enrichment of
experience we are unable to envisage now. Nor is this wholly
ruled out in what I have described as 'a world of thoughts alone'.
It might afford its own substitute and much compensation. In
addition, just as Spinoza thought of infinite attributes, though
we only know two of them, so there may be entertained the
possibility of various modes of existence, dimensions, if I may use
an over-exploited word, of which we have no conception at
present. We cannot rule this out on principle; and in other modes
of being there may be, not only the preservation of what matters
in a world of sight and sounds and sensations, which on the face
of it we would much miss, but also other glorious possibilities not
dreamed of now.

There is certainly no reason why someone who envisages some
form of future disembodied existence should take a dim view of
the body as some dualists, including Plato much of the time,
have done. Much less should the body be thought to be evil,
though that has also been extensively maintained.

It is implicit, however, in all that I have been suggesting in this
paper, that we can fully conceive of our own existence independently of our present physical state. Unless we can have an
acceptable idea of persons which does not involve identity with,
or dependence upon, our present physical bodies, there seems to
me little point in considering a possible future existence, whether
'future' be the proper term or not. Elsewhere I have defended the
view that mental states are of a different nature from physical
ones, and that they belong to a subject or entity that persists
through various states without being reducible to them. The
first seems an obvious prerequisite of any significant doctrine of
survival, but I attach almost equal importance to the second.
The most that I can add here is that, in considering such views
we should not father them wholly on the much maligned
Descartes. There are very great names in the same line of
country before him – and many after. It is to Kant perhaps, more
than any other, and to notable followers of Kant like James
Ward and F. R. Tennant fairly recently, that we owe our best
indication of the notion of a Pure Self or Subject.

Nothing has been said, in this paper, about the notion of an
identification of the finite person with some infinite or supreme

and absolute being. This is also a view which has widespread and impressive support. It does not seem to me consistent with what we must think about the distinctness of persons. But my reasons for omitting further reference to it are those, not of disrespect, but of space and the need to circumscribe our discussion.

For similar reasons I have said nothing about the grounds we may have for believing that we will in fact survive. My concern has been solely with the way we should think about it and how philosophical difficulties may be met – to keep the door open if you like. If challenged to adduce such grounds, I would not place much weight on general philosophical arguments or proofs. The best known traditional ones are notoriously inadequate. Nor is there any case to be made, in my view, for the inherent indestructibility of the soul. More may be said for the evidence from psychical research. It is not unimportant that philosophers as clear-sighted and cautious as C. D. Broad and H. H. Price seem convinced (especially Price) that some of the evidence invoked here points very strongly towards explanation in terms of some kind of survival. The layman is not in a good position to go further than this, and my own acquaintance with the subject is much too ragged for me to offer an opinion to which weight could be attached. I will however add the following comments.

(a) The weakness in much of the serious evidence for survival offered along these lines is that much of it could be accounted for in other ways, though often involving some paranormal element, such as telepathy or clairvoyance. The usual impressive case is that where information is obtained which would not be normally available to another living person or acquired in normal ways. If such information comes allegedly from a person now dead who would have had easy access to it, the presumption is that the dead person is now alive in some way and able to communicate with us, for example to tell us where he himself has concealed a will. It is possible however that the information, in these cases, has been obtained, whether or not of set intention by the communicant, telepathically from some living person who chances to have come across it, or, more plausibly, by clairvoyance. In itself, and allowing for other difficulties in the idea of survival, explanation in terms of a communication from the dead seems stronger and more direct. If the paranormal has to be invoked at all, why not go the whole way with the more inherently plausible explanation?

A considerable strengthening of the case along these lines could be made if one were able to obtain information, not about some relatively isolated fact, but about a spate of happenings to which we would normally have no access, but which in due course we were able to verify. We might, for example, have variation on the case I considered in my book in discussing reincarnation. Suppose a diary came to light confirming in great detail what a medium or the like had described about the hour-by-hour activities over a period of many days of someone long dead. If the medium claimed to remember this, there would seem to be a strong presumption of rebirth – that would seem to me much more likely than other explanations. If there were no distinct suggestion of memory, or if it seemed not in the least like memory to the medium, the explanation in terms of communication from a person now dead would appear irresistible. In either case some form of survival would be involved. I am not aware of a case that strictly measures up to this, but it would seem to provide a model of what would be required to set reasonable doubt at rest.

(*b*) If the evidence in question were to be found conclusive, or at least very strong, it would still be important not to give it the wrong kind of significance, or to suppose that it afforded some once for all clue to all major outstanding problems. Some, for example, have rushed to the findings of psychical research for the refutation of materialism. But the most obvious counter to materialist views of personality must be in terms of what we normally find to be the case, and if we cannot succeed at this level it is a moot point whether any other special evidence would defeat attempts to offer exclusively materialistic explanations.

(*c*) Any positive conclusions we may draw about survival from paranormal phenomena would still fall very far short of what religious persons usually claim. Little might be known about the permanence or the quality of future existence. It might be possible to deduce only that we 'hover around' in some form for some while after death. This would not be the 'life eternal' that Christians, for example, speak of, and there might be no more reason, in the accepted cases of survival, to invoke the idea of God and related religious ideas than is already available in present temporal existence.

There should, however, be a caveat here. The seemingly trivial or pointless character of much that seems to be communication from the dead, should not be taken straightway to discredit the soundness or the significance of such communication. As Price has pointed out on more than one occasion, there may be many reasons for the seeming triviality of the alleged communication and the rather discouraging impression it gives of a 'world beyond'. Much may be ascribable to faulty reception or the peculiar difficulties of such communication and the proper interpretation of it.

(*d*) Religious people, for the reasons instanced, often take a dim view of psychical research and its relevance to their claims. They are right if it is supposed that the findings of psychical research could do duty for the fulness of religious belief, and they may be justified in their suspicion that excessive preoccupation with the preternatural at this level could divert attention from more distinctly and centrally religious concerns. Religion has to do with much deeper needs than those which psychical research could satisfy, and the latter must be seen in its proper perspective. All the same, religious persons are very ill-advised to be contemptuous of psychical research or to dismiss it as of no importance for them. In many ways besides those concerned directly with survival (as in the study of religious symbolism for example) it could be most illuminating for their purpose.

In particular, in our present context, it would be quite absurd to dismiss any powerful evidence for survival, obtained from psychical or mediumistic sources, as of little importance. Most persons pay little heed to the matter at present, mainly, I believe, because the present state of the subject and especially of information about it, leaves it very uncertain for most people that there is anything in it. But suppose it were established, with the sort of firmness with which new findings in science come to be accepted, the nature and distance of remote heavenly bodies and the early formation of our own planet for example, that there was communication with persons known to have lived and died on this earth but therefore existing now in some form, what then? It would seem to me that this would be a most momentous event, and I can hardly conceive of its being passed without major widespread notice. It would certainly hit the headlines and might well have consequences for our future much more far-reaching than many of the remarkable scientific discoveries which have transformed so much of our lives today.

Nor would this be unimportant for religion. It would not give us the more fundamental claims which religious persons usually make, but it might well produce attitudes of mind and an outlook on our present existence which could very considerably bring us more within the ambit of properly religious concerns. It would be unthinkable that a firm belief, on the most objective grounds, that we do have some existence beyond the fleeting and imperfect present one, sobering or grim (as Broad suspected) though the prospect may be in some aspects, would make little difference to our main concerns and attitudes. It might well revolutionize them, and for that reason psychical research, even if presumed to be still in its infancy, should have the fullest respect of religious persons.

Having said this, I must add that the main positive reasons for belief in life after death seem to me to bc essentially religious ones. To deploy them is a vast undertaking in itself. Philosophy has certainly a part in such process, but religious insights would also be involved and need to be defended. Something might be made perhaps of the oddity, a little overlooked in religious apologetics, of a brief attainment of so much that is thought to be wholly obliterated. But to go further would require not only a general defence of religious claims, but the more precise commendation of a particular religious allegiance, in my case a Christian one, and a particular understanding of this. Indication of these tasks is all that can be given here. My concern has been solely with the way we may best understand the possiblity of life 'after' death. Envisaging this positively is in no way essential to having such expectations. We may hold on to our faith, if we have good reasons for it, while also affirming that 'it doth not yet appear what we shall be'. But specualtion may help, more I suspect than religious people appreciate and it is in any case of great philosophical interest on its own account.

NOTES

1. 'Is there a case for disembodied survival?' *Journal of the American Society for Psychical Research*, Vol. 66, April 1972, p. 129.

2. *The Ontological Argument*, p. 84. Mr Barnes strengthens his position by adding, 'If the conclusion is not allowed (on the dubious ground that Gods

are, by definition, *incorporeal*), then it follows that any God is *both* corporeal *and* incorporeal; so that it is a necessary truth that there are no Gods'.

3. *St Mary's Quarterly* (Journal of St Mary the Virgin, Bourne Street).
4. Op cit., p. 141.
5. *The Self and Immortality*, Chapter 9.
6. Chapter 8.
7. Chapter 8.

II ANTONY FLEW,
Professor of Philosophy, University of Reading.

1. *Some points of agreement*
I follow the the excellent example of Professor H. D. Lewis by starting with points of agreement. Since I am writing a second paper, I can pick out not one but several. Nor is the list below exhaustive.

(*a*) First, I wholeheartedly concur with his old-fashioned academic dedication: 'Notions which are not reconcilable with religious claims . . . must be considered on their merits. Our concern, whether religious or not, is . . . with the pursuit of truth' I could wish – to take an illustration from another but still topical controversy – that it was in that spirit and with that commitment that everyone approached the contested issue of whether there are in fact genetically determined differences between racial groups, genetically determined differences, that is, other than those by reference to which membership in such groups is itself defined. Too many – and, most scandalously, too many teachers in tertiary education – have recently felt called upon to denounce affirmative answers as racist, which they are not; without, apparently, being troubled by any pedantic concern lest the contrary doctrine, which they find more palatable, might not after all be false. ('A pedant', to quote one of Russell's mischievous yet salutary definitions, 'is a person who prefers his statement to be true'.)

But, having said this, I have to jib at a remark made by Lewis in considering the suggestion that we might 'survive without memories of our previous existence or any thought of it'. In a discussion of what, for better or for worse, may in fact be the case he is not entitled to help himself to the assumption that everything which occurs must have some satisfactory point: '. . . it is hard to see what purpose could be served . . . in this way'.

(*b*) Second, though this is a concurrence of another kind, Lewis and I have both written at greater length on the same subject elsewhere. Lewis mentions both his book on *The Self and Immortality* (*SI*) and my article 'Is There a Case for Disembodied Survival?' (ITCDS). I now have to ask the court to take into account also my recent collection of papers, *The Presumption of Atheism* (London: Pemberton, 1975). *PA* includes a revised version of ITCDS, as well as several other essays in the same area. I cannot avoid recycling some of this material here.

(*c*) Third, I agree with Lewis in linking the question of the essentially incorporeal nature of persons with the question of the existence of a God defined as both incorporeal and in some sense personal. If it makes no sense to speak of incorporeal persons, then it can scarcely make sense to speak of such a God.

I also agree with the parenthetical suggestion that Professor P. F. Strawson's remarks about '*former* persons' cannot be squared with Strawson's own fundamental contention that persons are tokens of 'a type of entity such that *both* predicates ascribing states of consciousness *and* predicates ascribing corporeal characteristics . . . are equally applicable to a single individual of that single type' (*Individuals*, pp. 115–16 and 102; italics original). By enunciating this basic proposition Strawson disqualifies himself from going on to say, as he does, that 'each of us can quite intelligibly conceive of his or her individual survival of bodily death. The effort of imagination is not even great' (p. 115). Really to imagine myself disembodied would surely have to be to imagine (the same person as) me; but disembodied. Now, either we really imagine a person or we do not. *Former* persons, if they are only *former* persons, are no more a sort of person than *ex*-wives, if they are only *ex*-wives, are a sort of wives. We cannot, therefore, allow Strawson these concluding manoeuvres: first, in his easy imaginings to assume that his putative disembodied beings would be persons; and then, when the going gets tougher, to sidestep the consequent charge of inconsistency by saying that they are *former*, and hence presumably not, persons. (Compare *PA*, XI 3 and IX.)

(*d*) Fourth, after insisting: that 'Unless we can have an acceptable idea of persons which does not involve identity with,

or dependence upon, our present physical bodies, there seems ...
little point in considering a possible future existence'; Lewis
warns that 'in considering such views we should not father them
wholly upon the much maligned Descartes'. Indeed we should
not. It is therefore perhaps just worth noting that the name
'Plato' does not occur in the Index to the first edition of *The
Concept of Mind*; although its first chapter 'Descartes' Myth' does
end with an 'Historical Note' allowing that 'Platonic and
Aristotelian theories of the intellect shaped the orthodox
doctrines of the immortality of the soul' (p. 23).

Now consider, as the occasion for a further scholarly note,
some remarks made by Mr A. M. Quinton in the opening
paragraph of his article on 'The Soul', first published in *The
Journal of Philosophy* for 1962: 'In the history of philosophy the
soul has been used for two distinct purposes: first, as an explanation of the vitality that distinguishes human beings, and
also animals and plants, from the broad mass of material objects;
and, secondly, as the seat of consciousness. The first of these,
which sees the soul as an ethereal but nonetheless physical
entity ... need not detain us. The second ... the soul of Plato and
Descartes, deserves a closer examination than it now usually
receives'.

So it does. But Quinton's will not serve. Certainly Plato did
not see 'the soul as an ethereal but nonetheless physical entity':
this view he ridicules at *Phaedo* 77D. Yet it is quite wrong to
suggest that Plato therefore did not conceive of the soul as a
principle of life, and hence possibly as some sort of 'explanation of
the vitality that distinguishes human beings ... from the broad
mass of material objects'. For both in *The Republic* (352D–354A)
and in *Phaedo* (105C9–D2) this clearly is at least part of Plato's
conception of the soul. In both places he fails to distinguish
sufficiently: between an idea of the soul as the (incorporeal)
principle of life; and the concept of the soul as the true (always
incorporeal) person. In *Phaedo* this failure is crucial to the
plausibility of his great set-piece argument for immortailty
(100B-105E). For more on this see my *Body Mind and Death* (New
York: Collier-Macmillan, 1964: Introduction and under Plato).

It is equally wrong to attribute what is in fact a distinctively
Cartesian emphasis on consciousness to Plato. For it was
Descartes who first, after concluding that he or his soul was

essentially an incorporeal thing, a spiritual or thinking substance, proceeded to define 'thinking' in terms of all and only
consciousness. So it is to Descartes that we owe the modern
problem of mind and matter, considered as the problem of the
relations of consciousness to stuff. In setting us this problem
Descartes prescribed his own factitious meaning for the word
'thinking', going against the grain of all established verbal
habits. So, almost inevitably, and almost immediately, he
becomes himself the first backslider: his 'two most certain tests'
of the presence of a thinking substance inside the machine of a
body are tests for rationality rather than for consciousness. The
price of Humpty Dumptysim for Descartes is heavy: he both
fails to uncover completely our twentieth-century problem of
other minds; and he concludes that the brutes, simply because
they are not rational animals, must be as it were permanently
anaesthetised.

(*e*) Fifth, I agree with Lewis about the possible religious
relevance of the evidence of psychical research. So, although my
own appraisal of the present state of that evidence is even more
discouraging than his, it is perhaps just worth adding two
supplementaries. First, it really will not do to dismiss conceptual
difficulties about the notion of survival in such supercilious
words as were used by the reviewer of C. B. Martin's *Religious
Belief* in *Mind* for 1961: 'Christians believe that they are to be
resurrected. They are not committed to any particular theory of
personal identity, e.g. "that there must be something that is
continuous and identical in this life that will survive into the
next" (p. 107), an insistence argued convincingly by Mr
Martin to be pointless. Christians do not have a theory here at all.
They believe that they are in for damnation or salvation, which
is something Mr Martin does not consider. The notion of
"looking forward to a life after death as a means of settling
questions concerning the existence and nature of God" which he
seems particularly concerned to attack smacks of "Spiritualism"
perhaps rather than Christianity' (p. 572). This evasive com-
placency is grotesque. Survival is not an alternative to, but a
necessary condition of immortality. It is, once again, the first
step which counts.

Second, we must not assume that a proof of 'communication
with persons known to have lived and died on this earth but . . .

existing now in some form' would necesssarily provide support
for all those 'systems of religion' which embrace some doctrine of
immortality. Certainly survival is, as I have just insisted, a
necessary condition of immortality. But the particular content of
such hypothetical communications could either count against or
even decisively falsify one or other particular system of religion.
The tales which some Spiritualists have told or been told about
the Summerland do not easily fit into any traditional Christian
picture of either Hell or Purgatory or Heaven. And, if Islam
really does promise that those who die fighting on the right side
in a Jehad pass straight into the eager arms of black-eyed houris,
then the disappointment of this stimulating expectation must
constitute decisive falsification for what would be humanly the
most attractive element in that religion.

(*f*) Sixth, Lewis and I agree about the crucial position,
though not about the size, of what I call the 'enormous initial
obstacle'. This, as Lewis says, 'is what sets the problem'. The
problem is to show how, if at all, any doctrine of personal
survival or personal immortality could get around or over the
obstacle. It is, I suggest, helpful to distinguish three sorts of way
in which this may be attempted. Many compounds of these
three elements are possible. But it is best to begin by distinguishing pure forms. I will now where necessary explain, and
examine, these three ways one by one.

2. The reconstitutionist way

What this involves becomes clear from two quotations. I have
used these more than once before. But they do bear repetition.
The first is an epitaph composed for himself by Benjamin
Franklin. I copied it from a plaque erected not on but beside his
grave in Christ Church cemetery, Philadelphia: 'The body of B.
Franklin, Printer, Like the Cover of an old Book, Its Contents
torn out, And stript of its Lettering and Gilding, Lies Here,
Food for Worms. But the work shall not be lost; for it will, as he
believ'd, appear once more in a new and more elegant Edition
Corrected and improved By the Author'.

The second quotation comes from Chapter XVII 'The
Night Journey' in *The Koran*, in N. J. Dawood's Penguin
Classics translation. As usual, it is Allah speaking: 'Thus shall
they be rewarded: because they disbelieved our revelations and

said "When we are turned to bones and dust shall we be raised to life?" Do they not see that Allah, who has created the heavens and the earth, has power to create their like? Their fate is preordained beyond all doubt. Yet the wrongdoers persist in unbelief' (p. 234).

Lewis is clearly embarrassed by such robust suggestions: 'That, in some Christian contexts at least, people have supposed that the graves and the seas will one day yield up their dead again is due largely to the highly unrealistic view men have been apt to take, with one part of their minds perhaps or in some moods, of decomposing bodies'. But Lewis seems not to have appreciated that and why this is the kind of mountain which even faith could not move. Though apologising a moment later for his apparent light-heartedness, Lewis writes: 'We may also ask, just what would be the point of this reconstitution . . . What of any significance could be accomplished? Could not God, as omnipotent, equally well have provided a duplicate, a new body, original cells and all, exactly like my present one? I would certainly not know the difference'.

The trouble here is that Lewis has simply not taken the measure of the reconstitutionist. For the reconstitutionist holds that a person just is a creature of flesh and blood, not an essentially incorporeal being who may happen to be equipped with a body. Suppose Lewis had been right thus to project his own view of persons on to the reconstitutionist. Then it would indeed have been a puzzle to find any reason why 'a duplicate, a new body' would not be acceptable. But, as things actually are, the reconstitutionist has to meet the crucial Replica Objection. This is the objection: that the 'new and more elegant Edition' would not be the original Founding Father, Signer of the American Declaration of Independence, but only a replica; and that Allah spoke more truly than his prophet realised when he claimed, not the ability to reconstitute numerically the same persons, but only 'power to create their like'.

In this context we can see why a reconstitutionist should 'invoke the omnipotence of God' in order to 'reassemble the scattered elements of our decomposed bodies to constitute again the body we have now'; although, of course, a pure reconstitutionist would not talk as Lewis does of our having or not having bodies in a putative life after death. One good reason for the reconstitutionist to make this particular appeal will be that he hopes – maybe rightly, maybe wrongly – to meet by this means the Replica Objection.

Pure reconstitutionism, as illustrated by my two quotations, has no doubt been rare, even in places and periods of more absolute faith. (One may perhaps take leave to wonder whether Franklin's suggested epitaph was itself the sincere expression of such a faith!) Usually spokesmen for the resurrection of the flesh or the reconstitution of the person – however strong their insistence that any truly human being must be corporeal – have wanted also to make some provision for a substantial soul. At least part, though surely only part, of the point of this provision has been to have another answer to the Replica Objection. See, for instance, the *Summa Theologica*, Part III (Supp.) Q.LXXIX A.2; especially the Reply to the first Objection. So long as there is a soul which is a substance, in the sense of something which could significantly be said to exist separately, then that soul can be called upon to remain in being between death and resurrection; and thereby to preserve the desired identity of the resurrection persons with their 'dead originals'.

In so far as we are dealing with an impure reconstitutionism, and in so far as (we believe) the Replica Objection is adequately met by reference to the impurity, we may well wonder – with Lewis – why there should be such a strong insistence upon having the same organism, and neither a perfect duplicate nor a new improved replacement. I think the answer lies in something which Lewis tries to minimise: namely, the importance within the Christian tradition of the notion that to be truly human is to be corporeal – that that is our proper ontological station. That this matters to St Thomas, for instance, comes out very clearly in the whole subtreatise 'Of the Resurrection', where the passage cited in the previous paragraph is found (Qq.LXIX-LXXXVI).

The first Article of the same Question LXXIX, incidentally, shows: that while for Thomas a human soul can be said to, and does, survive physical dissolution; still it could not exist or, rather, subsist before its body. It thus appears – no doubt to the surprise of both – that here Thomas in his own way anticipated Strawson's notion of *'former* persons'.

A more immediately relevant illustration of Christian concern with corporeality is provided by Lewis' – and my – former colleague Professor Eric Mascall. Lewis quotes Mascall as proclaiming 'that Christ has risen in his body', albeit a body 'unimaginably transformed'. Lewis is perplexed: 'But why, in this context or any other, should much be made to turn on whether his body actually came out of the tomb, as a transfigured body; whether it did or not'.

The answer again is, surely, that Mascall – good Thomist that he is – holds that to be truly human is to be corporeal. Hence, if Jesus is to remain man as well as God after his resurrection, he has then to be 'neither a ghost or a zombie, but a living and transfigured man'. Of course, as Lewis and I agreed in Section 1 (*c*) above, this is going to be an awkward commitment for the theist theologian. If human persons – the paradigm persons – are thus essentially corporeal, then it must be at least very difficult to show that there is room for a concept of God as a being both essentially incorporeal and also in some sense personal.

3. *The way of the astral body.*
The best approach to the present notion of an astral body is by thinking of those cinematic representations – as long ago in the movie version of Noel Coward's *Blithe Spirit* – in which a shadow person, visible only sometimes and only to some of the characters, detaches itself from a person shown as dead, and thereafter continues to participate in the developing action, at one time discernibly and at another time not. This 'astral body' is taken to be itself the real, the essential, person.

It is not, however, essential that an astral body be of human shape; much less that, even after the traumatic detachment of death, it should remain – as in those decent old days it did – neatly and conventionally clad. The crux is that it should possess the corporeal characteristics of size, shape and position; and that – though eluding crude, untutored, observation – it should nevertheless be in principle detectable. It it were not both in this minimum sense corporeal and in principle detectable, it would not be relevantly different from the Platonic-Cartesian soul. If it were not in practice excessively difficult to detect, no one could with any plausibility suggest that such a thing might slip away unnoticed from the deathbed: '. . . if the notion of an astral body is worth considering at all in this connection, as a distinct idea, it must be on the basis of its having physical properties of some sort, or being detectable in physical space'. For present purposes, therefore, we ought to classify corporeal souls as astral bodies. The notion which, as we saw earlier, Plato derided at *Phaedo* 77D clearly satisfies the present specifications; and that notion surely was, as near as makes no matter, that of the soul of Epicurus and Lucretius.

Lewis complains: 'There is however some confusion, and I feel that Professor Flew is in some measure guilty of it, about what we should understand by the idea of the alleged astral body. It could be thought to be some kind of non-physical "dream" or "image" body, or some quasi-body not in physical space and quite distinct from our present body, which we may have or enter when we discard the body we have now'.

Certainly there is confusion in plenty in the literature to which Lewis and I were both referring. But I plead 'Not guilty' to confounding my concept of an astral body, as explained in the two previous paragraphs, with that preferred by Lewis, and explained in the passage just quoted. I am sure that Lewis suggests that I am confused, where I am not, out of charity. He cannot bring himself to believe that I have knowingly kept company with so disreputable a concept as that of the astral body (Flew); whereas the astral body (Lewis) is, he allows, 'a notion we can take seriously'.

I am grateful for the kindness. Yet it is misplaced. In ITCDS I entertained only the Flew and not the Lewis concept, and I gave it this hospitality for the reason which Lewis himself notices. (See the quotation in my last paragraph but one.) Of course I agree with him about 'the inadequate character of evidence in support of it'. That is the good reason why I did not attempt any elaborate development – that 'much more careful analysis . . . needed if it is to be examined seriously and with some bias in its favour by philosophers of Professor Flew's standing'. The 'bias in its favour' which Lewis detects is grounded in my conviction that there are insuperable philosophical difficulties in both the alternative ways; whereas the way of the astral body, though certainly blocked, is blocked by empirical difficulties.

4. *The Platonic-Cartesian way*

This consists in two moves, not one. The first is to maintain that what is ordinarily thought of as a person in fact consists of two radically disparate substances: the one, the body, earthy, corporeal and perishable; the other, the soul, incorporeal, invisible, intangible and perhaps imperishable. The second consists in the contention that it is the second of these two substances which is the real, essential person. It is obvious that if this way will go, then what I call the enormous initial obstacle is really no obstacle at all: the death of the body is not necessarily the death of the soul, which is the true person; and such an essentially incorporeal entity cannot in principle be touched by the earthy corruptions of the graveyard, the inferno of the crematorium.

Lewis, it seems, right from the beginning takes this Platonic-Cartesian framework absolutely for granted. Without it, as he says in his first paragraph, 'there would be no point in raising the question of the possiblity of our survival of death'. Indeed Lewis appears to be unable even to describe my two alternative possible routes over or round the 'enormous initial obstacle' except in intrusively Platonic-Cartesian terms. Thus, as we have already noticed, in discussing reconstitution he asks: 'Could not God, as omnipotent, equally well have provided a duplicate, a new body . . . ? I would certainly not know the difference'. Obviously the referent of this 'I' is a Platonic-Cartesian soul.

The same deep assumption reappears in the distinction between two senses of 'astral body'. The second, approved, kind of astral body would be one 'which we may have or enter when we discard the body we have now'. That this enterer and discarder of bodies is none other than 'the soul of Plato and Descartes' becomes, if possible, even clearer when Lewis later notes 'the oddity of our having what might almost be called the encumbrance of an astral body when we have normally no consciousness of it and when it seems to have no function related to our normal transactions in this world. Why, if I may so put it, do we need it now? Will the soul come adrift in some way if it has not this spare bodily harness ready to contain it when we die?'.

Certainly Lewis makes a fair point in insisting that the spokesman for the way of the astral body has to establish not only that there are, but also that we are, astral bodies; just as, as I have to add, the protagonist of the Platonic-Cartesian way has to show not only that people contain, but also that really and essentially they are, incorporeal substances. What I feel that Lewis never fully recognizes is that there are serious, perhaps intractable, difficulties in his view of the nature of man: that, in Quinton's words, 'the soul of Plato and Descartes deserves a closer examination than it now usually receives'. I have elsewhere attempted a rather more systematic presentation of these difficulties (*PA*, X). Here, as befits a second symposiast, I will raise them in the form of occasional comments on the first paper.

(*a*) Lewis writes: 'Elsewhere I have defended the view that mental states are of a different nature from physical ones, and that they belong to a subject or entity that persists through various states without being reducible to them. The first seems an obvious prerequisite of any significant doctrine of survival, but I attach almost equal importance to the second'. References later in the same paragraph to 'the much maligned Descartes' and to 'the notion of a Pure Self or Subject' make it quite clear, even before referring to *SI*, that the crucial adjective 'incorporeal' should here be supplied to qualify 'subject or entity.' (Without that insertion I could myself happily assent to both claims!)

When I reviewed *SI* for *Philosophical Books* I made the inexplicable, but also inexcusable, mistake of attributing to Lewis himself, as an aberration, what was in fact part of his statement of a rival view. Inevitably therefore, and properly, I have qualms in reporting that I still cannot see that Lewis gives in that book any more or better reason than he gives in his present paper for thinking that mental states must, or even may, be the states of such a subject.

His aim is 'to break down the materialist presuppositions of much contemporary thought . . . by what we find to be the case in ordinary experience . . .' (*SI*, p. 204). But he in fact reaches the desired Cartesian conclusions by taking it that an exclusively Cartesian interpretation of various familiar ongoings is itself an essential part of our ordinary experience of these ongoings. Thus, for instance, he says: 'If my wife calls and I go downstairs, this is because I understand that dinner is ready, etc.; and surely my understanding counts, short of treating all purposive activity as some curious sort of reflex action' (*SI*, p. 64).

Certainly Lewis, and Mrs Lewis, and everyone else, knows that his understanding her call is on this sort of occasion a causally necessary condition of his going downstairs. But this familiar fact simply does nor begin to show that two substances, conscious mind and non-conscious matter, have been causally interacting.

Nothing has been done, therefore, to prepare for the question on the following page: 'But why should we expect that or suppose that proper scientific study of the brain at its own level precludes the recognition that the impact of our thoughts upon it alters considerably what would have happened otherwise?'

To argue on these Lewis lines does nothing to foreclose on the possiblity that consciousness can be significantly predicated only of living organisms. To insist that such 'ordinary experience' as that of my hands moving because I decide to move them, or of my suffering agonies because a weight is crushing my leg, proves 'a close interaction of mind and body', is not at all to show that in these cases extended physical entities are engaged in causal transactions with something 'of a radically different nature from extended or physical reality'. Absolutely nothing has been said to rebut the studiously simple-minded contention that the deciding agent and the suffering patient are one and the same flesh and blood person. Nor has anything whatever been said to show that either pure moments of consciousness unalloyed with anything material, or incorporeal subjects of consciousness, either have been, or could be, isolated as independent causal factors. In sum it seems to me that reference to *SI* does not help to show that mental states belong to incorporeal substances. Nor does it help to show, more fundamentally, that we possess a viable concept of this kind of substance.

(*b*) In discussing 'The relevance of the idea of the astral body . . . to personal identity', Lewis says: 'The requirement of bodily continuity is usually made, in reputable philosophy, in respect of a point of view and the confirmation of memories etc.' But the philosophical problem of personal identity, the reputable problem, concerns not the confirmation but the content of claims to be the same person.

It is not Locke alone who needs to take to heart Butler's terse, elegant and decisive statement of the reasons why – whatever persons may be – personal identity simply cannot be analysed in terms of memory. For instance: Quinton, in the paper cited in my Section 1 (*d*) above, not yet being fully seized of this objection, was still trying to develop a neo-Lockean account of the sameness of souls; these being there conceived as 'series of mental states identified through time in virute of the properties and relations of these mental states themselves' (p. 397; compare *PA*, X 3 (i)).

It is in the third paragraph of his 'Dissertation of Personal Identity' that Butler delivers what another Bishop would have called the killing blow: ' . . . though consciousness of what is past does . . . ascertain our personal identity to ourselves, yet to say that it makes personal identity, or is necessary to our being the same persons . . .' is a 'wonderful mistake'. For 'one should really think it self-evident, that consciousness of personal identity presupposes, and therefore cannot constitute personal identity; any more than knowledge, in any other case, can constitute truth, which it presupposes'.

Just so. Hence 'The relevance of the idea of the astral body . . . to personal identity' is: not that knowledge of the presence of a particular body might enable us to know that the soul 'harnessed' to that 'encumbrance' was also present; but that being the same astral body might be being the same person. That Lewis does indeed see the problem as one of how, rather than what, we might know is confirmed by a later passage: 'The question of a linkage, in a future existence, with our present existence, has further difficulties. They would partly be met by dependence on memory, and I see no reason to doubt that, if I became convinced that I was in another existence, and seemed to have clear memories of the present life, I could put considerable credence upon it, as I do now when I wake up and without any checking'.

That 'could' shows that Lewis is asking, as too many do not, the properly philosophical question: not 'What would we in fact say if so and so?'; but 'What should or, better, ought we to say if so and so?' Questions of the former form belong to what a Kantian might call hypothetical anthropology, not philosophy. But though the Lewis investigation is properly philosophical, it is still about how we might know, and when we might be entitled to claim to know. Yet the primary question here is precisely what we should know if we knew that this incorporeal substance at time two was the same as that incorporeal substance at time one.

The nature and importance of this most fundamental question is for many obscured by the extraordinary, and yet extraordinarily widespread, assumption that person words are ordinarily used to refer to substances which, if not essentially incorporeal, are certainly not essentially corporeal. Given this, and given, what is indeed the case, that we are all both acquainted with many persons and equipped with at least an everyday if not a philosophical understanding of what it is to be the same person; then there obviously is no difficulty about what could be, indeed is, meant by talk of such incorporeal substances, and of one of these being the same or not the same as another.

Almost every passage which I have already quoted from Lewis will also serve to show how unshakably he holds, or is held by, this extraordinary assumption. Perhaps the point came out most clearly when we saw him misdescribing the reconstitutionist and astral body alternatives in terms which were themselves still unquestioningly Platonic-Cartesian. But my own favourite illustration of the entrenched strength of this assumption is provided by Hume. For Ryle's 'ungullible Hume', Hume the lifelong Mortalist, Hume who had nothing except perhaps his philosophical scepticism to lose and everything to gain, even Hume, still never thought to question this. Instead, in rather self-conscious radicalism, he asked only whether we have any good reason to believe in the existence of a Self as the subject of all our 'loose and separate' experiences. Very soon – and to us significantly – he found himself entirely at a loss to provide any tolerable account of the bond which unites such collections of unowned experiences; a notion which in any case, surely, makes about as much sense as those of a harmony without any elements being harmonised or of a grin without any face to grin it.

I do not know how to begin here to show that this extra-ordinary assumption about the ordinary meanings of person-words is, though among philosophers both deep and common, false. In part my difficulty arises because those who argue on this assumption never seem to make any but the most perfunctory attempt to show that it is true. One of my hopes of the coming discussion is that someone will indicate the lines on which they think this might be shown. In the meantime I ask Lewis whether he is really prepared to maintain, as this assumption appears to require, that anyone who characterises someone as a person, while denying that that person, or any other, either is, or contains, an actually, or potentially, incorporeal substance, thereby contradicts himself. On the side of the Noes we have the whole weight of the evidence which led Wittgenstein in the *Investigations* to say: 'The human body is the best picture of the human soul' (p. 178).

The second subject – I can scarcely say matter – upon which

I hope the discussion may throw some light is that of incorporeal substances. So long as it is assumed that we ourselves are, and can easily know that we are, such substances it is hard to recognise this as the opaque and disputatious notion which it is. We may here recall how in *Phaedo*, wishing to establish that this is indeed what we are, Plato's Socrates appealed to what he took to be the known fact of the existence of Forms; though we should notice, as he did not, that if there were such paradigm incorporeal substances they would presumably be, not, as his supposed proof of personal immortality requires, eternal (everlasting), but eternal (makes no sense to ask when or where).

But now, once we have come to see the key notion, or pseudo-notion, as possibly problematic, it is easy to put the finger on the fundamental problem. Is an incorporeal spiritual substance any more a kind of substance than an imaginary or non-existent entity is a kind of entity ? I cannot put the crucial point better, or more politely, than by quoting Professor Terence Penelhum's *Survival and Disembodied Existence* (London: Routledge and Kegan Paul, 1970): 'Beyond the wholly empty assurance that it is a metaphysical principle which guarantees continuing identity through time, or the argument that since we know that identity persists some such principle must hold in default of others, no content seems available for the doctrine'; and, apart from serving as a subject to which mental characteristics may be attributed, it is 'merely an alleged identity-guaranteeing condition of which no independent characterisation is forthcoming' (p. 76).

The first adjective in the expression 'incorporeal spiritual substance' seems to negate the identifying content of the noun. Nor is this, I suggest, an emptily verbal point, to be parried by some equally verbal manoeuvre. For any stipulation making it possible to identify such a substance, must thereby make it correspondingly possible to show that in fact nothing of the sort either enters at conception or leaves at death. The often un-acceptable price of providing such identification is that it becomes by the same token in principle possible to falsify the claim that these substances exist. This is in part why, I think, many would be inclined to dismiss anything which was identifi-able as only an astral body, not a genuine Platonic-Cartesian soul; and certainly this was part of my reason for proposing to classify Epicurean corporeal souls along with astral bodies. My own friendliness towards the latter, a friendliness which I am afraid shocked Lewis, is not of course a mark of any inclination to believe that there are such. It is rooted in my preference for the identifiable and the falsifiable as against the unidentifiable and, it seems to me studiously unfalsifiable.

In order to concentrate discussion upon what is, surely, the most fundamental and crucial question, and because it is always a pleasure to reread the 'Monster of Malmesbury', I conclude with some rather rude words from *Leviathan*, Chapter V: 'And therefore, if a man should talk to me of "a round quadrangle"; or "accidents of bread in cheese"; or "immaterial substances"; . . . I should not say he was in error, but that his words were without meaning: that is to say, absurd'.

SUMMARY

1. *Some points of agreement* include: that our overriding concern should be with truth not comfort; that a view of persons as essentially corporeal threatens the idea of God as both incorporeal and yet personal; that what is called the survival evidence from psychical research could be relevant to religious beliefs; that the main philosophical battle must be about the Platonic-Cartesian conception of the nature of man; and that we must start from looking for ways round the 'enormous initial obstacle' of the facts of death.

2. *The reconstitutionist way* must be seen as, in its pure form, maintaining that people just are corporeal. This way is blocked by the objection that such a reconstituted person would be a replica, not the original.

3. *The way of the astral body* must again be seen as in its pure form, maintaining that people do not have but are 'astral bodies'. The decisive objection here is that there is no good reason to believe in the existence of such 'astral bodies'.

4. *The Platonic-Cartesian way* is in fact always taken for granted by Lewis, even where he believes that he is offering evidence in its support. The two crucial questions for discussion are: first, can we hope to show that at least part of what person-words are ordinarily used to refer to is a Platonic-Cartesian soul; and, second and more fundamental, is it possible to provide any positive identifying characterisation for any such incorporeal spiritual substance?

6 Immortality and Dualism

I SYDNEY SHOEMAKER,
Professor of Philosophy, Cornell University

1. Someone who believes in immortality is not thereby committed, logically, to believing in dualism and in the possibility of disembodied existence. Nevertheless, any anti-dualist who believes in immortality is committed to believing things which most anti-dualists would find even less plausible than dualism. Observe that if at some future time I die and then undergo bodily resurrection, or if I arrange to have myself deep-frozen and then thawed a few millennia later,[1] or if I have my brain transferred to a younger and healthier body, or if I have my brainstates transferred to a younger and healthier brain, or if I undergo rejuvenation at the hands of the micro-surgeons, then no matter how much my bodily existence will have been extended beyond three score years and ten, I will still have an eternity ahead of me. None of the imagined life-prolonging (or life-restoring) episodes would, by itself, bring one immortality, as opposed to mere increased longevity. If someone believes that these (will be?) immortal, but rejects dualism and the possibility of disembodied existence, he is committed to believing either (a) that beginning now or later he will live forever embodied in a body of the sort he currently has, one subject to all of the ills flesh is heir to, or (b) that at some future time his body will be transformed into, or replaced by, one that is imperishable and indestructible (by natural means), in which he will then be embodied forever, or (c) that he will undergo and survive an unending series of life-prolonging episodes (resurrections, brain transplants, rejuvenations, etc.). Even if none of these beliefs can be faulted on logical or conceptual grounds, most people would agree that there are overwhelming empirical grounds for rejecting all of them.

For anyone who wants to believe in personal immortality, dualism seems to offer obvious advantages over anti-dualism. A dualist can believe in immortality without clashing head-on with science and with the fund of experience which has made 'all men are mortal' a truism. While we have abundant empirical evidence of the perishability and impermanence of material substances, especially organic ones, we have none at all of the perishability and impermanence of immaterial substances. To be sure, we also have no empirical evidence of the *im*perishability and permanence of immaterial substances. But to many philosophers it has seemed that we are guaranteed the latter on *a priori* grounds. An undoubted attraction of the idea that persons are immaterial substances is the idea that such substances, being simple and without parts (a supposed consequence of their lacking spatial extension), will be incapable of going out of existence through dissolution of parts, and so will be 'incorruptible' by natural means. Nowadays, of course, such ideas do not have the following they once had. There are few who subscribe to the sort of 'rational psychology' attacked by Kant in the Paralogisms. But the effects of such ideas linger on, and the view persists that belief in dualism is appreciably more compatible with belief in immortality than is belief in materialism. One of my objects in this paper is to undermine this view.

2. Recent philosophers who reject dualism and deny the possibility of disembodied existence of persons tend to fall into one of two groups. Those in one group seek to show that the falsity of dualism can be demonstrated on conceptual grounds.[2] Those in the other group maintain that dualism is an intelligible and logically coherent doctrine, but that we have overwhelming empirical grounds for rejecting it as false.[3] On the first view there is no possible world in which dualism is true. On the second view dualism is true in some possible worlds, but not in the actual world.

I think that there is an element of truth in each of these views; roughly, they are true of different versions of dualism. There is a version of dualism, and one that implies that disembodied existence of persons is possible, to which there is, as far as I can see, no decisive logical or conceptual objection. This it seems reasonable to regard as a doctrine to be accepted or rejected (I opt for the latter) on empirical grounds. Once it is clearly distinguished from other versions, this version turns out not to be of much help to believers in immortality, and it is not, I think, the doctrine that such believers have ordinarily held. There is another version of dualism which at least some believers in immortality have held, and which seems in harmony with the doctrine of immortality. I believe that this second version is conceptually incoherent, but I shall content myself here with arguing that there is, and could be, no reason to believe it true.

Presumably any dualist who believes that it is possible for him to exist in disembodied form believes that there is an immaterial substance such that (*a*) what mental states he has depends on what states the immaterial substance has, (*b*) all causal connections involving mental states between his sensory 'input' and his behavioural 'output' are mediated by states of this immaterial substance, and (*c*) it is possible for him to exist, as a subject of mental states, without having a body, as long as the immaterial substance exists and has the appropriate states. Let us say that anyone of whom all of this is true has a minimally dualistic nature. I shall use the term 'Minimal Dualism' for the doctrine that all persons have minimally dualistic natures – but it is worth noting that there is no evident incoherence involved in holding that some persons have minimally dualistic natures while others are purely material creatures.

Notice the Minimal Dualism does not say either (*a*) that the immaterial substance associated with a person *is* the person, or (*b*) that the states of the immaterial substance *are* the mental states of the person. Neither does it deny that (*a*) and (*b*) are true. So two versions of Minimal Dualism can be distinguished. Both of these hold that the person is something distinct from (nonidentical with) his body, and that physical states (height, weight, etc.) belong to a person only derivatively – so, for example, a person has a certain weight in virtue of having (rather than being) a body having that weight. And both hold that the mental states of a person belong to him non-derivatively – that a person's being angry, for example, is not a matter of his being related in a certain way to something (non-identical to himself) that is angry. But one version affirms what the other denies, that a person is identical with an immaterial substance, the states of which are the mental states of the person. I shall call the version that says that persons are immaterial substances Cartesian

Dualism, and shall call the other Non-Cartesian Dualism. But these are only suggestive names, and I do not claim that Descartes consistently adhered to the doctrine I call Cartesian Dualism.

It is worth noting that what Minimal Dualism says about immaterial substances is the same as what many contemporary philosophers are prepared to say about *brains*. Many philosophers would hold that for each person there exists a brain such that (*a*) what mental states the person has depends on what states the brain has, (*b*) all causal connections involving mental states between the person's sensory input and behavioural output are mediated by states of the brain, and (*c*) it is possible for the person to exist, as a subject of mental states, as long as the brain exists and has the appropriate states. The only part of this that would ordinarily be regarded as at all controversial is (*c*), which is affirmed by those who think that a person could survive the destruction of his body if his brain were detached and kept alive *in vitro*. Now this view about brains does not seem to imply that persons *are* brains (and so weigh only a few pounds, are greyish in colour, and so on), and that the mental states of persons just *are* states of their brains. And no more does Minimal Dualism seem to imply Cartesian Dualism. It seems compatible with Minimal Dualism that an immaterial substance should be related to a person in much the way we ordinarily think of a person's brain as related to him – that it should be, in effect, a ghostly brain.[4] And this is what I shall take Non-Cartesian Dualism to hold.

It should come as no surprise that the version of dualism I regard as conceptually coherent (although empirically very implausible) is Non-Cartesian Dualism, while that which I believe to be conceptually incoherent is Cartesian Dualism.

3. Before I can go on I must explain some terminology and state some assumptions.

A substance, as I shall use the term, is a 'continuant' in W. E. Johnson's sense – something that can persist through time, and can have different properties at different times. A material substance I take to be a substance whose non-derivative and non-relational properties are necessarily limited to (*a*) physical properties and (*b*) properties it has in virtue of what physical properties it has (in the way a machine can have a certain computational capacity in virtue of having a particular physical structure, even though things having very different physical structures, and perhaps even immaterial things, could have the same computational capacity).[5] And I take it that physical properties can belong, non-derivatively, only to material substances. Beyond this I shall not attempt to define the terms 'material' and 'physical'. I shall simply assume, for the sake of this discussion, that the correct definitions of these terms (if there are such), or the ways in which their references are fixed, are not such as to make it self-contradictory to suppose that there might be properties and states that are not physical and substances that are not material.

It is misleading to treat the terms 'material substance' and 'immaterial substance' on a par. The relationship between them should be thought of as analogous, not to that between 'iron' and 'copper', but to that between 'iron' and 'non-ferrous metal'. If there can be immaterial substances at all, presumably there can be different kinds of immaterial substances, these being as different from one another as they are from material substances. For each possible kind of immaterial substances there will be a kind of properties which are essential to those substances in the way physical properties are essential to material substances. Just as physical properties can belong (non-derivatively) only to material substances, so immaterial properties of one of these kinds will be capable of belonging (non-derivatively) only to immaterial substances of the corresponding kind; and, conversely, the non-derivative and non-relational properties of immaterial substances of a given kind will be necessarily limited to (*a*) immaterial properties of the corresponding kind and (*b*) properties they have in virtue of what immaterial properties of that kind they have.

A term that purports to refer to a kind of immaterial substances, and to be on a par with 'material substance', is 'spiritual substance'. Spiritual substances are what Cartesian Dualists believe persons to be. They are (or would be if they existed) substances whose non-derivative and non-relational properties are necessarily mental properties (if you like, modes of consciousness); and anyone who holds that there can be such substances is committed to holding that mental properties can belong (non-derivatively) *only* to such substances.

It might be supposed that 'immaterial substance' could be

defined as meaning simply 'substance that is not a material substance'. A reason for not so defining it (one that would not, however, impress a Cartesian Dualist) is that this would make Non-Cartesian Dualism logically incoherent. Persons are certainly substances in the broad sense I have defined; they are 'continuants'. Now Non-Cartesian Dualism denies that persons are material substances, and so would be committed, by the proposed definition of 'immaterial substance', to holding that they are immaterial substances. But I have characterised Non-Cartesian Dualism as the version of Minimal Dualism which denies that a person *is* the immaterial substance on which his mental states depend; and if a person is not that immaterial substance, what immaterial substance could he be? No answer seems forthcoming.

But there is another reason, and one that even a Cartesian Dualist should appreciate, for rejecting the proposed definition. On any version of dualism which allows for the possibility of causal interaction between material and immaterial substances (and only such versions are under consideration here) there can exist systems which consist of one or more immaterial substances interacting causally with one or more material substances. Such systems (I will call them 'partly physical systems') will be continuants, and so substances in the broad sense. And such systems will have properties – dispositional properties at least – which they possess in virtue of what properties their material and immaterial components have, and of how these components are related to one another; something's having such a property will be a 'partly physical' state of it. Clearly such a system will not be a material substance. Yet it will not do to characterise such systems as immaterial substances; for obviously a system which has material as well as immaterial components cannot be immaterial in the same sense in which its immaterial components are immaterial.

Immaterial substances, if there are any, will be substances whose non-relational and non-derivative properties are neither physical nor partly physical. What we have just seen is that if we admit the possibility of there being immaterial substances as well as material substances, we must admit the possibility of there also being substances, or at any rate continuants, which are themselves neither material substances nor immaterial substances but whose existence in some way consists in the existence of material and immaterial substances. We cannot, I think, rule out *a priori* the possibility that persons, or even minds, will turn out to be such entities. [6]

4. I shall follow tradition by assuming that immaterial substances lack spatial properties, and so are not spatially extended, and that they do not have spatial location in their own right. Some philosophers have held that the non-spatiality of immaterial substances makes the very idea of an immaterial substance incoherent. Their argument has been that there could be no satisfactory way of individuating such entities; since immaterial substances are supposed to be particulars, rather than abstract entities, they could not be individuated by their non-relational properties (for it ought to be possible for two particulars to share all of their non-relational properties), and since they are supposed to be non-spatial they could not be individuated by spatial relations. Likewise, it has been objected that there is no way in which the notion of identity through time could be applied to entities to which the notion of spatiotemporal continuity is inapplicable.

Those who make such objections usually assume, as do most philosophers who write about dualism, that immaterial substances would be spiritual substances. It does seem logically possible that two numerically different persons should be exactly similar with respect to their mental or psychological attributes. And it may seem to follow that the notion of a spiritual substance, a substance having only mental (psychological) properties and states, is not a coherent notion.

Even if this constituted a valid objection against Cartesian Dualism, which takes persons to be spiritual substances, it would not refute Non-Cartesian Dualism, which is not committed to the existence of spiritual substances. And in fact it does not seem to me a convincing objection to Cartesian Dualism.

Both Cartesian Dualism and Non-Cartesian Dualism are versions of what I have called Minimal Dualism. And Minimal Dualism is committed to the claim that immaterial substances are such that they can interact causally with material substances; for it is essential to Minimal Dualism that the states of immaterial substances mediate the causal connections between the sensory input and the behavioural output of the bodies of living persons. [7]

Now immaterial substances are usually thought to lack spatial position, and spatial relations, as well as spatial extension. And this makes it difficult to understand how there can be causal connections of the required sorts between immaterial substances (and their states) and material substances (and their states). There can be no spatial relationship, such as spatial contiguity, which relates the immaterial substance which is my mind, soul, or ghostly brain to *my* body and not to any other, and which relates my body to *my* mind (soul, ghostly brain) and not to any other immaterial substance. Why, then, do the states of my mind affect only the states of my body, and why is it only my mind that is directly affected by sensory stimulation of my body? Since I am supposing that Minimal Dualism is coherent, I must suppose that this difficulty can be overcome. And to suppose this we must suppose, I think, that there could be non-spatial relationships between immaterial substances ('minds') and material substances ('bodies') which play a role in determining what causal relationships can hold between these substances which is analogous to the role which spatial relationships play in determining what causal relationships can hold between material substances. Let us speak of these as 'quasi-spatial relationships'. Now there seems no reason why a Non-Cartesian Dualist cannot hold that immaterial substances are, or can be, related to material substances by such relationships; there seems to be no conflict between this claim and the essentially negative characterisation of immaterial substances given by Non-Cartesian dualism. If it is incompatible with the notion of a spiritual substance that such a substance should stand in quasi-spatial relationships to material substances, then Cartesian Dualism cannot make intelligible the possibility of interaction between mind and body, and can be rejected on that account. But it is not clear that this is incompatible with the notion of a spiritual substance. What we know from the notion of a spiritual substance, beyond the fact that spiritual substances are immaterial, is that the *non*-relational properties of spiritual substances are mental properties. Offhand, this implies nothing about what relations such substances can enter into, except (perhaps) that they cannot enter into spatial relationships. But, and here is the point, if it is intelligible to suppose that immaterial substances can be related to material substances by such quasi-spatial relationships, there seems no reason why we should not suppose that they stand in quasi-spatial relationships to one another. And then their quasi-spatial relationships could play the role in their individuation, and in their identity through time, which spatial relationships play in the case of material substances. It seems that this could be held by Cartesian Dualists as well as by Non-Cartesian Dualists.[8]

5. Immaterial substances have traditionally been supposed to be 'simple', in the sense of being indivisible and without separable parts, and this supposition has figured prominently in *a priori* arguments for immortality. One basis for this view has been the view that *persons* are simple and indivisible, this being based on considerations which we can lump together under the heading 'the unity of consciousness'. Given the premise that persons are simple and indivisible, that properly speaking nothing can be a *part* of a person, plus the premise that persons must be either material substances or immaterial substances, plus the obvious fact that material substances are *not* simple and indivisible, we can derive both the conclusion that persons are immaterial substances and the conclusion that at least some immaterial substances (namely those that are persons) are simple and indivisible. In order to reject this argument I do not need to dispute the claim that persons are (in some sense) simple and indivisible. For I have already rejected the second premise of the argument, namely that persons must be either material substances or immaterial substances. A Non-Cartesian Dualist, who denies that persons *are* immaterial substances, cannot conclude from the (alleged) simplicity of persons that immaterial substances are simple, and cannot cite the simplicity of persons as proof that there are immaterial substances.

It may be objected that even if persons are not identical with either material or immaterial substances, their existence must in some sense consist in the existence of substances of one, or both, of these kinds. With this I agree. And it might further be held that if something is simple and indivisible, its existence cannot consist in the existence of substances that are not themselves simple and indivisible. But this further claim seems to me unwarranted. I can imagine someone arguing that the United States Supreme Court, for example, is in some important sense without parts and indivisible, and that the relationship of the individual Justices to the Court is not that of part of whole (since, arguably, the Court would continue to exist even if all of the Justices were simultaneously to die or resign and since, presumably, the question, 'How much does the Supreme Court weigh?' is one we should reject rather than answer by summing the weights of the individual Justices). But nothing that could plausibly be meant by this would persuade a materialist that he must choose between denying the existence of the Supreme Court and abandoning his materialist view that the things that exist in the world are either material substances or things whose existence consists in the existence of material substances and their relationships to one another.

There is, however, a traditional reason for thinking that immaterial substances would have to be simple and indivisible which does not rest on the claim that persons are simple and indivisible. For it is taken for granted (as I do here) that an immaterial substance cannot be spatially extended, and from this it is concluded that immaterial substances, if there be such, are necessarily indivisible and without parts. No doubt this consideration and those leading directly to the conclusion that persons are simple have tended to reinforce each other – if someone has been persuaded on independent grounds that (a) persons are simple and (b) immaterial substances are simple, it will not be surprising if he concludes that immaterial substances are just the right sorts of things for persons to be.

But this second reason for thinking immaterial substances to be simple is undermined by the points made in Section 4. We saw there that in order to make intelligible the possibility of causal interaction between immaterial substances and material bodies (as is required by both forms of Minimal Dualism) we must suppose that there are 'quasi-spatial' relationships which immaterial substances can stand in which constrain what causal relationships they can stand in to material substances, and do so in a way analogous to that in which spatial relationships constrain what causal relationships can hold between different material substances. Moreover, we saw that in order to answer the 'individuation' objection to dualism we must suppose that there are 'quasi-spatial' relationships that hold between different immaterial substances. But given all this, it is surely intelligible (if talk about immaterial substances is intelligible at all) to suppose that immaterial substances can interact causally with one another, as well as with material substances, the causal connections between them being constrained by quasi-spatial relationships holding between them. And if there could be causal interaction between different immaterial substances, surely there could exist, in virtue of the holding of causal connections, *systems* of immaterial substances which constitute causal units in much the way a (physical) machine is a causal unit in virtue of the causal connections that hold between its parts. And such systems would have parts, or at any rate components, some of these being subsystems and some (perhaps) being 'atomic' immaterial substances which are simple and without parts. Presumably such systems could have a quasi-spatial unity which goes with their causal unity in much the way that the spatial unity of material bodies goes with their causal unity.

Someone might allow that there could be such systems of immaterial substances, but deny that such systems would themselves be immaterial substances. If this denial stems from a stipulation that a substance, of whatever sort, must be simple and without parts, we can point out that this stipulation rules out talk of material substances (or at any rate excludes human bodies, and other macroscopic material things, from being substances). But there is no need for us to quibble here about the word 'substance'; if need be, we can abandon it in favour of 'thing', 'entity', or 'continuant'. The point is that if there can be immaterial substances at all, of the sort required by Minimal Dualism, there seems no reason why there should not be immaterial entities that have parts. More specifically, if Non-Cartesian Dualism is coherent, there seems no reason why the 'ghostly brain' of a person should not be a composite immaterial thing, a system of immaterial things which are so related as to constitute a causal unit, rather than an 'atomic' immaterial substance. Certainly the view that we have immaterial brains that are such systems is no less intelligible than the view that we have immaterial brains that are immaterial atoms.

Finally, and this is of course the point of all this, if it is possible for immaterial substances (or things) to have parts or components, then there seems no reason to suppose that immaterial substances are not subject to destruction through the dissolution of their parts. Clearly we have no empirical evidence of the indestructibility of immaterial substances. Let us suspend, for a moment, our scepticism about purported cases of communication with the dead, 'out of body experiences', and other spiritualistic phenomena. Even if such cases were evidence that there are immaterial substances, it is clear that they would provide no evidence that these substances are simple and indivisible, or that they are for any other reason indestructible. Likewise, if we discovered evidence that the structure of the human brain and nervous system is insufficiently complex to account for all aspects of human behaviour, then while this might be evidence that there exist immaterial substances which function as the 'ghostly brains' of persons, or which are the immaterial components of partly physical systems which function as 'partly ghostly brains', it clearly would not be evidence that these immaterial substances are simple and indestructible.

It is plain that support for Non-Cartesian Dualism, if we had it, would not as such be support for the doctrine of immortality. Moreover, it seems (and I shall argue later) that whatever empirical evidence we can imagine having for the truth of Minimal Dualism would be compatible with Non-Cartesian Dualism – assuming, of course, that Non-Cartesian Dualism is a coherent position. If so, dualism can be used to buttress the plausibility of the doctrine of immortality only if it can be shown on *a priori* grounds that Non-Cartesian Dualism is not coherent and that Cartesian Dualism is – in other words, that Cartesian Dualism is the only coherent form of dualism. It will turn out that in order to maintain this one must maintain that it can be established *a priori* not merely that Cartesian Dualism is the only coherent form of dualism, but that it is the only coherent philosophy of mind. In other words, one must maintain that it can be established *a priori* that persons are spiritual substances and that mental states are immaterial states of such substances. As will become clear in the following sections, I think that there are no sound *a priori* reasons for believing this to be true, and that there are strong *a priori* reasons for believing it to be false.

6. Let us consider what the status of mental states would be if Non-Cartesian Dualism were true. The brief answer, I think, is that their status would be much the same as it would be (or is) if materialism were (or is) true – where by 'materialism' is meant the view that whatever exists (apart from 'abstract entities' such

as numbers) is either a material substance or something whose existence consists in the existence of material substances, their states, and their relations to one another.

Materialists sometimes assert that mental states are neuro-physiological states of the brain. Now on one understanding of this, it implies something which many materialists would want to deny (and which, I think, any materialist *should* want to deny). Suppose that pain is said to be the firing of C-fibres. This might mean that the mental property, or attribute, *being in pain* is identical with the neurophysiological attribute *has its C-fibres firing*.

Now this ought to imply, not merely that in all actual cases, whatever has the mental attribute has the neurophysiological one, and *vice versa*, but also that this holds in all possible cases as well – for it is a principle of modal logic that if *a* is identical with *b*, *a* is *necessarily* identical with *b*.[9] And if every mental attribute were thus identical with some physical feature of human brains, it would follow (*a*) that disembodied existence of subjects of mental states is not even a possibility, and (*b*) that other physical creatures (e.g. the inhabitants of remote planets) cannot be subjects of mental states unless they have brains capable of having the relevant physical features, e.g. brains containing C-fibres. But many materialists would reject (*a*), and most would reject (*b*). There is, however, another way of taking the claim that mental states are neurophysiological states of the brain. To say that pain is the firing of C-fibres might mean that in the case of human beings (but not, necessarily, in the case of all possible creatures) being in pain 'consists in', and 'is nothing over and above', the firing of C-fibres. Or as it might be put, in human beings the attribute of being in pain is 'realised in' the firing of C-fibres – which is compatible with its being realised in other ways in other creatures. It is even possible to hold that in the case of human beings a given mental state sometimes has one physical 'realisation' and sometimes another. Of course, it needs to be explained what this relationship of 'being realised in', or 'existing in virtue of', amounts to. I think that this can best be understood if we adopt a causal, or functional, analysis of mental concepts. Roughly, to say that in a certain person at a certain time the attribute of being in pain is realised in the firing of C-fibres is to say that in that person at that time the firing of C-fibres plays the causal role which is definitive of pain.[10]

Now a Non-Cartesian Dualist will not hold that mental attributes are identical to immaterial attributes of immaterial substances. Just as it seems possible that there should be creatures which, given their behaviour, we would want to count as having mental states despite the fact that the physical make-up of their brains or 'control systems' is very different from ours, so it seems possible (assuming the coherence of Minimal Dualism) that there should be creatures to which we would be willing to assign the same mental states despite the fact that they have 'ghostly brains' having very different immaterial states. What the Non-Cartesian Dualist will hold is that the mental states of a person are realised in, that they exist in virtue of, immaterial states of an immaterial substance that functions as the person's 'ghostly brain', and that it is possible (in principle, anyhow) for the same mental attribute to be realised in different immaterial states on different occasions or in different persons. Indeed, just as a materialist can hold that there *could* be creatures (though in fact there aren't) whose mental states are realised in immaterial states, so a Non-Cartesian Dualist could hold that there could be creatures (though in fact there aren't) whose mental states are realised in physical states. And somebody could hold, although I doubt if anyone ever has, that the mental states of some creatures are realised in physical states of brains, while those of other creatures are realised in immaterial states of 'ghostly brains'.

While the Non-Cartesian Dualist holds that mental states are 'realised in' states of immaterial substances, he does not hold that they are themselves states of immaterial substances. They are states of persons; and just as a sensible materialist does not hold that persons *are* their brains, a Non-Cartesian Dualist does not hold that persons *are* the immaterial substances which function as their 'ghostly brains'. A person, according to Non-Cartesian Dualism, is an entity which normally exists, and has the properties it has, in virtue of the existence of a 'mind' and a 'body' which are related in a certain way and have certain properties, but which can exist in virtue of the existence of the mind (immaterial substance) alone. Perhaps the Non-Cartesian Dualist can say, harking back to the discussion in Section 3, that a normal, i.e. embodied, person is a 'partly physical system', but one whose identity conditions permit it to survive the loss of its physical components. But if he says this he must avoid saying that in becoming disembodied a person would become an immaterial substance; for immaterial substances are essentially immaterial, and nothing can become one or cease to be one. Likewise, a materialist who thinks that mental states are 'realised' in physical states of the brain will not think (or should not think) that mental states are themselves states of the brain; for he will know that they are states of a person, and that a person is not identical with his brain (for one thing, the size, shape, weight, etc., of a person are not normally the size, shape, weight, etc., of his brain).[11]

7. Now let us turn our attention to Cartesian Dualism. The Cartesian Dualist holds that mental attributes *are*, in the sense of being identical with rather than in the sense of being realised in, immaterial states of spiritual substances. This means that he must hold, not merely that neither materialism nor Non-Cartesian Dualism *is* true, but that neither of these positions *could* be, or *could have been*, true. If being in pain (say) were merely realised in some immaterial attribute (rather than being identical with it), this would not rule out the possibility of its also being realised (in other creatures, or in other possible worlds) in some physical attribute of a material substance. But if being in pain is *identical with* an immaterial attribute, it is plainly impossible that it should be realised in a physical attribute of a material substance. Likewise, if it is identical with an immaterial attribute (an attribute which can belong only to immaterial substances), it cannot belong to something which is *not* an immaterial substance (e.g. a person as conceived by Non-Cartesian Dualism), and so cannot do so in virtue of some immaterial substance (someone's ghostly brain) having some *other* immaterial attribute (one that is not mental).

This is not yet to say that the Cartesian Dualist is committed to holding that it can be established *a priori* that both Non-Cartesian Dualism and materialism are false or incoherent. For while he is committed to holding that neither of these positions could possibly be true (that neither is true in any possible world), this would be compatible with his holding that the truth of his own position, and the falsity of these others, is necessary *a posteriori* (in Kripke's sense) rather than necessary *a priori*.[12] Just as an identity like 'Hesperus is Phosphorus' is established empirically, despite the fact that if true it is necessarily so in the sense that it could not have been false (is false in no possible world), so it might be held that identities between immaterial attributes and mental attributes are (like all identities) necessary in this sense, but are known to hold *a posteriori*.

But this view has no plausibility at all. For suppose, first of all, that we wished to establish empirically an identity statement of the form 'Mental state M is immaterial state I'. Clearly we would need, to begin with, to have some way of identifying or picking out state I which guarantees that it is an immaterial state but which leaves it an open question, to be settled empirically, whether it is identical with M. In fact, of course, we lack any such way (or any way at all) of picking out immaterial states. But even if we had such a way of picking out immaterial states, what could we discover empirically that would show that a mental state M is identical with an immaterial state I, as opposed to being merely correlated with it, or being realised in it? We could rule out *mere* correlation if we could establish that effects (e.g. behavioural ones) which we confidently attribute to M are in fact due to I. But this would no more establish that M is identical to I than the discovery that pain behaviour is produced by the firing of C-fibres would establish that the attribute *is in pain* is identical (and so identical in all possible worlds) to the physical attribute *has its C-fibres firing*. At best such a discovery would establish that, in the creatures investigated, state M is realised in state I; and this in no way rules out the possibility that there should be creatures in which it is realised in some other state, either immaterial or physical (i.e. that there should be creatures in which behavioural and other effects which would correctly be regarded as manifestations of M are due to some state other than I). Yet if this would not establish that M and I are identical, it seems to me that no empirical discovery would establish this.

Of course, someone might maintain that we could establish empirically that mental states are immaterial states without establishing identities of the form 'Mental state M is immaterial state I' (just as many materialists would hold that we can establish that mental states are [realised in] physical states without establishing any statements of the form 'Mental state *M* is [realised in] physical state P'). But essentially the same difficulty arises about this. For in the absence of an *a priori* argument against the possibility of Non-Cartesian Dualism being true, it seems that any conceivable evidence that might be thought to show that mental states *are* immaterial states would be compatible with the claim that they are merely realised in them, and that the same mental state could (in principle) be realised in more than one way. This is true, for example, of the (perhaps) imaginable discovery that we need to posit the existence of immaterial substances in order to explain the behaviour that is attributed to mental states.

8. Let us turn, then, to the question of whether the Cartesian Dualist has any hope of establishing his position *a priori*.

The *a priori* arguments for dualism that I know of simply assume, and make no attempt to show, that Cartesian Dualism is the only viable form of dualism. I do not myself think that any of these arguments are sound. But what is relevant to our present concerns is that even if some of them were sound, and did establish Minimal Dualism, they would not establish Cartesian Dualism. For example, one typical argument goes (fallaciously, I believe) from the (alleged) fact that I can conceive of myself existing in disembodied form to the claim that it is possible for me to exist in disembodied form, where this is taken as a statement of *de re* modality to the effect that I am something that can exist in disembodied form,[13] from which in turn it is concluded (validly) that I am not a material substance. But even if this conclusion were established, we could not legitimately go from it to the conclusion that I am a spiritual substance (or, more generally, that persons are spiritual substances), for nothing in the argument excludes the possibility that I am (that persons are) as Non-Cartesian Dualism represents persons as being. Or consider the arguments that purport to show that mental states are not physical states. If the conclusion means simply that mental attributes are not identical with physical attributes (and that it is therefore possible for them to be realised non-physically), then even a materialist can accept it. If it means that mental attributes cannot be realised in physical states (that the having of a mental attribute cannot be 'nothing over and above' the having of certain physical attributes), than I do not think it can be established *a priori*. But even if it could be, this would not establish Cartesian Dualism, for it would be compatible with the truth of Non-Cartesian Dualism. Still another argument is from the alleged 'simplicity' of persons; we have already seen that this fails to establish Cartesian Dualism.

Moreover, I think we can see that there *could* be no sound *a priori* argument for Cartesian Dualism. For suppose (*per impossible*) I had such an argument, and knew *a priori* that all mental states are identical with immaterial states of spiritual substances. And suppose that, having this knowledge, I am faced with what looks like someone who is, with great ingenuity and resourcefulness, repairing a complicated machine; that is, I am faced with what, as things are, I would take without question to be a person having certain mental states. On our supposition, I could not be entitled to regard what is before me as a person having these mental states unless I were entitled to believe that the body before me is animated by a spiritual substance. Someone might argue that since I would be entitled to believe that there is a conscious person before me, and since, *ex hypothesi*, I would know that all mental states are identical with immaterial states, I would *ipso facto* be entitled to believe that the body before me is animated by a spiritual substance having the appropriate immaterial states. But here it seems more appropriate to argue backward, and to say that since one *cannot* be justified on empirical grounds in believing that something is animated by a spiritual substance, and since, *ex hypothesi*, I would know that all mental states are immaterial states of spiritual substances, I could not be entitled to believe that what was before me was (or was the embodiment of) a person having those (or any) mental states.

To elaborate this, suppose that I am confronted with *two* creatures, one from Venus and one from Mars, both of which are exhibiting behaviour which one would ordinarily take to show the existence of certain mental states. And suppose, what seems compatible with this, that the physical make-ups of these two creatures are entirely different (their evolutionary histories having been different), and that I know this. There are two possibilities here; either the causes of the observed behaviour are entirely physical, or they are at least partly immaterial. If I had good reason to believe the former, and was guaranteed on *a priori* grounds that mental states are immaterial states, I certainly could not be entitled to take the observed behaviour as evidence of the existence of mental states. So let us suppose that I have good reason to believe that the causes of the behaviour are at least partly immaterial. Now, given that the physical make-ups of these creatures are entirely different, it seems reasonable to suppose that they would have to be acted on by different sorts of immaterial states or events in order to yield the same output of behaviour (roughly, that there would have to be immaterial differences to compensate for the physical differences).[14] Moreover, if we can investigate immaterial substances empirically at all, it ought to make sense to suppose that we have investigated the immaterial substances that animate our Martian and Venusian and discovered that they have very different immaterial states. So let us suppose that I have discovered this. I would therefore know, given our supposition that I am guaranteed *a priori* that mental states are immaterial states of spiritual substances, that at least one of the creatures was not the subject of the mental states which seem to be manifested in the behaviour of both. And this would be true *no matter what* the behaviour was, and no matter how extensive it was. Moreover, given what I argued in Section 7, nothing I could establish empirically would show *which* creature, if either, is a subject of those (or any) mental states – that is, there is nothing that would show which body, if either, is animated by a *spiritual* substance. More generally. on the supposition that we are guaranteed *a priori* that mental states are immaterial states of spiritual substances, the behavioural evidence we would ordinarily take as establishing that a creature is a subject of certain mental states does not establish this, and there is no empirical data which in conjunction with this evidence would establish it. In other words, on this supposition mental states are unknowable. And this seems to me a *reductio ad absurdum* of the supposition.

It seems, then, that we could have neither good empirical grounds nor good *a priori* grounds for believing Cartesian Dualism to be true. It does not follow from this, perhaps, that Cartesian Dualism could not be true – that it is logically or conceptually incoherent. We could establish this stronger conclusion if we could establish that either materialism or Non-

Cartesian Dualism *could* be true. For as we have seen, if it is so much as logically possible that either of these positions is true, Cartesian Dualism cannot be true. And if the falsity of Cartesian Dualism follows from a true statement of logical possibility, then it is not even logically possible that Cartesian Dualism should be true. We could establish the logical possibility of materialism or Non-Cartesian Dualism being true if we could establish a causal or functional account of what mental states are – for such an account would allow for the possibility of mental states being realised in a variety of physical states or a variety of immaterial states. I believe myself that only such an account makes sense of our ability to have knowledge of mental states (our own as well as those of others). But I have not the space to argue this here. However, if I have succeeded in showing that there is and could be no good reason for believing in Cartesian Dualism, then, given what I argued earlier, I have shown that there is and could be no good reason for believing in a form of dualism that would make belief in immortality significantly more plausible than it is on anti-dualist assumptions.

NOTES

1. See Robert C. W. Ettinger, *The Prospect of Immortality* (New York, 1966).

2. I have not been able to find a unequivocal and unqualified statement of this view in the literature; but it is implicit in my own book *Self-Knowledge and Self-Identity* (Ithaca, N.Y. 1963), and in the writings of other philosophers who have attacked dualism on conceptual (or logical) rather than empirical grounds.

3. See David M. Armstrong, *A Materialist Theory of Mind* (London, 1968) p.19.

4. See my paper 'Embodiment and Behaviour,' in Amelie Rorty (ed.), *The Identities of Persons* (Berkeley and Los Angeles, 1976).

5. I owe this example to Richard Boyd.

6. Even on the assumption that there are no immaterial substances, and that the existence of everything in some way consists in the existence of material substances, there may be a sense in which persons are neither material nor immaterial substances. For even on materialist assumptions, it is natural to hold that stones, trees and automobiles are material substances in a sense in which corporation, nations, and political parties are not. If such a narrow sense of 'material substance' can be defined (and I shall not attempt to define it here), it may be that even a materialist should deny that persons are material substances in the narrow sense – for one thing, the identity conditions for persons seem to differ importantly from those for paradigmatic 'material objects', but not in ways that call materialism into question.

7. So I am not discussing Occasionalism, and other versions of dualism that deny interaction between material and immaterial substances. I believe, but

have not the space to argue here, that interactionism is the only coherent form of dualism.

8. Despite what I have said here, something must be conceded to the objection that there is no satisfactory principle of individuation for immaterial substances. In the sense in which we have a conception of material substance, which includes, as central to it, a partial specification of the identity conditions for material objects, we do not have a conception of immaterial substances, or of any particular kind of immaterial substances. The definition I have given of 'spiritual substance' does not specify such a conception, for it says nothing positive about what relationships would hold between spiritual substances (to say that some of these relationships would be 'quasi-spatial' is not to say what they would be). So it is in a rather thin sense that it is 'conceivable' that there should be immaterial substances. It is not that we have a determinate conception of some kind of immaterial substance, and can conceive of there being things that satisfy this conception. It is rather that we can conceive of having (or acquiring) such a determinate notion, and of believing, intelligibly and consistently, that there are things that satisfy it. However, in the remainder of this essay I shall write as if we do have a determinate conception of immaterial substance; this can be thought of as a concession to my opponents.

One other common objection to dualism should be mentioned here. It is sometimes urged that there are intimate conceptual, or logical, connections between mental states and their behavioural manifestations or expressions, and that because of these connections it is logically incoherent to suppose that a person might exist in disembodied form. In order to assess this objection we must consider in what sense, if any, mental states and behaviour are 'conceptually connected'. I cannot discuss this complex issue here; but I have argued elsewhere that what seems to me the most defensible version of the 'conceptual connection thesis' is compatible with the view that disembodied existence is possible – see my 'Embodiment and Behaviour,' op. cit.

9. See Saul Kripke, 'Identity and Necessity', in Milton Munitz (ed.), *Identity and Individuation* (New York, 1971), pp. 135–64.

10. See D. M. Armstrong, *A Materialist Theory of Mind* (London, 1968) and David Lewis, 'An Argument for the Identity Theory', in D. M. Rosenthal (ed.), *Materialism and the Mind-Body Problem* (Englewood Cliffs, N.J., 1971), and 'Psychophysical and Theoretical Identifications', in *Australasian Journal of Philosophy*, Vol. 50, No. 3 (December, 1972), pp. 249–57.

11. It may be thought that if a person's brain is kept alive *in vitro*, and is all that physically remains of him, then (on materialist assumptions) he will be identical with it – and, likewise, that if all that is left of a person is an immaterial brain, he will be identical with it. But this cannot be so if, as I believe, it is impossible for entities X and Y to be numerically different at one time and numerically identical at another (or if, what would seem to come to the same thing, identical entities must have identical histories).

12. See Kripke's 'Identity and Necessity,' op. cit., and his 'Naming and Necessity', in Donald Davidson and Gilbert Harman (eds.), *Semantics of Natural Language* (Dordrecht, 1972), pp. 253–355.

13. The fallacy in this, I think, involves a confusion of a certain sort of epistemic possibility with metaphysical possibility. In the sense in which it is

true that I can conceive of myself existing in disembodied form, this comes to the fact that it is compatible with what I know about my essential nature (supposing that I do not know that I am an essentially material being) that I should exist in disembodied form. From this it does not follow that my essential nature is in fact such as to permit me to exist in disembodied form.

14. See my 'Embodiment and Behaviour', op. cit., for an elaboration of this.

II HYWEL LEWIS

I am in entire agreement with Sydney Shoemaker on one main point. This is the point with which he begins, namely that we are reduced to desperate straits, in seeking to make any case for immortality, unless we can first make out a case for dualism – on the mind-body problem. I would indeed go further. I do not think that any case for immortality can begin to get off the ground if we fail to make a case for dualism. This has been extensively recognised by non-dualists. Immortality has normally been understood to mean that we continue to exist when the present physical body has been destroyed. In conditions of existence in the past, and in any condition we can reasonably forsee now, the body one now has is very completely destroyed, as a functioning organism, very soon after we draw the last breath. Usually today it is reduced to ashes, and even if preserved in some mummified form, the chances of revivifying it to function as it does when we are alive, are too remote to be taken seriously. There is indeed a little more prospect today, owing to the advance of science, that the deterioration of living organisms could be arrested or reversed or that there might be some other 'life-prolonging episodes' or devices which would ensure our literal bodily continuity without end. But even if this were a prospect we could entertain with some confidence, it would be rather far removed from the expectations usually entertained by those who believe in immortality. The latter has been thought to be available to human beings past and present, to the millions whose bodies have suffered complete disintegration already as well as to the fortunate ones, assuming they are so, on whom endless bodily existence may be conferred some day by the advance of science. Indeed, the case for immortality has hardly ever been made to rest on the avoidance of the reality of death; it concerns an expectation of something which holds irrespective of the normal accepted facts of death and decay, and, for many, the attractiveness of the prospect turns, in part at least, on our superseding the limitations as well as the ills to which flesh is heir and embarking on other, presumably richer, modes of existence.

Against this it may be urged that, in the Christian context at least, what has been largely expected is that, notwithstanding death and decay, there may still be a 'resurrection of the body'. This, we are told, does not mean the 'resuscitation of corpses', but it does then become difficult to know what it can mean. Some just invoke here the omnipotence of God with whom 'all things are possible'. But we still need to know in some measure what is contemplated, and what reason there could be for supposing that God would in fact literally recompose our bodies. I have, however, commented at more length on this issue in another recent symposium;[1] and have referred to the suggestion that better scientific understanding of physical bodies can make the present supposition more attractive. In the same context I have also discussed the relevance, not very great it seems to me, of the the notion of an astral body and its intelligibility. I will therefore leave this point here with the general expression of agreement with the view that immortality must at least be understood to involve such independence of our present physical existence as will make it intelligible to suppose that we continue to exist and function notwithstanding the destruction of the present body.

But suppose someone says: 'I agree, but surely you will need a body of some kind'. I do not think I would concede this, at least as an absolute requirement.[2] But if the point were conceded, it would still mean that my continued existence was independent of any particular body I might have at one stage. The body is replaceable while I remain the same. This commits us to dualism at least to the extent of making my own existence, in essentials, independent of my having a particular body, and especially my present physical body which, I have no doubt, will come to its end with the end of my 'allotted span'.

On this score then there is nothing seriously in dispute between Shoemaker and myself, whether or not we would put our points in quite the same terms. But immediately beyond this point a gap begins to open. For I consider a dualist position to be an

indispensable basis for belief in immortality in at least one
markedly different way.

For me the dualist supposition is a requirement of any
reasonable understanding of what it would be like to be
immortal, or of what this notion *means*. On most of the widely
held views of mind and body today, any kind of future existence
is ruled out, and for this reason it is essential for anyone who
wishes to defend the belief in immortality to counter the doctrines
which plainly preclude it. I do not expect to do more than this,
in the present context, in my defence of dualism. I only wish to
keep the door open, to rule out the essential inconceivability of a
future existence, in an immortal or more limited way. Nothing
is claimed, on the present score, to make it certain, or even highly
probable, that we shall survive the dissolution of our bodies.
Other reasons must be invoked to accomplish this further aim. I
an not concerned in this paper with what they are.

Shoemaker's attitude here appears to be different. He expects
the case for dualism, especially in its stricter Cartesian form, as
he labels it, to yield more positive results, indeed to establish
nothing less that the essential indestructibility of the soul.
Immortality is assured if the dualist case is made.

This is not because some of the obvious difficulties, for example
the indisputable causal dependence on the body in the present
existence, are removed or have the sting taken out of them.
Much more positively it is established that, in terms of what we
find ourselves to be, we just cannot fail to be immortal.

Furthermore, the way this is understood is that, in a dualist
view, we must be deemed to have a simple, indivisible nature,
and nothing which is thought to have such a nature can ever be
destroyed, on the grounds presumably that destruction must
take the form of the dissolution of some entity into its component
parts. This supposition, although it has never been central in
discussions of the subject in the past, is not without an impressive
ancestry. Plato has recourse to it, in the *Phaedo* and in the
Republic, although he turns also to some other rather formal
arguments such as the insistence that nothing is destroyed except
by its own evil, the evil of the soul being injustice which is far
from causing the death of the wicked. What is impressive in the
case of Plato is the sustained conviction that the individual soul is
immortal.

On the indivisibility argument, Plato would also find difficulty in his own sustained account of the tripartite division of the soul. The reply might be made that appetite and spirit, on Plato's view, come about through involvement with the body and do not belong to the true and essentially rational nature of the soul. But the famous myth in the *Phaedrus* at least ascribes both appetite and desire to the soul in its pre-natal state. It is worth noting also that the discussion in the *Phaedo* finds the clue to the simplicity of the soul in its affinity with the Forms and this gives the former a somewhat different character from its invocation in later traditions.

The idea of the simplicity of the soul has lurked in the background of much subsequent Western thinking, but it has also been prevented from making fuller impact by anxiety not to inpugn the essentially created character of all finite things. A soul that is, in virtue of its essential nature, not destructible would presumably have pre-existed, and while this in some form would be acceptable to Plato, it would cause some embarrassment to later theism by coming close at least to elevating one kind of being into a state of existence in its own right over against a purported Author of all things.

To pursue the last point further on our own account, and in closer relation to Shoemaker's view, it is not at all clear to me why anything should be deemed impervious to destruction just by having an essentially simple nature. Can we take it for granted that nothing can come to an end except by dissolution into its constituent parts? This would confer inviolate, and thereby it would seem necessary, existence on any finite entity that has the appropriate simplicity. But we generally assume that necessity does not characterise any statement of finite existence. Indeed, the principle has sometimes been generalised to apply to all existence, as in J. N. Findlay's celebrated reversal of the Ontological Argument.[3] Generally it is conceded that necessary existence belongs solely to God and that it is so essential a feature of God, where the being of God is at all acknowledged, that it is impious to place it elsewhere. Less piously, I repeat the question why should anything be thought essentially less destructible solely in virtue of the simple nature it is alleged to have.

That there is a sense in which the self does have a simple ndivisible nature seems to me true, although the point needs to be presented very carefully indeed to avoid the difficulties instanced in discussions like that of Shoemaker. To the last point we shall return shortly. But in the meantime it seems evident to me, irrespective of any understanding we may have of our own natures, that we are in no way exceptions to what seems evident about other finite existences, namely that, in the last resort, we just find that certain things do exist. Granted, of course, the order of nature as in fact we find it, then we may claim that certain things are required. Our common speech reflects this as much as scientific statements. 'It must have rained', we say, 'there must be another force at work somewhere, another planet drawing known ones from their anticipated orbit', but this holds only given the order of nature as we find it. There is no inherent ultimate necessity why the world should be as it is or why any particular entity should be; and anything we say in this respect in one finite context must apply in just the same way in all. There is nothing inviolable about simplicity, and if we do have some ultimately simple nature this does nothing at all to remove us from the class of things which, in the last analysis, we just find to be.

It may be that Shoemaker does not want to dispute what I say here, but is simply concerned to dispute the sort of grounds on which it seems to him the case for immortality is usually made, or has to be made. If he does take this line, then he seems to ignore the main course of the commendation of the belief in immortality, at least in Western thought, where ideas of worth, of moral requirement or the known will of God for certain of his creatures and so forth hold the centre of the stage. It is on these grounds, or in consequence of some alleged evidence of some measure of survival of death, rather than on *a priori* grounds, that most people, today and in the past, would wish to base a belief in immortality. Even if *a priori* grounds are invoked they are usually of a more wide-ranging kind than the insistence on alleged simple natures.

All the same, I agree, though on quite different grounds, that the maintenance of a dualist view is an indispensable part of any plausible case for immortality, and I also deem it an essential ingredient of a sound dualist view of persons that, in the last analysis, selfhood will be found to be ultimate and indivisible. This will become clearer if we now turn to the substance of Shoemaker's paper in the attempted refutation of dualism.

The case against dualism, as advanced by Shoemaker, involves the distinction he draws between two kinds of dualism, labelled for his purpose, without claiming historical accuracy, Cartesian Dualism and Non-Cartesian Dualism. The first he considers to be wholly untenable and the second is thought 'not to be much help to believers in immortality'. Both are said to be versions of 'Minimal Dualism'. In both the main forms, and thus in all Minimal Dualism, it is affirmed that there is an immaterial substance, a 'continuant' which 'can have different properties at different times' and such that our mental states must depend on those which the immaterial substance has. The states of the latter mediate all causal connections involving mental states between sensory 'input' and behavioural 'output', and we may exist without having a body as long as the immaterial substance exists and has the appropriate states. But, on Cartesian Dualism, the person *is* the immaterial substance, on the other view he is not. That is the crucial difference.

So, just as some philosophers say that a person may exist 'as long as the brain exists' but without implying that persons *are* brains, Non-Cartesian Dualism holds that we have 'a ghostly brain', the immaterial substance, which is not however the person.

There are difficulties in this view which I shall try to bring out in due course. In the meantime let it first be noted that Shoemaker attaches very great importance to the notion of Non-Cartesian Dualism. The main weight of his arguments seem to rest, at the crucial points, on the availability to us of this alternative to Cartesian Dualism. The latter is not shown in this paper (though Shoemaker thinks it can be done) to be strictly incoherent. But we have no reason 'to believe it', for all the considerations that might seem to require it are equally consistent with Non-Cartesian Dualism which has in addition attractions of a further sort, though not such as to induce Shoemaker to accept it. It seems then to follow that we can have no *a priori* argument for Cartesian dualism, there can be no strict requirement of its being sound, for all thought directed to it leaves us with the rival version; and it seems thus to be shown that we are not bound to think of ourselves as simple immaterial substances which can thus be deemed, in virtue of what they are, to be incapable of destruction, in the only way deemed relevant, by dissolution into further components.

This seems to me the gist of Shoemaker's central thesis. Let us look at the details. The arguments turn much here on the questions of individuation and identity. This is in line with much that has recently been said by philosophers opposed to Cartesian views, even those who would not wish to give a behaviourist or a physicalist account of mental processes, for example Ayer, Strawson and, very explicitly, Bernard Williams. What they say, in brief, is that, if it were not for the body, we could not be individuated, and Williams at least appears not unsympathetic, in that context, to the notion of a universal mind, at least as what we would have to think if we retained the notion of mental processes without bodies. The idea of a universal mind or some strictly shared, unindividuated consciousness has appealed to many religious thinkers and to psychologists from time to time – it is a widely held interpretation of mysticism. Many post-Hegelian idealists subscribed to it, and there might for that reason be some grounds for rebuking Shoemaker for not reckoning with this possibility – it is the approach that many who would defend the belief in immortality would be disposed to take. I do not myself, however, wish to make much of this point, partly because no one can deal with everything in one paper, and Shoemaker has his distinct target in Cartesian Dualism, but even more because there are few views which seem to me more mistaken than the notion of unindividuated finite minds, and I have done my own share of blowing upon it, in itself and in its ethical and religious consequences.

There must, then, I agree, be individuation. But how is this possible if the immaterial substances in question cannot, as the thought of them would seem to imply, 'be individuated by spatial relations'. This problem, I must now add, does not worry me a great deal, and it never has. It has always seemed evident to me that everyone knows himself to be the being that he is in just being so. We identify ourselves to ourselves in that way, and not in the last resort on the basis of what we know about ourselves. The reaction to this is sometimes to retort that we seem to be running out of arguments, and we must surely make our case by argument. This is a trying situation for a philosopher to have to meet; quite clearly he does not want to seem unwilling to argue. But argument is not everything, we have also to reckon with what we just find to be the case, we cannot conjure all existence into being by argument and we cannot, as I hope does not sound portentous, argue against reality. There is a way of looking at what there is, and wisdom in philosophy has been thought, from Plato to Wittgenstein, to depend largely on knowing how to look. The bane of much philosophy, past and present, has been the supposition that we must provide arguments for everything, and Shoemaker himself seems to be in some measure a victim of this, as may perhaps become plainer later. Admittedly, famous dualists, Plato and Descartes, have been apt on occasion to fall back on very formal arguments little worthy of their proper attainments, and I suppose Descartes must have regarded the *Cogito*[4] as a strictly rationalist *a priori* argument; but the real strength of the *Cogito* lies elsewhere – the 'I think' refers to experience and what we find it to be. This does not commit us to dogmatism or an unthinking commitment to this or that view, or the lack of taught thinking. It is just a caveat about the *a priori* and the wrong sort of exclusive reliance on argument. I shall not pursue this further, and I have indicated more fully elsewhere[5] how, without any quasi-empirical looking in on ourselves, we find ourselves to be the distinctive beings that we are in the fact of being so, and in the same way are aware of having the experiences we do have.

It is quite otherwise when we think of how we know, not ourselves but one another. I am not convinced that spatial media, or their like, are altogether essential for knowledge of other persons, and I have tried[6] to sketch how, taking telepathy as a possible partial clue, we might communicate in what I have called 'A world of thoughts alone'. But I readily admit that, in identifying other persons, normally at least in present conditions, we require observable evidence, though what we do establish is not itself observable. I shall not develop this further now, and must leave it with what I have said elsewhere, although a brief reference will have to be made to the same point below. But let us return to the way Shoemaker proceeds.

He does not think that the requirement of 'spatial relations' is altogether fatal even to Cartesian Dualism, although he notes that this has often been thought to be the case. But this is for very different reasons from those I might adduce.

He observes that we have to admit, and on the whole may do so without jeopardy to Cartesian Dualism, that immaterial substances can interact causally with material substances. That was certainly Descartes' intention and that of any Dualist who claims to make sense of common experience. Shoemaker does indeed here touch upon the somewhat hoary objection of how minds having, *ex hypothesi,* 'no spatial relationship; such as contiguity' can affect material bodies and, in each case, one particular body – one recalls Passmore observing[7] that minds do not push and bodies do not persuade. But he thinks we 'must suppose that this difficulty can be overcome'. The difficulty is not to my mind all that serious. It is indeed strange that minds do affect bodies, and vice-versa, and peculiar, though generally fortunate, that one mind affects just one body. There seems to be no way in which we can account for this (and to postulate 'mysterious transactions' as Ryle and others would require of their opponents is only to make matters worse). But here again we must not go against the facts because we have reached the limit of further explanation – no causal relation can be quite exhaustively explained. We must again take the world as we find it, and we do find that states of mind affect bodies (one particular body normally at least) and bodies minds. But granted this how do we proceed?

We come here to the crux of Shoemaker's thesis. If the difficulties in the supposition that immaterial substances can interact causally with material substances 'can be overcome' (and if it cannot what do we say to the out-and-out materialist?), then we can establish relationships between substances of these two sorts, analogous to the spatial relationships which have their role in determining causal relationships between material substances and establishing their identity; and on the basis of these 'quasi-spatial relationships' we can establish further 'quasi-spatial relationships' between the immaterial substances themselves and, on this basis, determine their identity and continuity through time. This can furthermore apply to Cartesian Dualism and to Non-Cartesian Dualism, and it is for this reason, it seems, that the former cannot be rejected expressly by its failure to cope with the question of individuation. But in that case, how does Cartesian Dualism come to grief?

It comes to grief, as Shoemaker seems to hold, because of the availability to us, on the basis of what has just been outlined, of the notion of immaterial substances which can *have parts*. As he sums it up: 'Finally, and this is of course the point of all this, if it is possible for immaterial substances (or things) to have parts or components, then there seems no reason to suppose that immaterial substances are not subject to destruction through the dissolution of their parts' (p.120). There are further points in the elaboration of this to which I shall return. But first we should have the core, or central theme, of the argument clear. And the sum of it seems to be this. We might be tempted to object, as our first move, that the argument could cut in another way than the one intended by Shoemaker, that is, we might argue that, because Cartesian Dualism is available to us, we can reject Non-Cartesian Dualism. For all that has been shown that might be true. But I do not think this would quite take the force of Shoemaker's special contention here. What he seems to be holding is that, since Non-Cartesian Dualism is available we cannot claim that immaterial substances as such are bound to be without parts and indestructible. And the presupposition of all this, in turn, seems to be that we need to establish in an *a priori* way the essential indestructibility of immaterial substance, and that by dissolution into parts. But how is this requirement itself established? Even within the ambit of Shoemaker's own procedures it could be urged that, as Cartesian Dualism has not been shown to be incoherent (and Shoemaker fully admits that) a person could, for all that has been shown, be a Cartesian substance in the present sense and so, *ex hypothesi*, indestructible.

In other words, why, on the argument as we have followed it hitherto, does anyone who hesitates to go along with Shoemaker have to show 'that Cartesian Dualism is the only coherent form of dualism' (p.121)?[8] If I have missed something vital here I shall be relieved to be shown what it is. It will not, of course, be enough to bring forward other reasons for rejecting, or having doubts about, Cartesian Dualism.

Let me now refer to other points of difficulty in the elaboration of Shoemaker's main thesis. I would like first to reflect further on the way the notion of a person must be understood in the context of Shoemaker's notion of Non-Cartesian Dualism, and, in particular, to be clear how person and substance are taken to be related here. First of all, what would an immaterial substance, not itself the person, be in this case? Is it a Lockian 'something we know not what', and do we then just have to 'suppose' it? Or a Kantian 'thing in itself', and on which of the many versions of this? I do not by any means rule out the possibility that there may be types of existences of which we know nothing at present, as implied in the celebrated notion of 'infinite attributes'. We know only mental and physical reality, at least explicitly. The universe may have other things in it of which we have no conception. Is Shoemaker thinking along these or kindred lines? I doubt it. In that case, the immaterial substance, in the present context, must be some combination of mental states, on which more in a moment, and the quasi-spatial relationships indicated – or perhaps some combination of the latter alone (but where, in that case, would mental states come in?). Is the substance in the latter case to be defined exhaustively in terms of such combinations – if not what is left over? And where, in all this, does the person, which is not the substance, figure?

I suspect that the answer to the last question is that a person is a further combination of immaterial substances, and their relationships, and perhaps material substances. If so, it begins to be a far cry from what we normally think of persons. But it will certainly help to have this matter clarified. Moreover, when we are told that there could '(perhaps)'[9] be 'atomic' immaterial substances, is this intended seriously, and where does it figure, if it does, in the account of persons and substances, if the latter at least require the quasi-spatial relationships for their identification?

The only clear example we are offered, to help us to determine how persons must be understood – or what constitutes a person – is not very helpful in fact. It is that of the Supreme Court on page 118. This is brought up in the context where it seems to be admitted that persons may be 'simple and indivisible' although the relevant substances need not be so. One reaction to this would be to point out that, when people concern themselves with questions of immortality and survival of death, it is persons that they have especially in mind – it is persons who are immortal, etc. – and if persons may after all turn out to be 'simple and indivisible' they would qualify without more ado for Shoemaker – what is simple cannot be destroyed. But let us look more closely at the example itself.

The Supreme Court, it appears, is 'in some important sense without parts and indivisible.' This is, apparently, because it would continue to exist if all the members died or resigned at the same time. Now it certainly would be true that the Supreme Court, as part of the American constitution, would continue in these sad circumstances, and it could function as before as soon as new members were appointed – and so indeed for any committee. A committee does not lapse when all its members leave. But what is it that remains? Surely a system of rules and procedures, for the appointment of members and their rights and duties – terms of reference, the rights of the chairman, etc. And while these are not manifold in the case in which the individual members are, they certainly involve some complexity and inter-relations of parts. The Supreme Court is a fairly elaborate part of an elaborate constitution.

But in any case is this a proper model for our concept of a person? There are indeed doctrines of corporate personality, but when they are not explicitly taken to refer to legal or quasi-legal fictions, they seem to be misleading and, in fact, mischievous doctrines. Post-Hegelian idealists welcomed them, though in some cases with reluctance, and the sinister consequences of entertaining them were effectively exhibited by L. T. Hobhouse in his celebrated *The Metaphysical Theory of the State*, as relevant in its day as it is in ours. Professor Hannah Arendt has taken up the same cause with vigour and eloquence in our time. This is a topic in itself, and having made it a central theme of some of my own writings, I must leave it there now. But the meeting of extremes in this way is not, perhaps, so unimportant a feature of current philosophy as some might suppose. When it appears in the work of highly professional and cautious thinkers like Shoemaker and Strawson[10] one wonders whether they appreciate whither their thoughts may be tending.

I should maintain by contrast that the person is the distinct individual, and to think of persons by analogy with abstract systems seems to put us gravely in danger of substituting hypostatised abstractions for individual beings. As a rule, in Western thought at least, it is of oneself as a particular being and not of some abstract constitution of one's individual existence, that one is thinking in relation to the prospect of immortality, whether that is attractive or not. The constitution of my own nature, or my 'values' as some have supposed, are repeatable, presumably *ad infinitum* and in diverse conditions. But will *I* live again?

Even in Oriental thought, the position, if properly scrutinised (as, alas, rarely happens) may not be as accommodating to Shoemaker's notions as some might be inclined to assume. But that is also a theme in itself.

Let me now add a brief word on mental states as they figure in Shoemaker's paper. Here we come closer to a materialist position than I thought previously he wished to go. The status of mental states is, we are told, the same as it would be if materialism were true, the view that whatever exists 'is either a material substance or something whose existence consists in the existence of material substances, their states, and their relations to one another' (p.121). But this does not apparently mean that mental states are just neurophysiological states of the brain. A person could in fact be in pain without having the neurophysiological states of my brain, or indeed of brains and bodies like ours at all when we are in pain. A mental state may have 'sometimes one physical "realisation" and sometimes another'. If this merely meant that the same mental state could conceivably be caused by different physical states, I would not dispute it. But it seems to mean more. There is no admission that the mental state is essentially (perhaps I could be allowed the word 'ontologically') other than its physical conditions. It is rather that we must adopt 'a causal, or functional, analysis of mental concepts'. The causal role of certain neurophysiological states could be taken over by others. Pain may thus be 'realised' in different sorts of physiological states. But just what is it that is being 'realised'? What is being caused, what function is exercised – an exclusively physical or behavioural one? This seems most implausible.

Indeed, I must confess here to head-on collision with my cosymposiast. For while he could admit (and this makes him appear to concede a great deal more than he does) that pain could be 'merely realised' in some immaterial attribute of an immaterial substance, in what may seem by now a rather unusual view of the latter, the pain could not be '*identical with* an immaterial attribute', for then it could not be realised in a physical attribute of a material substance. Against this, which appears to be essential for Shoemaker's system, I should want to insist that pain, like all other mental states, is essentially an immaterial attribute and that a causal or functional definition does not begin to do justice to the facts. There are normally physical conditions of pain, and there is pain behaviour. But I had hoped that it would be evident to philosophers by now that pain is neither of these, or their like. It is what I *feel*. I know it in experiencing it and in no other way. I could learn to recognise the physical accompaniments and the behaviour but this would not tell me what pain was. I might also have pain without any awareness of conditions (a wound perhaps) which would normally induce it – or any disposition to behave in the way normally expected of people in pain. And so, even more obviously, of thoughts, the ones that go on while writing this paper or speaking to it. These are what I find them at the time to be, and that is essentially non-spatial reality. I have no independent proof of this, I can only reflect and invite you to reflect on what I find my experience to be like, and if this is not allowed, then I must protest against being put out of court before the only proper case can be stated.

The same goes for our knowledge of one another. Shoemaker reverts to the stock objection to a Cartesian account, namely that empirical evidence cannot tell us anything about a 'spiritual' or non-empirical substance. But why not? Shoemaker himself notes that if I saw 'what looks like someone who is, with great ingenuity and resourcefulness, repairing a complicated machine' he would take it without question 'to be a person having mental states'. But if this is so obvious, is it not equally plain that the mental states, far from being merely causal or functional, are ongoing thoughts and purposings such as each of us would be aware of in the process of having them in his own case? Admittedly, in knowing other persons, we do not proceed through correlations of behaviour and directly inspected states of mind of other beings, as that is *ex hypothesi* out of the question. But that, as Ryle and others have overlooked, is no bar to our finding the observable behaviour explicable on the assumption of designs and purposes such as we have in our own inner life. It is sheer unwarranted dogma that empirical evidence can only establish empirical things.

This shows us what is wrong with the example of the Martian and the Venusian at the end of the paper. It is of course possible to be mistaken about one another, and we can never wholly eliminate that. With a different 'evolutionary history', etc., the same outward behaviour may reflect a different state of mind, but this is something we could only discover if we had very elaborate evidence. In these peculiar circumstances we certainly could not know from the limited evidence of the present occasion that one of the creatures had not the thoughts and purposes we would normally ascribe to it. But in due course, from sufficiently comprehensive evidence we would expect to discover this. And if for some reason we did not discover it, that would be just too bad, as in the case where we are, as often happens, at a loss in the case of identical twins. Such confusion, or failure of identity, is no bar to the confidence we otherwise have about identity and the ascription of mental states. But if the only course were to establish by some direct independent inspection a causal relation between physical and non-physical states, the sort of quandaries that Shoemaker envisages would present insurmountable problems.

It may be urged at this point that I have not said much in a positive way myself about the possible simplicity of the self or subject and the relation of this to the obviously varied and changing mental states that we have. My reaction is that I find this is a peculiarly difficult philosophical question, though in a very different way from Shoemaker. There seems to me to be a very unique or distinctive way in which everyone finds himself to be the being that he is, whether he reflects on that or not. We are also aware that certain states of mind are ours in the fact of having them. I do not, to keep to the relatively simple stock example of pain, infer that I am in pain – I do not have to tell myself, or note my bleeding finger or swollen limbs or hear my own cries. These are the ways in which I know that someone else is in pain, and if a coach were blacked out in an accident I might wonder which of my companions is in pain. I would not wonder about myself. I would know that I had the pain in having it, it is very much myself; I do not know first that there is a pain, and wonder about the ascription of it as in the case of other persons. I know it immediately as mine, and by this token, though not certain always in other cases who is in pain, I have no conception of a pain that is not in this immediate sense someone's pain. There could not be just a 'floating' pain. But to find adequate terms for this is peculiarly difficult – 'belong', 'owned', etc., have associations with physical belonging (or with rights) which are quite out of place here, though we may have to be content with a cautious use of such metaphors. A hasty and oversimple use of terms in this sort of context is the bane of sound philosophy, and it is better to say nothing at all than be too hasty. There is, all the same, a peculiarly intimate sense in which a pain, or any other mental state – thoughts, purposing, etc. – is me or mine; and at the same time this is also not strictly correct.

It is not correct, not just because there is more to any of us than just being in this particular state, having this pain, etc., but also because I would be the being that I am, and know this, even if I did not have the actual states of mind I do have, or if all my experiences were different. The latter would make a difference in one sense to my identity, the sense in which I do not know who I am in loss of memory or split personality. But basic to all this is the sense of my being the one I find myself to be, an ultimate irreducible sense, in those or any other contingencies. Even if I should be born again, as on reincarnation theories, in some entirely different conditions, and with no knowledge of my present existence, I would have, in this new state, the same basic sense of being the being that I am in my present state, though *ex hypothesi* I could not know this, having no way, on our supposition, of knowing, by memory or other evidence, what had gone on previously.

There is in this way a simplicity and finality or ultimacy about personal identity to which no proper parallel is to be found elsewhere, though philosophers go astray, as many do today, by neglecting this and looking too closely for models or parallels in other cases of identity external to ourselves. At the same time our ongoing mental states are also, as was stressed, ourselves in a very distinct sense; and I am not at all happy about any way of presenting this situation. Perhaps there is not much more that we can say, but in granting the tension between similar, but not quite reconcilable, things we are forced to say, we may here be getting as deep as we can into the philosophical apprehension of the subject. I certainly want to say that the self is simple in the sense that it could not be or become another, however much the kind of experiences we may have may overlap or be shared. Nor is a person just the experiences he happens to have. At the same time, a self is not to be too sharply dissociated from the actual experiences or mental states it does have.

With this, and the awareness that much harder thought may

have to be given to this subject to take it further than I have done, I return to the points I made at the start, namely that the most immediate relevance of the view of persons and identity which I advance to the question of immortality lies in the disassociation of the self, in its essential nature, from the bodily state which we have every reason to expect to be completely ended in due course. The issue of simplicity or finality does indeed relate very expressly to questions of absorption in some more complete or universal existence, which is how some think of immortality. But the alleged indestructibility of the simple has not, on my view, much significance at all. If it came within God's purpose that a tree should be conserved for ever, I see no reason in logic, from the fact that a tree obviously has parts, why this could not be. But if I am identical with my body I cannot expect to be conserved in the absence of what seems altogether unlikely, namely the conservation as well of this seemingly mortal coil. But to dissociate a person, in essential being, from any material state is not to make the case positively for either survival or immortality; it is to remove an obstacle and make a start, but there is a long way to go beyond that.

NOTES

1. *Proc. Aristotelian Society Supplementary Vol. LXIX* 1975.

2. See my *The Self and Immortality*, Chapter 9.

3. *Mind*, 1948.

4. As also the Ontological Argument, although what remains is an initial insight into there having to be some necessary being.

5. *The Elusive Mind*, Chapter XI and *The Self and Immortality*, Chapter 5.

6. *The Self and Immortality*, Chapter 9.

7. *Philosophical Reasoning*, Chapter iii.

8. It could, I suppose, be argued, that the Cartesian Dualist has to hold that mental states are necessarily identical with those of an immaterial substance and that, in consequence, his position becomes untenable even if we can consider an alternative view. But the Cartesian Dualist would only hold his view on reflection on what he finds to be the case, not on some independent *a priori* ground.

9. Page 120.

10. *Individuals*, page 113.

7 The Belief in Life After Death

There can be little doubt that the greater part of mankind has believed, in some way or at some level, that they have a destiny beyond the fleeting transitory existence we have in the present life. This belief is deeply rooted in most of the great religions, and most persons in the past have subscribed to some kind of religion. Even Shinto, although a very secular religion in some respects, makes much of the worship of ancestors who are thought to be still 'around' in some form. Theravada Buddhism, in spite of its scepticism, at least leaves the matter open and, while presenting special difficulties for any view of personal survival, has drifted into forms of belief and practice which involve at least some notion of a round of various existences; Mahayana Buddhism makes it very explicit. The so-called primitive religions seem also to centre on the expectation of some kind of further existence. How profoundly religious allegiances have affected people's attitudes and how firmly religious persons have adhered to their professed beliefs is a more debatable matter. But few things have affected the general life and culture of people in the past more than religion: it has been a main determinant of attitudes, a shaper of major presuppositions; and it would not be incautious in the least to affirm on this basis that, at some level, by far the greater part of mankind has committed itself to the expectation of a life besides the present one and has shaped its activities accordingly.

Could the same be said today? There can be little doubt that most communities today have become much more secular than at any previous time. How deep or permanent is this change may not be easy to settle. Some, like myself, regard it as a phase in the profounder and more intelligent recovery of religion, although this by no means involves commendation of secular attitudes or the canonising of them as inevitable stages in some dialectic of religious progress. But without going further into this particular question, I would hazard fairly confidently the guess that, where the question of belief in life after death is concerned, most persons, if a poll of some kind were taken, would still return a fairly firm positive answer, even in countries where vast material changes have brought about considerable secularisation. What importance we should ascribe to that I leave unanswered for the moment.

Beliefs can be held in a variety of ways and at different levels. There are at least two main ways in which this is true in respect of the present theme. A belief can be held at one level only when we adhere to it in spite of the fact that the evidence for it (or other reasons for holding it) is not very strong. There are some beliefs which we can hold with much more confidence than others. They need not be the most important beliefs. If I believe that it is fine and sunny at the moment, I have only to look up from my desk or step out into the garden to be sure of this, and anyone who calls will confirm it. I am equally certain that I have a pencil in my hand and am writing with it. I see and hold it, and that is about the greatest certainty we could have. Philosophical questions could be asked about the status of things like pencils or the nature of perception. But for all normal purposes I am as certain as anyone could wish to be that I am holding a pencil and that the sun is shining. I am not so certain that the point of this pencil will not suddenly break or that the weather will hold for my walk this evening. But the pencil looks firm enough and the weather seems set for a glorious day. I make plans accordingly. I am not quite so certain of what falls outside my immediate purview, though in many cases as certain as makes no difference. I am quite certain that King's College still stands in the Strand. In principle there could have been some weakness in the structure causing it to collapse this morning, but having heard no hint or rumour of this, I do not give the possibility serious thought. But there are a host of other matters, ascertainable in perception, of which I am less certain. A road near my home in North Wales was closed recently, but I only learned of this when I got there.

In more serious matters we are often a good deal more certain of some things than of others. Some of my acquaintances I trust absolutely, but I am cautious about others. Confidence is sometimes misplaced, and we must go on the strength of the evidence at the time. We likewise adhere with varying degrees of firmness to certain principles, socialism or pacifism for instance, and some are swayed more than others by evidence and rational reflection. But clearly, when a strong case can be made out for something and objections met, we are normally disposed to think favourably of it and try to put prejudice aside. One reason therefore for the weakness of a belief and oscillation in the firmness of our adherence to it is the difficulty of making out a simple overwhelming case, as I can for my belief that it is not raining in my garden at the moment. The belief in a future life cannot be established with that kind of conclusiveness. If it could only idiots would doubt it.

This is what has set many persons searching for some foolproof way of ascertaining that the dead do in fact live again. The most obvious approach here is parapsychology and mediumistic evidence. Some religious people are very contemptuous of this. It will not, so they say, prove the resurrection but only the survival or immortality of the soul, of which some religious people take a curiously dim view. But this is, in my view, a very great mistake. The evidence may not give us all that we want to establish in a religious context – it certainly cannot provide all that the Christian means by 'the life eternal'. But if it did the trick it would certainly give us a great deal. It might not prove that we live for ever; but if some kind of mediumistic or kindred evidence could be found which made it tolerably certain (as certain as we are about conditions in some of the planets we can more easily study, for example) that someone whose lifeless corpse we had seen put in its coffin and buried or cremated was now all the same unmistakably in communication with us, in whatever trivial a way, this would be momentous.

I can in fact think of nothing that would startle people more, or have greater news value. A journalist who failed to report it would obviously be falling down on his job. The trouble is that there is much to dispute about mediumistic evidence, and most people take the line that, while 'there may be something in it', it is all too uncertain to be taken seriously – and in the meantime there is much to tell against it, including the lifeless corpse. I repeat therefore that if confidence could be established in the psychical approach to the question of survival, it would be a matter of enormous importance. The issue is not, of course, the straightforward one of finding conclusive or very impressive evidence; there are peculiar difficulties about the interpretation of the evidence available, as critics are not slow to point out. Some views about the nature of persons would rule out from the start the interpretation of any evidence in terms of actual survival, and those who defend the possibility of survival must reckon with such views as a vital part of their undertaking. But apart from this, and even allowing for some psychical phenomena, there are differing ways in which it is proposed to interpret the available evidence. Clairvoyance and telepathy among the living might cover much of it. I myself find much of the evidence impressive, and I am even more impressed by the fact that very clearsighted investigators with the highest philosophical competence like C. D. Broad and H. H. Price have thought it worth taking very seriously, the latter being fully convinced of its adequacy to establish at least some form of survival.

There are, admittedly, some people who would prefer the evidence to be negative, and Broad is perhaps the most notable example. There are indeed disconcerting aspects to the possibility of another life. It may not by any means be all that we expect now; but even so, and allowing fully for the sombre side of those possibilities, my own expectation would be that most people would be immensely relieved and excited if they had firm assurance comparable to that which we may have about ordinary matters of fact that the friends they had lost were alive 'somewhere' and might even be contacted, and that their own existence would not come finally to its end at the close of their earthly life. This assurance could in fact make a vast difference to the way we think of ourselves and our lives at present. We do not have to think of morality in terms of rewards and punishments to appreciate what a change it would make to our present attitudes and restlessness if we were certain that this life is 'not all.'

For these reasons I do not think that religious people should be as contemptuous or suspicious as many seem to be of the investigation of the alleged paranormal evidence for survival. They are indeed entitled to insist that this will not give them any of the essentials of a Christian faith or the reasons for holding it, and we need thus to be warned not to confuse major issues or draw attention away from the sort of assurance on which the Christian faith depends. All the same, an assurance that men do live after they are dead (even if it extends to only a limited period) would make a very considerable breach in the hard wall of scepticism which confronts us now and open men's minds to further possibilities which come closer to the profounder and more exhilarating insights which the Christian claims. It has been said in a classical context that philosophy can 'make room for faith'. This has sometimes been understood in a way that implies that philosophy has no place in faith as such, and it is, alas, this travesty that appeals most to those who invoke the distinction most often today, thus maintaining an unholy alliance between religious dogmatism or uncritical relativism and philosophical scepticism. This was certainly not Kant's idea, and without pretending to follow him further in how he thought of faith, we can insist that there are rational ingredients capable of philosophical refinement at the centre of a religious faith. Nonetheless, philosophical and other secular assurances which do not affect the core of a Christian commitment can help to open men's minds to possibilities which prepare the way for a deeper religious understanding.

There are a great many ways in which this holds today, and there are many important and exciting tasks for religious philosophers who rightly understand their prospects and have the energy and courage to persist. But I cannot investigate these now; I must content myself with the insistence that philosophical and scientific investigation of the religious implications and possibilities of psychical research is a respectable and important part of seeking a better understanding and acceptance of Christian beliefs. The pitfalls are many, but that is no reason for avoiding the subject as many religious thinkers do today. If the results prove negative no harm is done, for this is not what faith turns upon; if positive, a great deal is gained. In any case, our first concern is with the truth, disconcerting or otherwise.

I come now to the second main way in which a belief may be held 'at one level' of our minds only, namely when we believe, as it is sometimes put, with 'one side of our minds' or 'one part of us'. To some extent, this is true of all of us, and it needs to be reckoned with more than is commonly the case in matters of belief. In extreme cases we have the situation memorably described by Plato in his account of what he called 'the democratic man'.

Day after day he gratifies the pleasures as they come – now fluting down the primrose path of wine, now given over to teetotalism and banting; one day in hard training, the next slacking and idling, and the third playing the philosopher. Often he will take to politics, leap to his feet and do or say whatever comes into his head; or he conceives an admiration for a general, and his interests are in war; or for a man of business, and straightway that is his line. He knows no order or necessity in life; but he calls life as he conceives it pleasant and free and divinely blessed, and is ever faithful to it.

This is not, in the main at least, a case of insincerity or hypocrisy. In certain moods men genuinely do believe what they do not believe at all at other times. This is how some well-known public figures leave the impression of a deep insincerity of which they may not really be guilty. They really do believe, perhaps quite fervently at times, what they also seem to reject or disregard, though there may be insincerity as well. We are, all of us, more of a mixture than we care to admit.

There has, on occasion, been serious commendation of this frame of mind, as in some doctrines of a dual standard or in the nineteenth-century notion of a 'truth of the heart' which could ease the intellectual strain for us by being entertained alongside an incompatible 'truth of the mind'. I hope no one today encourages this kind of intellectual schizophrenia. But we must all be on our guard against the insidiousness of our temptation to lapse into it in subtle ways.

It is here also that we may find the element of truth in John Baillie's famous account of believing something 'at the bottom of our hearts' which we deny 'at the top of our minds'. Baillie's mistake was to suppose that this must be true of all unbelief. That is certainly not the way to take the measure of unbelief or the magnitude of our task in resisting it. But it may well cover many cases; and even notable atheists, like Bertrand Russell, come sometimes very close to the substance of what the believer professes.

The sum of this, for our purpose (it is a theme of great importance which needs to be treated more fully on its own account), is that our beliefs need to be cultivated. That is not a commendation of wishful thinking or of naive refusal to look serious difficulties in the face. But profound and precious beliefs about spiritual matters can neither be achieved nor maintained in a casual way. This is again what we learn from Plato, who spoke eloquently about 'the long and toilsome route' out of the cave and how easy it is to lose a true belief or to substitute for it a merely superficial opinion. We have to be like athletes, a comparison to which St Paul was also very prone, resisting 'the softer influence of pleasure' and 'the sterner influence of fear'.

The saints have indeed been well aware of this: they are constantly wrestling with doubt and despair; the pilgrim sinks deep in the Slough of Despond; our hymns are full of varieties of mood, from triumphant certainties to deep despair, from the hilltops to the valleys and the shadows; and this is as it should be – we have to win our way through doubt to firm belief and the renewal of belief. But this is no mere intellectual matter; it is more a maintaining of the set of our thoughts and dispositions, of living with the evidence which leads to spiritual discernment; and for this reason we should welcome the importance that is accorded today to contemplation. Meditation has its discipline, and there are those who can guide us. This is often travestied and sometimes almost equated with physical exercises or mechanical stimuli. We need to understand much better what contemplation means, for it is in the fullness of meditation, which extends to thought and practice alike, that faith is renewed. This will have rational ingredients among which philosophical thought has a prominent place.

The belief in life after death is not an easy one. There is much to induce us to identify ourselves with our bodies, and philosophers today find it hard to avoid that. This is not the place to put the case against them – I have tried to do that elsewhere. But we all know what will happen soon to our bodies. They will rot or be burned. To believe seriously that we can survive this needs some very clear thinking, and I do not discount in this context the oddity we all feel, I imagine, of the notion of our own total extinction. But what I most wish to stress at the moment is the strenuousness at the intellectual level, and at the level of committed religious living, of maintaining a genuine belief. Belief in life after death is a momentous one, and the burden of our witness to it has come to be taken too lightly.

In the sophisticated thinking relevant to a belief in afterlife, there is one item of exceptional importance to which I wish to draw attention and which will be my chief concern for the remainder of this discussion. It is at this point that I find myself sharply at odds with Plato and with the vast range of philosophical thinking for which he has been largely responsible. Plato, you will recall, maintained that genuine reality consisted of certain general principles, the ideas or the forms, as we call them. These are not concepts, though the best way for us to begin to understand them is in terms of universals; they are in his view real, indeed the only true reality. They are also closely interrelated, and in the progress of Plato's own thought there is a deepening insistence on the essential interrelatedness of the forms. At the centre and transcending all is the form of the Good; and it is in our glimpse or vision of this at the end of our toilsome route that we find our clue to the ultimate necessity of all the rest.

Particular things, it is thus affirmed, 'the choir of heaven and the furniture of earth' (in the words of a kindred but more down to earth spirit), in the rush and travail of our own lives derive such reality as they have from the forms themselves; they have a questionable borrowed reality. The wise man will seek to draw away from the insubstantial fleeting world of particulars and centre his thought not on 'shadows' but on the only true realities, the forms. He will in this sense seek what is 'above'. It is significant that, in spite of this denigration of the particular and the seeming exclusiveness of the bifurcation into the world of particulars and the world of forms, Plato continues to think of the soul as essentially individual. Exactly where it fits is not clear, but it is certain that Plato never wavers on this – the soul is the individual, now and always; and it is also for Plato immortal because it is essentially indestructible, and it is indestructible because it has an essential affinity with the forms; the eternal world of forms is its home.

It is this affinity with the world of forms that Plato stresses most of all in claiming the immortality of the soul. The inadequacy of his other argumentation has often been exposed, but his main considerations provide a not unimpressive view of the immortality of the soul. It has many of the ingredients we would also stress: the sense of the inevitable transitoriness of our present existence, the urgency with which we are pressed to look to the things 'above' (almost as the Bible tells us to 'lay up treasures for yourselves in heaven, where neither moth nor rust doth corrupt'), the abiding conviction that at the heart of all is the absolute transcendent Good, the source of our being and our home. We must not despise this understanding; it is never monistic, 'soul is soul' whatever else we say, and it has helped extensively to shape Christian understanding at various times. But it has one radical weakness. It does not take proper account of the here and now. This is not because Plato adopts an unmitigated other-worldly view as in extreme monism. He set the course, on the contrary, for the effective rebuttal of the arguments of Parmenides, whose force he well appreciated. The philosopher, in some ways like the *avatar*, has to return to succour and provide for others. In the world of forms there is an essential variety. Nonetheless the particular, whether in the world of nature or in our own lives, tends to count solely as a reflection of the true reality of eternal verities. The persistence of this view is the source of the main points of disagreement one would have with Plato.

This is seen to good advantage in Plato's treatment of the family and personal relations. He did not think physical enjoyment in any form an evil thing, but he rated it very lowly, not appreciating how physical enjoyment enters into a fuller experience to make it more meaningful. The intimacy of full personal encounter and a rounded friendship seems to give way before the idea of the blueprint and the pattern laid up in heaven (which is surprising in view of Plato's own enjoyment of excellent friendships and his great regard for Socrates). Appetite tends to remain brute appetite; it does not become an ingredient in a richer experience. For the same reasons, the morally or physically handicapped receive very harsh treatment. If they do not play their proper part in the fulfilment of 'the pattern', they are dispensable. The same clues yield us the secret of Plato's famous perversity about poetry and the arts. A very great literary artist himself, and very consciously attracted to poetry, he would have none of it officially. This is because he understood well that poetry does not deal in essences or universal notions –

a point about which our late and gifted friend Dr. Austin Farrer was peculiarly confused.[1] Art is some illumination of the particular, even in its rarefied and abstract forms, and it is for this reason that literature, music, painting and all the other arts are accorded such a very lowly place in a scheme of things which puts all its premium on the impersonal and eternal aspect of things.[2]

This is where true religion provides its corrective, and that is why Plato can never set the model for a truly religious philosophy. For religion, as I understand it, has always an element of revelation at the core of it; and in revelation the transcendent discloses and shapes itself for our illumination in a peculiar involvement of itself with a particular situation, a time and place at which the revelation happens notwithstanding that it may not always be precisely specifiable. The disclosure is to someone, and may well include some transmutation of what is presented immediately in his environment. It speaks of the 'beyond', but it is also altogether of the here and now. Others may appropriate it, and it takes its place in the exchanges of committed religious living as the gradual refinement of our understanding of God and the sense of his presence.

This puts immeasurable worth on particular things, on an essentially created world in which the divine splendour shines, and on the lives of all. All the earth is holy, a 'sacramental universe' as it has been boldly put, and personal existence as the peculiar centre of divine involvement acquires a significance which nothing can efface, a place at the heart of the life of God. This is what the mystic perceives and this is why he speaks of an absorption in which God is all in all. This is a travesty if, as often happens, it is taken neat. God is God, but the point of true religion is the discovery of our place in the life of God himself, and as the disclosure deepens and the essentially self-giving character of it reveals itself, as the bond tightens, we know that we are 'of God' and have no home but God. The inestimable worth that is placed on each, even 'weak things' and 'things that are despised', puts the question of the elimination of anyone out of the question. This is in some ways a terrible truth for us to realize, for whatever is evil in our lives or persons is present there in this holy relationship. It is no wonder, therefore, that outstandingly saintly persons have been so peculiarly tormented by the sense of sin as to seem to others obsessed and unbalanced. We may much resent the words 'sinners in the hands of an angry God', and indeed few things have been more travestied and misdirected, in theory or experience, than the sense of sin and the fear of God. But there is a certain horror, and an abysmal consuming wretchedness – the worm that does not die – in the spectacle of one's own life aglow in all its forms in the life of God. That is where the costliness of redeeming love begins to be seen.

In the peculiar claims of the Christian religion, the unfolding of divine love in history and the manifold experiences of men is alleged to come to a finality of fulfilment in Christ. Here God himself comes as a man to put the seal of his redeeming activity on the indissoluble bond of our own lives in his. Of the way we must understand this, and of the infinite sadness of the many travesties of it, we cannot speak here. But the Christian should have no doubt about 'the price that was paid'. Christianity without sacrifice does not begin to get off the ground, and it is in the sacrifice we celebrate in a holy communion that we find the ultimate seal on our own abiding destiny as sons of God. There can be no elimination of what is so completely of God himself.

These assurances in no way dispense with the need for thought; they have thought at the core of them. The wise Christian will come to terms with this, most of all in a developing culture. Insight is not random, and faith is not blind. Both are at the opposite poles to unreason. There is much work also in preparing the ground: in dealing, for example, with problems about the nature of persons, as indicated earlier, in sifting the evidence of psychical research, and in hard thought about the peculiarly tantalising problem presented by extensive evil in a world governed by divine love. The latter problem does in fact find some easement in the present case in the very substance of what faith affirms; for, in the affirmation of a life beyond, we do have a broader canvas on which to view the various ills men endure now. Compensation in afterlife could afford a partial solution at least to the problem of evil, and some of the most impressive writers on the subject of late, such as C. A. Campbell, A. C. Ewing and John Hick, give it particular prominence. I go more cautiously with it, as indeed do Campbell and Ewing, because I wish to stand firmly on our present assurances. In these the feeling we have that it would be strange for personal existence to be eclipsed for reasons incidental to what our natures properly are and what we do deserves more prominence than is often accorded to it; and here the study of other religions could be very relevant. But the main weight has still to be placed on the peculiar assurance of faith through divine disclosure.

This lends particular urgency at the present time to the proclamation of Christian truth and our witness to it. This should include at centre the affirmation of a life beyond, and if we fail in this we shall place a serious limitation on any renewal of faith in our time. The relevance of our proclamation to present ills will be much weakened. This is not because the new problems of today spring directly from irreligion; they come about largely through the complexities of a changed situation and marked advances in our understanding of ourselves and our environment. At the same time the limiting of our horizons to the here and now is not without profound effect, and, on the positive side, the transformation in attitude and expectation which could be induced by a detached and objective sense of illimitable possibilities of richer experience would be hard to calculate. The palliatives and substitutes would easily dwindle beside it.

It is in the context of this expectation and the renewal of faith in its fulness that the Christian should consider the question of a life after death. The hope we have in this precise sense is not a luxury, a secondary consideration to be investigated on its own account; it belongs to the essence of a Christian commitment. To tie that to some isolated doctrine of the Resurrection, or make the Resurrection stories pivotal on their own account, is a bad mistake. The work and person of Christ must be taken in its fullness, but it seems to be unthinkable that it should not be thought to include, in explicit word and in implication, the affirmation of our abiding place at the heart of God's love. We can form little conception of what this will be; the new dimensions of it go far beyond our present limitations and boldest speculation, involving transformations of the quality of life as much as its formal scope. It does not yet 'appear what we shall be' but we shall be 'like him', and that, to any who consider the matter seriously, is about as remarkable an expectation as that we shall exist without our present bodies. Indeed, it is in many ways the most bewildering item of our faith, as sober realistic theologians appreciated earlier in this century, however muddled in other ways. This is nonetheless the bold truth the Christian must proclaim, and in the long run we do better with the daunting character of the full Christian assurance than with half-hearted humanist travesties of it. That is one reason why narrowly dogmatic Christians succeed better, for a time at least, than the rest of us. Other reasons are less estimable. An enduring faith must be open and reflective. But it must be *faith* and the fulness of it, and that unmistakably includes our own conservation, sanctified beyond our dimmest understanding and renewed in the knowledge of the price that was paid, at the heart of the life of God. 'For God so loved the world, that he gave his only begotten Son, that whosoever believeth in him, should not perish but have everlasting life.' There is no Christian faith without 'everlasting life', and it is in the fullness of faith, as a rounded personal apprehension, that this life of 'the world to come' becomes also our proper possession 'in this time now'. In essentials it is all a matter of the right kind of faith.

NOTES

1. See *The Glass of Vision* (Westminster: Dacre Press, 1948), Chapter 7, pp. 113-31, and my comment in *Our Experience of God*, Chapter 7, pp. 131-45.
2. Cf. my paper 'On Poetic Truth', in *Morals and Revelation* (London: Allen & Unwin, 1951), Chapter 10, pp. 232-55.

8 The Person of Christ

One of the distinctive words of our times is 'relevance'. Everything has to be relevant. Some of our students will not begin, or continue, their courses without constant assurance of their relevance. I have often wondered, in a mildly whimsical way, how things might have gone if I and some of my friends, in my student days, had called upon that notable scholar, the late Professor James Gibson (author of a well-known work on John Locke), or his remarkably versatile colleague, Professor Hudson Williams who taught us Greek, to tell them that what they taught us, about the ancient Greeks and their ways, was hardly relevant to us today. They were both very courteous and kindly persons, and both in their ways rather remote and shy. They would certainly have been much embarrassed, and there would have been much coughing and floundering. Perhaps it is best not to speculate further.

At the same time it is important that anything we teach or think about should be relevant in the sense of taking its proper place in the modes of thought and conditions of our time. We cannot live wholly in the past and must come to terms in some way with what we find the world to be like today.

What then is the relevance of Jesus? Who was he? What do we know about him? Almost everything, indeed everything of any substance, that we know about him comes from a collection of writings that we know as The New Testament, four gospels, the story of the early Church in Acts and letters. The earliest complete copy of these comes to us from the Fourth Century A.D., but there are fragments identical with the later version which strongly suggest that the rest was in circulation at their own date, a hundred years earlier. Some find all this disconcerting, but I do not think we have any serious cause for anxiety here. There are good reasons, both of scholarship and common sense, for concluding that most of the New Testament was available, substantially as we have it, within the century in which Christ lived, and most of it not very far from the time when he died. Scholars will no doubt continue to debate the precise dating of parts of the New Testament, but I do not think there is any likelihood of serious doubt about the placing of most of it, including the first three (synoptic) gospels, at a date not very far removed from the events they purport to describe. It is well known also that the gospels exhibit patterns and other features which reflect some earlier records that were in circulation still nearer the time. I shall not go into further detail on these matters – they can be left to the appropriate experts. But I do not think there can be serious doubt about what I have hitherto maintained. The available records do unmistakably take us fairly close to the events in question – at least in point of time.

So far the Christian has no serious worry. Even so there is a gap. The evidence, even on the most optimistic view, comes to us from some time, a few years at least, after the events. The Muslim has the advantage of the Christian here. When Muhammad spoke what he claimed to be divine revelations communicated to him, and on other occasions too when, like St Paul at times, he gave more his own opinion, his words were immediately taken down on whatever was available. The record of the revelations given to him (in what manner is a further point not relevant now) was available in four nearly identical copies which were speedily conflated and edited to give us 'the Glorious Qu'ran' as it is often described. There can be little doubt that the Qu'ran gives us the words of Muhammad himself.

We can say nothing strictly comparable of Christian scriptures. Professor W. D. Davies, in his excellent short study, *The Sermon on the Mount*, has noted recently the familiar 'phenomenon of the retention and repetition of sayings and speeches by worthy men in the Semitic world of the first and other centuries'[1] and adduced other reasons which make it 'credible that the "words" of Jesus were preserved and transmitted with some degree of faithfulness'.[2] In other cultures our confidence in the authenticity of sacred scriptures owes a great deal to highly developed techniques of oral transmission operative long before there were written texts. There may have been nothing strictly comparable in Palestine, but we can certainly give some weight there also to habits of oral transmission which we lack.[3]

Even so we have, on the most optimistic view, to reckon with a gap. What we have is the evidence or recollection of witnesses some time after the event, some of it at second hand, and most having passed through the mill of public and social transmission. It is worth recalling how many witnesses have sworn in a court of law, often with the greatest sincerity, that they have seen something which it can be shown they could not possibly have seen from where they were standing. Our eyes deceive us and imagination plays tricks on us. Legends grow up quickly around charismatic persons and events, the story of St David when the mound sprang up under his feet to facilitate his preaching to the multitude, St Francis and the birds, nativity stories and 'transfigurations', and, in our own time, the story of the Russian soldiers, in the First World War, who landed in the North of England and were seen marching south on their way to help our troops in France *with the snow still on their boots*. Most of us have a subtle streak of credulity in us and have to be much on our guard against wishful thinking. We have also read much today about 'the life of images' and the way the great myths and their themes live on in some renewed way in new cultural settings. The writers of the New Testament had moreover a case to make, they were not detached, uncommitted witnesses.

In the light of this and like considerations can we place firm reliance on the New Testament *as history?* Is not 'the quest of the historical Jesus' a vain one from the start, as so many Biblical scholars have themselves maintained? The actual Jesus of history never emerges from the mass of culturally conditioned representations of him. Whose evidence do we trust?

At this stage I should like to make one point very explicit. In my view, if it is not possible to get at the historical Jesus, if the records are some kind of fabrication or the work of inspired imagination or literary genius, then the bottom goes out of any distinctively Christian affirmations. For me, it is 'the Jesus of History' or nothing. Bonhoeffer has maintained that God was *incognito* in Jesus and that the actual historical Jesus, for all we know, may have done some bad things. He does not indicate what the bad things might have been, consistent with the record as we have it. I am not clear what is meant altogether by saying that God was *incognito* in Jesus, but presumably it implies that we claim that 'God was in Christ' independently of what we feel we know about Jesus; and along these lines it is hard to see why we should make these claims about Christ rather than anyone else, any notable figure or even a disreputable one like Hitler. We would think it absurd to say that God was incarnate in Hitler, but this is because we know what Hitler was like. Bonhoeffer was a brave and notable person and died the death of a martyr, but that is unhappily no guarantee of sound religious understanding. For my own part, if I feel I had to admit that Jesus had done some bad things, then while I might feel inspired and helped by his teaching and example, as with other outstanding but erring and fallible human beings, I could not worship him or make the claims about him that seem to be central to the Christian faith. But how then, when there is so much room for scepticism, can we place reliance on the Biblical records? Can we take these firmly as history?

I answer with every confidence that we can, not because of any independent confirmation of substance, but because the records themselves, in their substance and character, authenticate themselves, as history as well as the essentials of faith. But this does not in the least mean that everything must have happened or been said exactly as described. There is much variety in the stories themselves from one report to another, and what Census was that which figures in the nativity story? What we have is a picture of a person, but not the picture of the eye of the camera, a portrait rather but a portrait which altogether convinces us as history and as saving truth.

What then do we find in this portrait? Let us pause to consider this. In the first place, we encounter in the portrait a young man of quite extraordinary gifts and powers. It is not at all a case of some relatively ordinary person on whom some peculiar status is conferred by divine ordination, as might happen, it might be thought, to anyone. By any computation Jesus was a most remarkable man and it is hard to think that he would not have made his impact on his own times and afterwards in some exceptional way even if his life had not taken the course it did take. This may seem obvious but it needs stressing today when it seems implied, in some theological attitudes and procedures, that the doctrine of 'the person of Jesus' does not rest at all on what we know him to have been like in historical fact.

What then was he like, what do we find in the portrait? First of all, unmistakably, a man with the eye of a poet to note the world around us coming alive, stark and distinctive, in its familiar unfamiliarity, the 'lilies of the field' in all their glory, the red sky at night, the fields white for the harvest and the tares also sprouting among the good seed, the ravens which neither sow nor reap and other fowls of the air lodging in the mustard tree, the sparrow limp in the dust, the foxes slinking to their lairs ahead of his solitary step on the mountain, the shepherd leading his flock; the gift to hear also the wind blowing where it listeth among the reeds and, with his own peculiar penetration and sensitivity, the widow's mite dropping into the treasury. He would not be the first to note these and their like, and to speak of them, but they come before us, notwithstanding our own great familiarity, with a peculiar starkness and freshness of their own.

The eye of a poet, but also the skill of the artist and his unfailing touch to convey it all with neatness and without false embroidery, a remarkable literary genius. Even if we had only the parables, and without the peculiar spiritual significance we give them in their full Christian context, what a treasure they would be for art and literature. We grow up with them as part of our talk, they are vital elements in the modes of our thought and culture – the prodigal son and his elder brother, the lost sheep, the good Samaritan, the talents, the pearl of great price, the wise and foolish virgins, the broad and the narrow way, the camel and the eye of the needle, the vineyard, the rich man and Lazarus, the great feast, and many more. These would undoubtedly take their place of themselves as part of a rich and classical culture, and as Jesus was so given to telling such parables, there may have been many more of which no record is left. A good parable is in some way very simple, but that is their glory and where the craftsman-ship shows, everyone can follow them and they are peculiarly whole and apt. To be so unfailingly ready with them was no little thing.

What else do we find? It seems to me that we have in Jesus someone who must have had an exceptional home. We know little about this, barely more than the names of his parents and

the story of the boy Jesus in the temple. And yet in one sense we
know all. The very silence is most revealing here. Joseph and
Mary, bringing up this strange child, would not have been unaware of what came to be described as his growing in favour with
men and God. He must have astounded people greatly long
before the start of his 'public ministry'. But his parents seem to
have been wisely restrained and unobtrusive in it all. They might
easily have thrust themselves forward and made the way hard for
him. By contrast we read that his mother 'kept all these sayings
in her heart'. The implications of this simple and tender observation seem to me more remarkable and revealing than a virgin
birth.

Admittedly we do have one observation that seems rather
harsh – 'Who is my mother, and who are my brothers?' But the
context makes it very clear here that this is not a lessening of
tenderness but the all-inclusive character of his public commitment. His personal life was bound to be deeply affected by his
special ministry. We recall by contrast his moving care for his
mother from the Cross. It is to me inconceivable that we should
have such central reference to 'my heavenly father' if Jesus had
not known in the fullest way what it is to have a fine father. I
shall not elaborate this but simply note how difficult it would be
to make sense of the story in disregard of the sensitivity and
tenderness bred in a home which would have entered deeply into
his character and outlook, and which in due course became part
of the full significance of his work – and the divine disclosure.

The very sharp intellect of Jesus and his general understanding
is also very evident at every stage. He was steeped in the
Scriptures of his own people and their culture, and could hold
his own in controversies about them or in meeting questions of
shrewd and learned people with a hostile intent. Everything
about him has the stamp of the profound insights and experience
of an exceptionally gifted person. He could have made a place
for himself with ease in learned religious circles in his own time –
and this, as the records again hint very strongly, is what many
expected of so remarkable a religious teacher. He mixed with ease
with the highest in the rich world of thought in his time. It is, I
must repeat, not a case of just anyone singled out for a peculiar
charismatic role.

Consider next the impact Jesus made on those around him,

and his influence. His popularity was obviously great at times, he drew the crowds, and there must have been much in his manner which charmed them. There seems little reason to doubt that this pleased him, although it wearied him also in more ways than one. He certainly did not go greatly out of his way to win or retain it, least of all at any cost. Much of the enthusiasm for him was cheap aud meanly motivated, and he made it evident himself what little value he put on that. But he clearly liked to move among the people, the warmth of genuine response meant much to him, and also the loyalty and companionship of his closest friends, though he could dispense with that also at need – 'Will ye also go away?'

But there is a great deal more involved than easy companionship or superficial popularity. That has happened to many, but what is of greater account here is the more profound impact which Jesus made on those around him, that which made the evangelists speak of people being astonished, amazed, dumb or filled with fear, not fear of something immediately impending, but the sort of awe which goes with the sense of great sanctity and holiness. Men could be much at ease with him, but they could also be quite subdued, he spoke 'with power' and as one having 'authority' very different from that of the scribes. When they wondered who he might be their thoughts turned to John the Baptist, alleged by Jesus himself to be the greatest of the prophets but who in turn is said to have declared himself unworthy to perform the meanest service for Jesus, and to Moses and Elijah, the great charismatic prophetic heroes of their remarkable moral and spiritual tradition. There could have been none more eminent with whom to compare him, it looked as though the greatest of the prophets had come again. And let us not forget to whom this happened. The Jews, like other nations, stoned the prophets, but the prophets are *par excellence* of the Jews, it was among them that they appeared, they produced them if you like to put it so, and they could recognise a prophet. It means something when they speak of teaching with authority and of being overcome in his presence. We are certainly not dealing with just anybody in the Gospels.

But is this all? By no means. As yet we have barely got beyond the periphery, although the matters with which we have dealt have their distinctive and important place in the pattern. The

weightier considerations have still to be noted. Among these is
the peculiar ethical penetration of Jesus, the scope of it, its being
so unerringly right when it is most unexpected, the balance and
precision of it in so many different settings. We see this in part in
general declarations, because their tone and their relation to one
another bring us to a very different world from similar pro-
nouncements before them and elsewhere. We find the Golden
Rule, to love others as ourselves, in many places, but I do not
think one is likely to be thought guilty of any bias in claiming to
find a peculiar penetration and sensitivity in the enunciation of it
in the Sermon on the Mount, as it is called, and elsewhere in the
New Testament. But it is not in general exhortation that we find
the peculiar glory and distinctiveness of the moral teaching
ascribed to Jesus.

We find that in the special way the whole is presented in
response and reaction to all sorts of occasions and to people of
such vastly different natures and circumstances. This is why so
many of the descriptions of Jesus and the labels, convincing and
illuminating enough up to a point, are also so very inadequate
and misleading – 'Jesus, the Agitator', 'the man for others'. He
was of course an agitator, a rebel, like his followers shortly afterwards 'turning the world upside down'. But he does not begin to
fit our normal picture of an agitator. There was so much gentle-
ness, patience, respect, conformity too of its kind and up to a
point. He could be stirred, but he was never a wild man. Categories and labels may help but they may also miss the main point
and be gravely misleading; what in fact we find is some quite
remarkable way of being so exactly right, most unexpected as his
reaction often was but also when it comes so amazingly right, not
in precise formulations to be mechanically applied in all other
circumstances, but as the disclosure of a way of life and attitude
of mind for us to try to follow. It is not that precise practical problems are evaded so that we are left without explicit guidance,
much less, as has indeed sometimes been thought, that we are
offered some kind of Christian spirit or attitude or some un-
defined acceptance that is compatible with almost anything and
everything in outward demeanour – that sort of antinomianism
has been the bane of Christian witness down the ages. The precise
practical challenge is a very bold one, and it often asks more, in
sacrifice and selflessness, than we sometimes begin to realise. It

can be quite revolutionary and make devastating demands. But it does not always take the same form. On the one hand, we have the story of the rich young man who went away 'sorrowful', for he had 'great possessions', and, on the other hand, in the same context, the curiously paradoxical promise to his followers that they 'shall receive a hundred-fold now in this time', and shall lack nothing, though 'with persecutions'. No one should take this promise literally, it did not happen that way to Christ or his disciples, but neither is it just words; and in a context only slightly later we have the story of the anointing of his head with costly oil – 'A man for the poor', the 'friend of outcasts and sinners', and as such the disciples expected him to condemn 'this waste'. It all went differently. With profound sensitivity and graciousness Jesus saw much deeper and praised this action as one peculiarly appropriate to his Kingdom and Gospel – 'Wherever this gospel shall be preached in the whole world, there shall also this, that this woman hath done, be told for a memorial of her'. How remarkable and how significant. The action of the woman was wholly in line with the gospel, as the sorrow of the rich young man was so far from it.

Thus at every point, surprise and novelty and in all cases so exactly right, wholly convincing even when it remains bewildering, in all sorts of conditions and with all manner of people, with old and young (his fondness for children was obviously deep and natural and his observations show how easily he entered into their world – few notable persons have approached him in this), with sick and maimed people, some of whom were in shocking and revolting conditions of deterioration with no provision for care or relief, with outcasts whom most people shunned if they could (and who would have gone so far as to *kiss* the leper?), with poor or simple or naive people, with people in all sorts of distress, with prominent and sophisticated people (he clearly increased in favour with them also), with happy people and those engaged in some special celebration, making a feast or killing their fatted calf and making sure to please their host by wearing the appropriate dress (proud of his own seamless garment notwithstanding that he also said we should take no thought for raiment), with foolish people and wise people, with kind and simple people and some devoted to him and mindful of his comfort, with troubled and perplexed people and those earnestly seeking, with the over-confident and with the reluctant, with vicious people and those cunningly trying to encompass his downfall or openly hostile, with the few who were spiritually, though not always with full awareness and discernment close to him and to whom he showed a special tenderness – in all this, and in an astonishing variety of situations, this extraordinary man, at an age we would still consider immature for many purposes, seemed to take the often surprising but so exactly and unfalteringly right stance; he knew what was in a man, he understood unerringly men's attitudes to one another and to himself and was quietly firmly certain of his own response in this very wide compass of his dealings with all sorts of people.

The episodes we have are not complete, the gospels are not strict or researched biographies, but surely we have enough to set before us a teacher of altogether profound and unfailing, challenging and demanding, practical wisdom, neat and explicit in an astonishing variety of live situations, and such that it is very hard indeed to think of anything in the history of moral thought and insight that begins to approach it, a phenomenon all of its own, an inexhaustible wonder.

If this does not give us the immediate answer to all our practical problems, and no one need claim that it does, it certainly gives us the way of life, if only we follow it, in which the answer must be sought. It is also amazingly distinctive, notwithstanding all that went before it, in the same setting or elsewhere.

From time to time, in the course of presenting this theme, I have been reminded of other distinctive ethical insights and of other scriptures for which uniqueness may also be claimed. During a recent lecture tour in India the *Gita* was often mentioned to me in this way. Most of us are quite familiar now with the *Gita*, though less so than people in other cultures are on the whole with our scriptures. There is no doubt much nobility in the *Gita*, and it certainly speaks to the condition of those who are attracted to its peculiar form of transcendence; the note of personal involvement, in the love of God and of man to each other, becomes very moving and challenging, but much of the splendour is also external and magical, the many eyes and mouths and so on, however symbolical; and the perplexed young warrior is left with very little explicit guidance at the end. The final impression is that, provided one fulfils the duty of one's station, one need not worry. Whether we live or die, whether we are ill or well, prosperous or hungry or troubled, none of this matters, not even duty itself, worship and devotion are all that count.

However we qualify this, as is also done in some transcendentalist forms of Western religions, by insistence that the right things will in fact be done, the centre of gravity is the devotion itself. 'Even if he is a very evil liver, but worships me with single devotion, he must be held good, for he has rightly resolved.' Contrast this with the one who moved as a man among men, who sups with us and us with him, and who discerned, with astonishing sensitivity and insight, just what this precise human condition required, who leads in the ways of life as we know it, the master as much at ease with his friends as when kissing the leper, aware of joy and sorrow and despising neither, fully in the world even if not of it, pointing the way as certainly in matters of inner intent as in outward performance, and in all this so unerringly, surprisingly right.

But this itself is not a matter to be formally established, any more than it is a blind determination to allow no fault on one's own side, to go on waving one's own banner, confessing one's own loyalty, whatever the facts. It is a matter of living thoughtfully in the world of these insights, of keeping in the way ourselves, until the authority of it imposes itself in our own convictions. He becomes the Way for us.

But also more than the Way. For these astonishing ethical responses take their shape for us in the context of the profoundest spiritual awareness. They are of this world but also deeply embedded in the life beyond. The sense of the presence of God pervades the whole story. This is not peculiar to Jesus. God had made himself known before; 'in diverse times and places', and I have discussed elsewhere[4] how these disclosures are to be recognised and established. But to any who are sensitive to such disclosure, who recognise the modes and distinctiveness of it, it becomes also very apparent how much all this is present in its finest, roundest form in Jesus. Do we know of any place where the life beyond is so finely intertwined with the here and now? This appears sometimes in explicit references to what comes to us 'from above', to 'my Father's house', 'your heavenly father', the fleeting, transitory character of earthly attainments. But it is equally evident, and in some respects more impressive, in the withdrawal into solitude and meditation, by the lake, or in desert places or the mountain. This profound inner spiritual life is surely one of the main themes of the story, and we cannot possibly get a fair picture of Jesus without careful heed to the abiding place of prayer in his life, prayers of the serene inner flow of spiritual awareness and the constant sense of the peculiar closeness of God, and the very distinctive 'My Father' and 'my Father's house', as well as the disturbing, explosive agitations of spirit, the agonising cry of dereliction which is not heard solely from the Cross, the rupturing of present existence by a power 'from Beyond' which at the same time leaves the serene sense of the proper place of present things undisturbed, the calm confident flow of the concerned understanding of this world and how it should be minded.

The finest, simplest prayer that we have was taught us by Jesus, it is a prayer that is perfectly blended with his own life, and although this life of deep spiritual awareness was so much a matter of course to him, as natural as breathing, no one stressed more the need for effortful cultivation of the life of prayer. To remain reflectively aware of this and the sense of the sacred which is also intimate and blended with present existence, as the story moves from the temple and the synagogue to the city and the countryside, to do this is an essential part of coming to see what is in the picture.

Is there more in the picture? Before I reply let me pause here to note how very remarkable a picture it is, in all its aspects and in its distinctive wholeness. We begin to understand already how people who do not wholly share a Christian viewpoint, like Martin Buber, admit that they find it extremely difficult to know how to classify Jesus. He seems to be already almost breaking out of the framework of our finitude and beyond any ordinary pattern we can convincingly shape. But we are still not quite beyond the periphery. There is one thing that matters yet more decisively, the best wine, to vary our metaphor, which we bring out last, and that is the *Obedience*, the total and unfaltering commitment of Jesus himself to all that he commended and his own way of life.

The marvel of this becomes all the more evident when we consider the pitfalls that lay in his path. How easy it would be for a young man of such extraordinary powers and insights, and so obviously winning favour in high places and in low, to adopt or bend his expectations on occasion, not for personal gain, but to win the closer co-operation of others, especially those in high places and positions of influence. There were good men as well as hypocrites among the leaders of his people, he himself never failed in his regard for the temple and the synagogue and the scriptures, he was not a ruthless iconoclastic revolutionary but a highly sensitive man capable himself of pointing out narrow excesses. Why not move more cautiously within the recognised media, how much more effective might it not be in the long run to compromise a little, what influence for good might he not have if he worked along with other good men in high places where he could easily win the greatest esteem himself and promote high and holy ends. His gifts would easily win him respect and influence, and out of that great and certain good could come. Why not move a little, like Bunyan's pilgrim, to the somewhat smoother path that might seem to go exactly in the same way – but in fact to the slough? He saw, in fact, very clearly the perils of this alluring shift and resisted it in all his ways.

He was likewise impervious to the false allurements and claims that might seem involved in his own deep affections and friendships. His friends undoubtedly thought at times that he was making things needlessly difficult for himself; how trying it must have been to have to stand at times against their own susceptibilities and their fondness for him; Jesus was a person in whom tenderness of feeling was peculiarly marked, and it must have gone hard with him to disappoint the expectations of those to whom he was peculiarly close, his disciples, his friends and his family, and even to stand aloof at times. But at no stage is there any hint of wavering or the slightest deviation from the course to be followed.

This, and more, is very evident in the stories of the Temptation, and Luke does well to note that it was only 'for a time' that Satan left him. The Temptation was not a once for all event, but a continuing feature of his life, more so for him than others on account of his remarkable gifts and powers and because of the exceptional strain and exhaustion of the course he had set himself and the unutterable loneliness it would involve in some respects, all of which would have been much relieved by relaxing a little of the demands of his total commitment and self-giving. The foxes have lairs but the Son of Man not wherewith to lay down his head, not of course because he was literally destitute, there were many homes where he was loved and welcomed and many were eager to serve him, but there were aspects of his life and commitment where no one could carry his burdens for him or even know what they were. But however evident the strain, there is no sign of weakening, not even in the terrible hours when he prayed that the cup should be removed from him. The completeness of his commitment, in sanctified assurance, without either ostentation or an affected show of humility, firm and gentle in the same instant, easy and natural in his dealings with those most dear and close to him, this seems to set him altogether apart, fully man indeed but one in whom also there is no shadow of turning; neither kindly gesture nor despiteful use, neither the marvel of the flowers of the field nor the loyalty and care of those devoted to him, caused the slightest deviation from the way to be followed. There is an astonishing wholeness about the short life so lived to its terrible end. We do not indeed have the whole story, but what need is there? We have enough to see, beyond the remarkable maturity of judgement and wisdom, a total mastery of his own movements and spirit; and the picture is so complete in all essentials that we can confidently set aside any possibility of anything inconsistent with it. This is a story, in the area of all our most crucial concerns, in which everything that happens is so unexpectedly right as to spell out its own finality and vindicate itself with an authority inherent to itself.

To what then does it come? What are we finally to say? In the first place, it would seem highly implausible now to suppose that the entire story was invented by some quite extraordinary genius. There is no hint of any or the slightest indication of who he might be; and although some works of creative literature, most notably of all in my view Shakespearean drama, are astonishingly rounded and convincing, the main characters having almost the reality of genuine history for us, yet it would seem just impossible to ascribe the quite peculiar blend of major insights and attitudes, in their rich particularity, as they come in the Gospel narrative, to the ingenuity and inventiveness of some genius of great originality, least of all when we bear in mind the immediate impact of the story and its far-reaching influence directly at the time. Surely the early witnesses were talking about things they

remembered, however imperfectly and however distorted in the
telling; if they did not at least seem to themselves to be talking
about things they had themselves seen and heard they could
hardly have remained so unshaken and courageous about it
under quite exceptional stress. Their devotion and commitment
is not the kind they would bring to the service of a fable, and if
they were being imposed upon in all this, in the presence of so
many who could have challenged their claims outright from the
start, how did the original inventor manage to conceal his
identity or have it totally concealed for him? The narrative has
at least the stamp of being taken at the time to be a report of
actual events and it can hardly be thought, with any plausibility,
to be, in its context and the circumstances of the time, a complete
fabrication or a fraud, deliberate or otherwise.

We need not therefore pay much attention to the supposition
that the story is the deliberate invention of some individual of
genius who somehow imposed his invention as actual history on
credulous minds, though this is undoubtedly something which,
in other forms and conditions, can be conceived and has almost
certainly happened from time to time. Could we then suppose,
more plausibly, that the story somehow grew up or shaped itself
in the consciousness of the first witnesses or the alleged 'experience of the early Church'? But how could any of that have
happened, without something to induce or stimulate it? What
produced their conviction? 'Divine inspiration', it may be
replied. But is not this even more incredible? No doubt some
remarkable things have sometimes been composed seemingly
out of nothing, and have been ascribed to direct divine intervention. The *Book of Mormon* is a good example. This book has some
remarkable features, its vastness and the swing and flow and
occasionally very genuine eloquence of its style, for example. It
was presumably produced within a short time, a matter of
months, either by John Smith himself or a very small group of
collaborators, making the claim, as we all know, which few
accept, that it was a copy of Golden Tablets from Heaven, since
withdrawn. There is certainly some mystery about this book,
even allowing for the very close familiarity with Biblical narrative
and language on which it is based. If one man poured it all out in
a short time it was an astonishing feat, for in point of literary
style it is certainly not rubbish. But what this book contains after

all is extensive imitation of the narrative parts of the Old Testament, often in the crudest and, out of context, cruellest parts, with much actual reproduction from the Old and the New Testament, in great measure, in a shapeless jumble and without any reference at all to established history before or after. Whatever mystery attaches to this composition, it is hardly possible for us, with any intelligence, to ascribe it to direct divine inspiration, least of all with the New Testament as a model for us of what is usually ascribed to divine inspiration. But what then of the New Testament itself? Is the notion of direct inspiration plausible here, and in a form which by-passes all historical evidence? I can only say that, if someone can believe that God gave the words of Scripture to particular persons – and nothing besides – he can believe anything. Indeed, we must ask: 'Would it be consistent with the character of God to deceive us in that way and miraculously induce a small number of people, but countless others through them, to believe something which never happened at all?' 'Quite so', it may be answered, 'but that is not properly what is being claimed here'. What then?

The most plausible suggestion here seems to be that the 'experience of the early Church' was formed by embroidering and imaginatively expanding some hard core of genuine fact or history that was available. But how much fact was required for this purpose and how precisely is 'divine inspiration' supposed to operate? If the substance of the narrative itself is only the result of subsequent inspiration and reflects nothing that men had reason to believe had in fact occurred, then we are back with the earlier situation and God again becomes a deceiver inducing men to believe something that had no foundation in fact. In short, is there any point at all in talking about the 'experience of the early Church' without a secure historical foundation for what is testified? To claim otherwise would certainly be a radical departure from the substance of traditional Christian faith and would in the eventual result give us a very attenuated and wellnigh secular form of Christianity.

But, someone may add, with more scepticism and also, I would claim, more integrity; it is not with divine inspiration at all that we have to deal here but simply that all that came to be affirmed took shape and ripened naturally in the consciousness of the first 'disciples' on the basis of some things at least which they remembered. This seems to be the real challenge, and we have to bear well in mind that to concede it and fail to meet it would involve the surrender of the essentials of a Christian attitude. Perhaps we have to make this surrender, for we certainly cannot today affirm and commend our faith, out of grim determination to cling to it come what may, on the basis of assumptions we can no longer accept on their merits. That would only be another lapse into dogmatic fundamentalism, and the time for that is long past; it is idle to try to induce people to believe contrary to reason, for the cause of true religion can never be served by religious brain-washing of any kind, and intelligent youngsters will not thank us for trying. There must be essential integrity in all worthwhile conviction.

The real answer to the more modest and rational scepticism I have just been noting has to be found, as I have already intimated, in the essentials of the narrative itself. Can we reflectively read this story and continue to suppose that it may be only inspired legend? That is the final test. Admittedly we have to make allowance for many of the forms of thought and assumptions peculiar to a very different age. How do we determine the dispensable contemporary ingredients, where does illuminating legend and provisionally conditioned expectation end? I shall make no attempt here to answer that question closely, except to note how Jesus himself has given us the essential clue. It is not the signs and wonders that matter most of all, however we view them, but rather the more essential features of the personality that is disclosed. Can we ascribe these to credulity and legend? Fable and legend are curious things, often a mixture of the fine and the trivial and indeed the unworthy, and they are often very crudely of this world. The style and character of legend is not what we find in the essentials of the 'testimony' with which we are now concerned, they are too amazingly apt in their variety and fullness for that, in detail and as a whole; and we could hardly expect anything so inherently fitting and coherent to take shape in the attitudes and responses of a large company of people, however fine and committed – and that was certainly not true of all members of the earliest Christian bodies, as the Epistle to the Corinthians makes very plain. To suppose that the most distinctive features of the story just grew up in the form that we have it in some collective experience with no important items of actual history behind it is much more incredible than the less-sophisticated supposition that there had actually been at the time such a person as is presented. In short it is very hard indeed, in the light of what the story itself is like, to understand how any-one can believe that the New Testament, and not just the Gospels, could have come into existence at all without there also having been a little while earlier the kind of person around whom the account revolves from start to finish. Disbelief is sometimes harder to explain than belief. The credulity of scepticism is sometimes the most incredible.

Very well then, suppose it is agreed that a historical person is reflected in the New Testament along the lines indicated earlier, what in addition can we say of him? At this point we have, I submit, to be very cautious and perhaps find ourselves in the position of seeming to prevaricate or be evasive ourselves in turn. It is certainly not a case, at this point, of drawing further con-clusions formally from the peculiarities of the figure that appears in the portrait. On the contrary we have to stay, to 'wait' in the term recently familiar here, in alert contemplation in the world of the evidence, to live with the testimony in the sense of conform-ing with the way and requirements of it as far as our initial convictions allow; and we should do this, not in the expectation that we can will to believe or bemuse ourselves into accepting what we would like to accept, much less to drift easily into the consolations and comfort of traditional belief and practice – that would be most out of accord with the spirit of the Gospels themselves – but to discern truly what is shaping itself in the variety and richness of the testimony; this was after all the appeal of the first disciples: 'come' and see.

What I see is the portrait of a person whom we just cannot contain entirely within the framework of a finite understanding. He is in one way wholly of this world and yet not of it. He extends beyond the limits of all we expect. Martin Buber, himself not a Christian, declared that he found it impossible to place Jesus in any special category. But to appreciate this, to cultivate the kind of contemplation that yields the proper insight here, we have also to be attuned to what had already been disclosed about God and his enactments in the world and history. Jesus did not appear in a cultural and religious void, and I find myself constantly remind-ing my own students of the wise observation of the late Austin

Farrer: 'Men knew that God was God before they knew that he would send his only begotten son into the world'. Indeed, they knew a great deal more, for God had already spoken 'at sundry times and places', there had already been divine disclosure in experience and history. The mode of this, and the reasons we have for acknowledging it and discriminating between the genuine and the apparent, is a vast subject in itself; and I have tried, in my book *Our Experience of God*, to indicate what the main considerations should be in estimating the soundness of the claims made for allegedly divine disclosures. I shall not repeat here what I have said at more length elsewhere,[5] I can only insist now that, to appreciate the full significance of Christian witness we have to heed carefully the way in which God had already become a living presence in the world of men and his dealing in a particular way with a 'chosen people', not mainly in the externalities of their life and history, but in the hearts and understanding of men, notably in the high peaks of prophecy, and the effect of this on their stance and attitudes in the good and ill turns of their fortunes. Christ, we are firmly told, came 'in the fullness of time', with the impression that what had been astir in the life of this remarkable people was now getting close to some exceptional denoument – for them and for all. No one saw clearly the form this would take, though some came very close. But with the coming of Jesus, and in knowing him moving amongst them, they found him, as we may do also, filling the pattern of divine disclosure so completely that we can no longer regard him, like the prophets and others before him, as one further stage in a process of disclosure to men and their under-standing of the special ways of God and of the love which is of his very essence, but rather as one in whom the complete pattern concentrates itself, the image of the invisible God becoming so markedly clear now, filling this strange personality with all that pertains so distinctively to himself, the image of all we come to recognise as most essential to infinity itself, that we can no longer say anything convincingly about him except as was said by the first doubter to be overcome in the presence – 'My Lord and my God'.

But Thomas said this when the Resurrection had also happened. Have I overlooked that victory and its significance? By no means, but it has also to be viewed in relation to the story in its entirety. It is not just any 'appearance' that will do, not any Empty Tomb, indeed, not an empty tomb as such at all, but the unmistakable presence, however that came to be, of the man they had already come to know in the cities and by the lake. Otherwise there would be no more than being stunned by some amazing supernatural occurrence; and although the circumstances of this strange appearance, and its like, and the profound experience of the Pentecost, were indispensable for the first disciples to convert their dismay and disappointment into a triumphant vision, this could only happen as an appreciation of what had already occurred in their midst, of what they had already found, somewhat more dimly, in the person of Jesus. It was not just in the Upper Room that Thomas found in him his 'Lord and God', and he would not have addressed him so without having been in his presence already.

It is what we 'see', as it emerges from the fullness of the testimony that matters, and that does not come lightly to anyone. The saints have made that very plain, it is only by persistent effort that the vision is attained, obstacles and hindrances have to be cast aside, there is a discipline of looking and maintaining spiritual concentration, but this has little to do in essentials with physical postures or psychological exercises as such, though no doubt holy people may have stumbled on aids of this kind, including restraint or suppression of grossly materialistic concerns which hinder spiritual awareness and sensitivity. What matters, and it is a supremely difficult business in itself, is that we should live our rounded lives, pursuing our necessary and legitimate aims, in the spirit of the testimony and with our thoughts often centred expressly upon it in enlivened imagination, looking and waiting for the essential features of the story to renew themselves for us in their full and proper significance. This is what we should mean by prayerful seeking and commitment. It has many pitfalls and many easy sentimental substitutes. The yoke, in one sense, is easy, but for a proper Christian insight we need to be wholly committed people, as very few seem to be today. In an increasingly sophisticated age such commitment must also be alert and critical of itself, but it is not beyond our reach.

The vision that men have had in the past is also available to us today, provided we can break through the habits of merely formal and superficial worship and bring a rounded intelligent

Christian commitment into the service of 'spiritual discernment', the discernment that begins and ends with the evidence and has no place for pseudo-spiritual esoteric religious pastimes. The time for trivial religious indulgences is past, and the state of the world is too serious for religious exercises that are not both consistent with our intellectual advances and demanding at the same time. Subject to that warning the vision, enriched by the experience of Christian people down the ages, is as fully in our reach as for men in times past.

In essentials, it is the vision that was crystallised formally for us many centuries ago at Chalcedon, however we may need to vary some of its modes of expression. What we also find ourselves saying, in the final analysis, is 'Very God, Very Man'. I commend this, not out of regard for tradition as such, but because that is how the matter seems to me. We must respect tradition without being tied to it. I have myself been highly critical of a great deal of traditional theology. But on the present central issue I find myself, in thought as in meditation and prayer, never very far from the centre of the path that leads from the traditions that culminated in the 'Apostle's Creed' through Nicea to Chalcedon.

But how, it may well be asked, is it possible for anyone to be 'Very God' and also 'Very Man'? To this there is only one answer we can give – 'We do not know'. And with that I may appear myself to be the most slippery of customers. Having made the boldest affirmation possible, I am, it may appear, not willing to defend it but just slip away slyly from the field. That, however, is not wholly so. There are certain things, in the world of thought, which, as I have maintained at more length elsewhere, we have to recognise without being able to explain them further, our awareness of our own identity for example. We have to hold on to this principle without becoming, or seeming to become, dogmatic and unwilling to discuss and argue, and with a good understanding of just where argument is proper. How much more in dealing with the mystery which is inevitable at some point in matters of faith? In the present concern, we just seem forced to recognise something of which it is not possible to give a further account. It must have been possible somehow for God, while remaining God (as was inevitable for God to be God), to subject himself also to the limits and consciousness of a finite being, we must take this to be somehow possible, for that is just how we read the evidence. We know that it must have been that way, although we do not know how. We may perhaps find some shadow of what must have happened in the strange limitations that occur at times in our own consciousness, in dreams for example, or in childhood or senility and forgetfulness. But these are dim shadows, and the mystery remains. It is a truth to be believed without being comprehended, but the belief does not become shaky for that reason or less firm and explicit. It is as highly rational beings that we come to recognise what is beyond our understanding – 'beyond', it should be stressed, not contrary to or irrational.

One of the most regrettable features of religious thought and theology has been that men, understandably indeed, have persisted in trying to provide explanations at precisely those points where explanation ends. How was Christ related to God in eternity, had they distinct centres of consciousness or how, in other ways, are the two natures related? Did Christ simply appear to be man without being so in fact, did he become God by some kind of adoption? This is how the heresies begin, and although they were anathema to many and the occasion of bitter conflict and hate, we can well understand their attraction. What we have to bear in mind, as wise men have often stressed, is that we are in the present matters always moving very close to the edge of the precipice. We certainly do not ascribe two selves, two persons to Christ. He is one being, and we certainly must not waver on that. Indeed, I have stressed very much elsewhere that persons are essentially distinct and that we cannot merge or fuse two persons in one, as a drop of water becomes part of the sea. The point to which we must cling is that we have no need to be cast down or finally perturbed, or suppose that we bring our reason into contempt, when the substance of the appropriate evidence compels us to recognise something which goes entirely beyond our comprehension. 'Great is the mystery of godliness' and great also is the mystery of the unending wonder of what is disclosed to us in Scriptures and the experience of the saints.

But having got thus far the rest follows. What was the purpose of this special intervention? We have again to remember that we are moving along a very narrow path at the edge of the precipice. Traditional theologians have been most regrettably bold at this point. The Gospel is essentially Reconciliation, between God and man and between men and one another in the bond of their fellowship with God, and this came about by God himself becoming one of us. He did so because our inclination to put ourselves first, to make ourselves the main, sometimes the exclusive, centre of interest gets the better of us so often, though we are free to do otherwise. This has happened so extensively in the past and in the community by which we are much conditioned, that each one is forced back upon his own resources, which are soon exhausted. We are left in the inner loneliness of one's own spirit, however full and sociable our existence may be on the surface. Our sensitivity to the true reality of 'the other' is enfeebled, and we are confined to that small inner world of our own in which we cannot properly nourish and sustain ourselves. This is that 'sombre solitude' of which even an agnostic of such varied and exhilarating interests as Bertrand Russell is found complaining. 'The way of the ungodly shall perish' and, as I once vividly heard it presented by a notable Welsh divine, it comes to perish by being abandoned; and it is we ourselves, comporting ourselves in ways that do not accord with the divine presence and proper fellowship, that bring this appalling fate upon ourselves. It is this death that is the 'penalty of sin', and the only way in which we can be finally restored and brought again to the unsearchable riches of the wholeness of our fellowship with God – and, thereby, with one another – is for God to disclose himself to us as one whose love is such that he is himself with us in this appalling wretchedness. He does not just feel for us in the remoteness of his infinitude, but sups with us on the bread of our sorrows; and thus we have him, in Jesus Christ, despised and mocked and made visibly an object of revulsion in death and rejection, coming to the limit of our own need and darkness till the darkness is lightened and the wound healed in the marvel of this humbling and the unsparing totality of the commitment. As the Lord Jesus himself – and how else can we now think of him? – dispensed with all external aids at need, yielding nothing to the establishment and not depending on it or even on the affection of those closest to him, so also in him God dispenses with the supports of his own infinitude, except in so far as that itself is unlimited love, and taking on him the form of a servant, being himself 'abandoned' in the agony and total dissolution of death, 'obedient unto death, yea, the death of the Cross'.

Jesus did not pretend to die, lapsing into unconsciousness and awakening in a few 'hours. Whatever death is for us, and it certainly has a finality all its own, and whatever we make of the mystery of the Third Day, Jesus died as we also die. Our vain presumption must not obscure that. And whatever else the victory over death may involve, it is one with the victory of the obedience.

The tragic thing is that, instead of holding to our deepest awareness of these astounding things (and sustaining that in all that we do) we persist in seeking to theorise on the mode and meaning of this redemption in a very earthly way and with very little appreciation of its mystery. That is how there came to be the most distressing heresies and the ones furthest removed from the spirit of Christ and the light of the Gospel. In particular, profound truths have been lifted out of their context in the fullness of the testimony, and analogies or figurative terms have been taken, again out of context, in a very literal mechanical way as the main and most final test for faith and doctrine. The symbol has become oppressive and a snare instead of a help, and in this way we have come to fashion and commend strange and needlessly offensive doctrines – about the total and unavoidable corruption of our nature, about the sinfulness of our under-standing and our gifts, about the most tender and self-sacrificing acts of human beings being only the filthy rags of their self-seeking and their pride, and about the way all this, including the sincerity of the honest doubter or his unorthodoxy, calls for retributive punishment in the form of eternal torment, were it not that Christ came to save at least the elect by bearing the punishment in a vicarious or substitutionary way for us and in this way, victim of the wrath of God himself, 'paid the debt'. Have there not been furious debates about the mode of this 'payment', payment to God or to the devil?

I readily agree with the distinguished philosopher and historian of thought, Professor F. C. Copleston when he observed that there can be few things less compatible with the spirit of Christ and his Gospel than the idea of eternal punishment. This is hardly the place to discuss this and like topics closely. But I would much like to urge that we approach the basic affirmations of our faith, and all questions of doctrine, in the light of what happens to us in our own most intimate and personal relationships. The Christian religion is a theistic one, and this means that we think essentially of God as a person, notwithstanding his transcendence, and of his dealings with us as personal ones. We should therefore consider what happens in our dealings with one another, how good personal relations are maintained, and what destroys them, how do things go wrong in our relations with one another and how even love and endearment can convert themselves into estrangement and hate, and above all the mode and conditions of restoration and the price that must be paid by someone somewhere to ensure genuine reconciliation. What does forgiveness mean for us, and what is the cost of it for him who gives it and for him who receives?

These considerations are no doubt but pale shadows of profounder spiritual things. Talk of God can never be wholly secularised, and we must not ignore the mystery. But the hints I have noted will serve us much better than dwelling on the images of the court, the judgement seat and the condemnation. Admittedly, the marvellous truth of the Gospel itself may shine resplendently sometimes through these comparisons, and there are of course very sombre aspects of the way the Son of Man came to seek and to save that which was lost. It is not for nothing that there is a strong apocalyptic element in the Gospels and the reference to the fear that came on all. The shadows deepen, if they fail to recede, in the Presence. It is not a little thing to become aware of 'so great a love' and stand in the presence of its holiness. The Cross is a place of dread as well as release. All the same, a great deal of the work of evangelism and mission and the powerful preaching of the past has lost much of its virtue and its efficacy for lasting good by dawdling too much, sometimes in the luxury of an easy emotionalism, on the very mechanical dramatisation of what is to be distilled out of the symbolism of 'the Great Assize' and its like. Jesus Christ is the judge of all as he is the saviour of all. But in all this also we have to remember carefully that we are again moving very near the edge of the precipice.

I shall make no attempt to pursue these matters further here, this address being a good deal longer than was intended. But I would like, in closing, to present the substance of what I have been maintaining in terms of a somewhat personal analogy.

I remember one occasion when I was with my father on one of his pastoral visits to a home in our village. My father, if I may say this myself without impropriety, was a very gifted man. He won open scholarships to both Oxford and Cambridge and, choosing the former, distinguished himself there in mathematics before, as one of his friends put it, he lapsed into the Ministry of the Presbyterian Church of Wales. He spent forty years in the village near Caernarvon where my brother and I were brought up. He gave himself fully to all aspects of the life of his community; and did so in a quiet unassuming way. He was many things besides the local minister, as was customary then, and was much loved and respected. He was a very serene and genial person, not easily ruffled – unlike his son some might say – and people still talk of the warmth and the kindliness of his smile. I do not know how I came to be with him. Ministers know well enough that it is not the place of their children to be with them on their pastoral visits, except by some special invitation. We preferred to be at our own work or play, mostly play. But for some reason I happened to be with my father that day.

He had certainly no idea what was awaiting him. There was a woman in the house in very great distress. I am not certain what had caused this, the loss of a child or a husband I believe, and it could be that my father had failed in some way. The picture I have is of this unhappy woman, in extreme agitation, with both her fists drumming at his chest – 'Why me, why me'? And that is a question which most of us have asked, inwardly if not overtly, at one time or another. My father remained calm, he, the gentle, if anything rather soft person, firm and unshaken that day, like a stout oak tree, and that wisp of a remarkable smile just wrinkling the edge of his lip. The woman became quiet, and I like to think that she received the blessing and comfort of the sacred ministry in which some of us still believe; and we left the house to climb the hill and take the turn for our home, when I chanced to look up and saw his face – tears! It was news to me that grown-ups cried. I said nothing, but, in my little boy's way, I began to see very deeply that day into some of the profoundest and most precious things in life: 'the chastisement of her peace' was upon him.

It is in this way, if I may compare small and ordinary things with sacred, that I see Jesus, moving from the intimacy of the home in Bethany, and a solemn ritual supper with his closest friends, straight to the tempest of betrayal – what is worse than betrayal – the hostile questioning, the beatings and being hustled bound from one court to the other at dead of night. It is well for some of our younger friends to remember that Jesus also stood trial, with neither minister nor friend to witness or speak for him, and no question of press or other publicity, just a verdict on the spot for immediate execution, the sorry little procession and the thrust to his place between the thieves. And when I see him in this way and call to mind who he was in the light of the total evidence, I have no difficulty, at least not an intellectual one though there are plenty of other things, in speaking, not just in the solemnity of public worship and the company of the faithful but in any company, however sophisticated – the difficulty is not to speak – of the price that was paid and the costly sacrifice.

NOTES

1. Op. cit., p. 127.
2. Op. cit., p. 137.
3. Professor Davies' treatment of the topic in Chapter 5 of the short work cited can be warmly commended to the layman.
4. In *Our Experience of God*.
5. *Our Experience of God*, Chapter V-VIII.

Index of Names

Aaron, R. I., 6–10, 21, 26
Aquinas, St Thomas, 57–8, 100
Arendt, H., 142
Aristotle, 5, 73
Armstrong, D. M., 129–30
Aurobindo, Sri, 81
Ayer, A. J., 2, 137

Baillie, J., 5, 153
Barnes, J., 77
Berkeley, G., 21–3
Bonhoeffer, D., 163–4
Boyd, R., 129
Bradley, F. H., 1–2
Broad, C. D., 13, 39, 82, 90, 93, 151
Buber, M., 27, 172, 178
Bunyan, J., 173
Butler, J., 105–6

Campbell, C. A., 2, 158
Cook Wilson, J., 4–6, 13, 21–2, 26–7
Copleston, F. C., 184
Coward, N., 101

David, St, 163
Davies, W. D., 162, 187
Dawood, N. J., 98
Descartes, R., 14, 76, 89, 96–7, 103–4,
    113, 138–9

Elijah, 167
Epicurus, 102
Ettinger, R. C. W., 129
Ewing, A. C., 2, 14, 158

Farquharson, A. S. L., 4
Farrer, A., 157, 178–9

Fawkes, G., 84
Findlay, J. N., 134
Flew, A., 31–2, 94–109
Francis, St, 163
Franklin, B., 98–100

George IV, 61
Gibson, J., 161

Hegel, G. W. F., 1
Hesperus, 125
Hick, J., 158
Hitler, A., 164
Hobhouse, L. T., 142
Hume, D., 11, 107

John the Baptist. 167
Johnson, W. E., 113
Joseph, 166

Kant, E., 7–9, 111, 152
Kripke, P., 125–130

Leibnitz, G., 63
Lewis, D., 130
Lewis, H. D., 49–55, 57–74, 94,
    97–107, 109
Locke, J., 7, 105, 161
Lucretius, 102
Luke, St, 173

Malcolm, N., 20–1
Mars, 127
Martin, C. B., 97
Mary, 166
Mascall, E. L., 78, 80, 101
Mill, J. S., 20

Muhammad, 162
Moore, G. E., 3–4, 6, 16, 22, 25–6
Moses, 167
Munitz, M., 130

Parmenides, 156
Passmore, J., 139
Paul, St, 154, 162
Penelhum, T., 108
Phosphorus, 125
Pickard, Cambridge, 25
Plato, 7–8, 13–15, 18, 33, 70, 89, 96, 102–4, 108, 133–4, 138, 153–6
Price, H. H., 38–9, 82, 86, 90, 92, 151
Pritchard, H. A., 4, 13

Quinton, A. M., 49, 55–9, 61–74, 96, 104–5

Rorty, A., 129
Rose, W. D., 4, 13, 24–6
Rosenthal, D. M., 130
Russell, B., 26, 94, 153, 183
Ryle, G., 56, 59, 76, 107, 139, 144

Shakespeare, W., 174
Shoemaker, S., 31, 86, 110–31, 133–45
Smith, J., 175
Socrates, 108, 156
Spinoza, B., 15, 54, 70, 89
Stout, G. F., 11
Strawson, P. F., 26, 31, 76–7, 95, 100, 137, 142

Teilhard de Chardin, 35
Temple, W., 76
Tennant, F. R., 89
Thomas, St, 179–80
Toulmin, 24

Venus, 127

Ward, J., 89
Watson, J. B., 50
Williams, B., 49, 56–70, 72–4, 137
Williams, H., 161
Wittgenstein, L., 14, 20, 64, 107, 138

Index of Subjects

Abstract entities, 121
Abstract forms, 157
Abstract systems, 142
Accidents, 109
Accountability, *see* Moral accounta-
    bility
Adoptionism, *see* Christian heresy
Allah, 98
Alternative logic, *see* Logic
Ancestor worship, *see* Worship
Anthropology, 106
Anti-dualist, *see* Dualist
Antinomianism, 168
Apocalyptic Gospels, *see* Gospels
A priori, *see* Knowledge
Art, 45, 48, 156–7, *see also* Christ as
    artist
Association of ideas, 2
Astral body, *see* Body
Astronomy, 39
Atheism, 95
Atheist, 153
Attributes, 68
    infinite, 15, 89, 141
Authority, 174
Avatar, 156

Behaviour, 36, 121, 123, 125–30, 144
'Behavioural output', 112–13, 116, 136
Behaviourism, 56, 57
Behaviourist(s), 50, 137
Belief, 5, 8, *see also* Christian belief,
    Belief in Life After Death
    contrary to reason, 177
    real/notional, 75
Berkleyan – view of external world,
    see World

Bethany, 186
'Beyond', 45, 157, 172, 182
Bhagavad Gita, *see* Gita
Bible, 79, 156, *see also* Christian
    scripture
Bible – as history, 164
Biblical scholarship, 79, 156
Body/bodies, *passim*, 10–11, 37, 41, 49,
    52–3, 56–63, 66–7, 70, 75–109,
    110–13, 117, 131–4, 137, 139,
    143, 154, 159
    astral, 36–7, 52, 80–4, 95–7, 101–9,
    132
    biophysical components of, 80
    dream, 52–3, 60, 81, 102
    image, 10, 81–2, 86–8, 102
    scriptural, 79
    subtle (or aura), 81
Bodily characteristics, 101
    continuity, 27, 36, 68, 83, 105,
    131
    duplication, 67, 99
    identity, *see* Identity
    out-of-the-body experience, *see*
    Experience
    recomposition/reconstitution, 78,
    80, 99–100, 132
    resurrection, 51, 58, 76, 78, 99–101,
    110, 150, *see also* Christ
    Resurrection
    transformation, 80, 101, 110, *see*
    also Transfiguration
Brain, 55–6, 59, 68, 105, 110, 113,
    117, 120–4, 130, 136
    specialists, 83
    states and processes, 59, 113, 122–4,
    143, *see also* Mental processes

Buddhism, 84
  Mahayana, 148
  Theravada, 148

Cartesian, 31, 104, 137, 144
  Dualism, *see* Dualism, *see also*
    Platonic Cartesian
Causation, 11, 12, 41, 122, 136, 139,
    143, 145
Causation at a distance, 41
Central state theory of materialism,
  see materialism
Certainty – primal, 10, *see also* Primal
    and absolute knowledge
  subjective, 9, 10
'C-Fibres' (Fictitious neurophysi-
    ology), 122, 125
Chosen people, 179
Christ – Jesus, person of, 161–87
  as artist, 165
  his commitment, 172–4, 183
  his disciples, 169, 173, 176, 178, 180
  his ethics, 168
  his historicity, 163–6, 178
  his impact, 166–9
  his obedience, 172, 184
  his relation to God, 182
  his resurrection, 78, 101, 132, 179,
    184
  his sacrifice, 187
  his virgin birth, 166
  the way, 171
Christian(s), *passim*, esp. 5, 39, 50, 84,
    100, 150, 158–60, 162, 165,
    178, 181
Christian, attitude to death, 76–7, 91,
    93, 97, 132, 159
  belief and faith, 5, 7, 9, 151–2, 156,
    159–60, 163–4, 169–72, 176–7,
    179, 181–2, 184
  commitment, 152, 159, 175, 180–1,
  creeds, 181
  Evangelism, 185
  Early Church, 161, 175–6
  heresy, 182, 184
  its authenticity and historicity,
    161–3, 174–8
  saints, 180, 183
  scripture, 79, 161–3, 166–70, 173–8,
    182–5, *see also* Old and New
    Testament Gospels
Clairvoyance, 41–2, 90, 151
'*Cogito*' (*ergo sum*), 138

Common Sense – philosophy of, 2–4,
    6, 12, 22, 27
Communication, 53–4, 70–1, 86–8, 138
  with the dead, 37–8, 41, 87, 90–2,
    97, 121, 150–1
Communion – Holy, 158
'Conceptual Connection Thesis', 130
Conditioned Reality, *see* Reality
Consciousness, 6, 9, 11, 36, 48, 85–6,
    105–6, 118, 176, 181–2
  modes of, 114
  unindividuated, 137
Conscious being, 62, 65, 127
Consequentialists, 26
Contemplation, 154, 178
Continuant (in relation to substance),
    113, 115, 120, 136
Contradiction – law of, 9
Corporealism, 36–7, 55
Corporealist, 83, *see also* Persons –
    corporealist view of
Cross, the, 166, 172, 183, 185
Culture(s), 158, 162, 165–6, 170

Damnation, 97, 184
Dementia, 63
'Democratic – The . . . Man', 153
Demonology, 46
Dialectic, 13
Discipline, 180
Disembodied, *see* Existence
Dispositions, 50, 56, 58–60, 62, 66,
    154
Dispositional properties, 115
Distinctness of persons: *see* Persons
Dogma, 144, 177
Dogmatism, 19–20, 138, 152, 160, 181
Dream(s), 9–10, 21, 24, 41, 52–3,
    58–60, 68–71, 182
  image, *see* Images
  body, *see* Body
Dualism, 10, 32, 110–47, *see also*
    Mind/body problem
  Cartesian, 112–31, 136–40, 147
  Minimal, 112–29, 136
  Non-Cartesian, 113–31, 133, 136,
    139–40
Dualist(s), 89, 138–9
  Anti-dualist, 110–11, 129, 131
Duty, 25, 170–71

Ecstatic states, *see* Experience
Ego, 32

Emotions, 62–4, 73, *see also* Feeling
Emotionalism, 185
Empiricism, 7, 20, *see also* Materialism
Empiricist, 7, 16
Esoteric religion, *see* Religion
Essenes, 156
Eternal, 108, 157
Eternity, 110, 182
Ethical principles, 5
  theory, 5
Ethics, 12–16, 24–6
  Christ's, *see* Christ
  meta–ethics, 12
Euthanasia, 63
Evangelists, 167, *see also* Christian
  evangelism
Evil, 2, 89, 133, 156–8, 171
  agencies, 46
Evolution/evolutionary, 17, 35, 127, 144
Existence, *passim*, 9–10, 13, 17, 41,
  43–5, 51–2, 68, 70, 79, 84, 88,
  106, 110, 121, 131–7, 141–3,
  146, 148, 151, 156, 172, 183
  disembodied, 54, 56, 69, 77, 88–9,
  95, 108, 110–12, 124, 126,
  130–1, *see also* Life after Death
  future, *see* Life after Death
  of God, *see* God
  modes of, 89, 132
  necessary, 134
  pre, 85–6, 95, *see also* Reincarnation
  universal, 147
Experience(s), *passim*, 7, 9–16, 21, 31,
  36–7, 43–4, 46–7, 53, 64, 73,
  86, 104–5, 107, 111, 138–9,
  144, 156, 159, 166, 179
  continuity of, 84
  dream, 53
  ecstatic, 42–3, 47
  of the future, 59
  out of body, 41, 121
  of pain, 50, 53, 122, 124, 143–6

Faith, 100, 152, 158–60, 164, *see also*
  Christian belief/faith
  renewal of, 154, 159
Feeling, 11, 26, 64
Forgiveness, 185
Forms/form of the good, *see* Platonic
  forms
Freedom, 2, 3, 24
Free will, 24
Fundamentalism, 177

Genetics, 94
Gita (Bhagavad), 170
God, *see also* Christ Jesus, 5–6, 17, 21,
  33, 39, 45, 48, 51, 70, 73, 77–8,
  80, 91, 95, 97, 99, 101, 103,
  109, 132, 134–5, 147, 157–60,
  163–4, 166, 170–2, 175–6,
  178–83, 185
  his disclosure, 171, 175–6, 179
  'Incognito in Christ', 163–4
  as incorporeal, 95, 109
  infinite, 179, 183
  his love, 157–9, 170, 179, 183,
  185
  necessary existence of, 134
  his omnipotence, 77–8, 80, 99, 103,
  132
  personal, 77, 95, 109, 185
  his presence, 171, 179, 183, 185
  his purpose, 147, 178
  his reconciliation, 182
  transcendence, 185
  his will, 135
Good – the form of, *see* Platonic forms
  utilitarian principle of, 25
  transcendent, 13
Goodness – non-natural quality of, 25
Gospel(s), *see also* Christian scripture,
  Testament (New), 79, 90,
  161–2, 167, 169–70, 174–5,
  178, 182, 184–5
  apocalyptic, 185
  authenticity, 174–5
  synoptic, 162

Heaven, 98, 156, 175
Hegelian idealism, *see* Idealism
Hell, 98
Hinduism, 84
Holy Communion, *see* Communion
Humanists, 40–1, 160
Humpty Dumptyism, 97
Hypostatisation, 3, 142

Iconoclasm, 1, 116, 130
Idealism, 1–2, 22, 35
  Hegelian, 35
  post-Hegelian, 22, 137, 142
Identity – personal or self, *passim*, 2–3,
  6, 10–11, 16, 21, 26–7, 31–3,
  37, 49–74, 75–109, 110–31,
  132–47, 148–60, 181, *see also*
  Persons, Self, Soul

Identity – personal or self–*continued*
  bodily, 11, 26, 51, 75, 80, 89, 95, 100–1
  non-corporeal, 52, 95, 104, 139
  through time, 116, 139
Identity – embodied and disembodied, *see esp.* 49–75, 75–109, 110–47, *see also* Dualism, Life after Death
Identity thesis, 36, 50–1, 75, 77, 130
Idolatry, 45
Images, 53, 163, 185
  body, 10
  dream, 71
  mental, 53
Immaterialism, 22
Immaterial properties, 114
  states, 123–8
Immortality, *see* Life after Death
Induction – principle of, 11
'Inner Eye', 24
Intellect – Platonic, Aristotelian theories of, 96
Intellectual, 68–74, 181
Intentions, 26, 27, 50, *see also* Purpose
Intuition(s), 4, 13–14, 24–6, 45
Intuitionism, 5
Intuitionist, 25–6
Islam, 98

Jesus Christ, *see* Christ
Jews, 167
Justice, 85

Karma, 85
Knowledge, 7–10, 21, 23, 106
  a priori, 14, 31, 85, 111, 116, 118, 121, 124–7, 135–6, 138, 147
  a posteriori, 124–5
  absolute, 8
  certain, 149–50
  of others, 10, 26–7, 53–4, 56–7, 71, 86–7, 138, 144
  primal, 8
  of self, *see* Identity
  theory of, 12, 57
Koran, *see* Qu'ran

Language, 7, 16, 24, 55, 130
  figurative, 47
Laws – of nature, *see* Natural
  physical and non-physical, 87

Life after Death, Immortality, Survival, 10, 35–41, 47, 49–74, 75–109, 110–47, 148–60, 171
Life eternal (everlasting): 110, 150, 160
Linguistic – analysis, 35
  convention, 23
  practice, 24
Logic, 147
  alternative, 3, 9
  Bradley's, 2
  modal, 122
Logical principles, 9

Magic(al), 41, 43, 170
Martyr, 164
Mathematics, 14
Matter, 54, 78
Materialism, 35–6, 50, 55, 57, 59, 91, 111, 119, 121, 124, 128–30, 143
  central state, 55, 59
  theory of, 35, 57
Materialist, 119, 122, 124–6, 129–30, 139, 143, 180
  view of persons, *see* Persons
Meditation, 43, 154, 172, 181
Memory, 54–6, 59–65, 68, 84–7, 91, 94, 105–6, 146
  loss of, 63–4, 146, 182
Mental concepts, causal analysis of, 122, 143
Mental images, *see* Images
Mental states – processes, 37, 49–51, 56–7, 59, 67, 89, 104–5, 112–16, 121–9, 136–7, 141–7
  properties, 58–9, 108, 114, 116, 122–6
Meta-ethics, *see* Ethics
Metaphysics, 2, 10, 12, 14–16
  methodological, 16
  rationalist, 2
  revisionary, 15–16
Mind(s) *passim*, 10, 21, 26, 53–6, 87, 96–7, 104, 116–17, 121–3, 129–30, 137, 139, 145, 147, 152
Mind/body problem, *see also* Dualism, Platonic/Cartesian way, 10, 35, 49–75, 97, 103, 105, 110–33, 139
  causal interaction, 129–30, 139, 145
Mind – universal, 137
Minimal dualism, *see* Dualism
Modal logic, *see* Logic

Monism, 156, *see also* Mysticism
Morality, 151
Moral accountability, 15, 24
  certainty, 8
  distinctions, 15
  obligation, 5
  requirement, 135
  thought, 170
Mormon – The Book of, 175
Muslim, 162, *see also* Muhammad,
  Qu'ran
Mystery, 175, 181–5
  ultimate, 11
Mystic, 157, *see also* Perception,
  mystical
Mysticism, 137
  monistic, 43
Myth, 96, 163
Mythology, 79

'Naturalistic Fallacy', 25
Nature – law of, 55
  order of, 135
  world of, *see* World
Neurophysiology, 121–2, 143
New Testament, *see* Testament
Noesis, 18
Nominalism, 3
Non-Cartesian dualism, *see* Dualism
Non-contradiction – principle of, 17
Non-identical, 112
Non-phenomenonalist, 79
Non-spatial relationships, 115–17

Objectivist, 79
Occasionalism, 129
Old Testament, *see* Testament
Omnipotence of God, *see* God
Ontological argument, 77, 134, 147
Oral transmission, 163
Oriental religion, *see* Religion
'Other', The, 183

Pacifism, 150
Parables, 165
Paradigm case, 24
Paralogisms (of Kant), 111
Paranormal, 41–8, 52, 90–1, 151
  communication, 87–8, *see also* Com-
    munication with the dead,
    Experience-ESP, Perception,
    Precognition, etc.
Parapsychology, 35, 150

Pain, *see* Experience
Pentecost, 180
Perception, *passim, esp.* 2, 6, 12, 15–16,
    22–3, 51, 69, 149
  extra sensory (ESP), 83
  mystical, 157
Person(s), *see also* Identity, Personal or
    self, 6, 26–7, 33, 37, 49–74,
    75–109, 110–29, 136, 140–51,
    157–8
  concept of, 52, 142
  Corporealist/materialist view of,
    50, 75, 83–4, 91, 99, 110–29,
    see also Materialism, etc.
  distinctness of, 2, 90
  essential or real, 101, 103
  'Former persons', 95, 100
  individuation of, 58, 116, 137, 139
  shadow, 101
  simplicity – indivisibility, 118–19,
    127, 133–6, 141
Personal encounter, 156
  relations, 156, 185
Personality, corporate, 142
  split, 146
Perspectival distortion, 21, 24
Perversity, 156
Phenomenalism, 3
Philosophical doubt, *see* Doubt
Physical body, *see* Body
Physical properties and attributes,
    101, 113–14, 126–8
  reality, 3, 105
  states and processes, 52, 59–60, 89,
    104, 112, 123, 125–6, 143, 147
  world, *see* World
Physicalist, 27, 137
Physics, 80
'Platonic – Cartesian Way', 81, 102–3
Platonic – Cartesian Soul, *see* Soul
Platonic forms, 3, 108, 134, 155
  the form of the good, 18, 154, 156
Plurality, 73–4
Poltergeist, 82
Positivist, 3
Post-Hegelian, *see* Idealism
Prayer, 43, 172, 181
Precognition, 41–2
Pre-existence, *see* Existence, *also*
    Reincarnation
Preternatural, 45–6, 92
Process philosophy, 35
Prophets/prophecy, 167, 179

Psychical research, 35–41, 47, 55, 81, 90–3, 97, 109, 151–2, 158
Psychic phenomena, 41, 151
Psychological states, *see* Mental states
Purpose/purposing, 50, 144–6, *see also* Intentions

Qu'ran, 98, 162

Radicalism, 107
Rationalist(s), 14, 138
Rationality, 97, 182
Realism (and realists), 1, 3–4, 21–3, 26–7
  epistemology, 4
Reality, 138, 155
  conditioned, 43
  mental, 141
  non-spatial, 144
  physical, 141
Reason, 8, 14, 21, 177, 182
Reconstitution(ist), 98–9, 100, 103, 107, 109, *see also* Bodily reconstitution
Redemption, 158, 160
Reincarnation, 50, 52, 55–6, 58, 84–5, 91, 146, 148
Relativism, 152
Relativity, 17
Religion, *see also* Buddhism, Christian, Hinduism, Islam, Shinto, 5, 35, 40–50, 72, 77–9, 91–3, 97–8, 148–9, 157–9, 177, 185
  esoteric, 181
  oriental, 33
  primitive, 148
  theistic, 43, 46–7
  transcendalist, 171
  western, 171
Religious belief, *see also* Christian belief, 91–2, 94, 109, 148–9
  symbolism, 92
  understanding, 152, 164
  thought, 79, 182
'Replica Objection' – the, 99–100
Resurrection, *see also* Bodily/Christ's Resurrection, 97, 100, 159
  spiritual, 78
Retribution, *see* Punishment
Revelation, 157, 158, *see also* God's disclosure
  of Allah, 98, 162

'Sacramental universe', 157
Sacrifice, 158, 169, *see also* Christ's sacrifice
Scepticism, 2, 33, 107, 148, 152, 164, 176–8
Schizophrenia, 153
Science, 43, 92, 105, 111, 131, 135
Scripture, *see also* Christian, Gospels, Testaments, Qu'ran, etc., 162–3, 166, 170, 173, 176, 183
Secular/secularisation, 148–9, 152, 176
Self, *see also* Identity, personal or self, 10, 21, 31, 33, 51, 62, 68, 85, 89, 95, 107, 129, 134–7, 145–7
  essential nature of, 147
  as pure self, 89, 104
  simplicity and indivisibility, 134–5, 145–7
  'substantial view of', 85
  as subject, 32, 89, 104, 107–8, 112, 145
Semantics, 130
Sensation(s), 10, 26, 50, 51–3, 66, 89
Sense datum, 7, 24
Sensory deprivation, 71–2
  'input', 112–13, 116, 136
  stimulation, 117
Shinto, 148
Sin, 158, 183–4
Sixth sense, 42
Socialism, 150
Solipsism, 26–7, 88
Soul, 38, 81, 83, 95–6, 100, 102–3, 105, 107–8, 117, 133–4, 136, 150, 155–6, *see also* Identity – personal, *also* Self
  of Epicurus, 102, 108
  indestructibility of, 90, 133–4, 136, 155
  of Lucretius, 102
  Platonic conception of, 95, 133–4, 155–6
  Platonic/Cartesian, 101–3, 107–9
  pre-existence 134
  simplicity of, 134, *see also* Self-simplicity and indivisibility of
Space, 10, 15, 40, 43, 78, 81–2, 87, 102
Spatial, contiguity, 117, 139
  extension, 111, 116–17, 119
  location, 116–17
  quasi-spatial relations, 117–19, 130, 139, 141
  relations, 117–18, 137–9

Spirit, 78, 134, 172, 174, 183
Spiritual, awareness, 171–2, 180
 concentration, 180
 discernment, 154, 181
Spiritualism, 72, 97–8
State – metaphysical theory of, 142
Substance(s), 32, 108, 113–14, 117–19, 139, 141, 143
 corporeal/material, 103–4, 106, 111, 113–20, 122, 124, 126, 129–30, 139, 141, 143
 incorporeal/immaterial, 97, 103–6, 105–9, 111–21, 123–4, 126, 128–30, 139–41, 143
 spiritual, 97, 108, 114–16, 121, 126–8, 130, 144
'Substantival view of self', *see* Self
'Summerland' – the, 98
'Supreme Court' – of US, 118–19, 141–2
Survival, *see* Life after Death

Telekinesis, 41
Telepathy, 53–4, 72, 87, 90, 138, 151
Testament – New, 79, 161–3, 168, 176–8
 dating of, 161–2
 as history, 79, 163, 176–8, *see also* Christian Scripture, Gospels
 Old, 176
Theism, 134, 185, *see also* Religion – theistic
Theologians, 159, 182
Theology, 79, 165, 181–2
Theory of knowledge, *see* Knowledge
Thing in itself, 141
Thought(s), *see also* Mental states and processes, 11, 26–7, 50–1, 54, 71–2, 89, 105, 144–6. 154. 159, 165, 177, 181
 materialist view of, 50
 oriental, 143
 western, 135, 142

'world of thoughts alone', *see* World
Time, 67, 78, 86, 105, 113, 118, 160, 162
Transcendence, 5–6, 11, 43–7, 156–7, 170, *see also* God, Good
Transcendalist religion, *see* Religion
Transfiguration, 78, 163
Truth, 77, 94, 106, 109, 111, 124, 152, 164, 182, 184–5
 'truth of the heart', 153
 'truth of the mind', 153

Ultimate(s), 17, 25, 32–3, 43, 54, 61–2, 66, 68, 78, 146
Universals, 155–6
 theory of, 3
Utilitarian – principle of greatest good, *see* Good
Utilitarianism, 25–6

Values, 142
Verification, 91
'Vision – the glass of', 160

Wisdom, 138, 170, 174
World, 13–14, 45, 55, 67, 83–4, 87–8, 135, 165, 171–2, 177, 181
 Berkleyan view of, 79
 of children, 169
 as created, 157
 dream, 70
 external, 5–6, 9, 11, 21–2, 79
 of images, 53, 70
 of nature, 14, 22, 50, 156, 165
 of particulars, 155
 physical (material), 3, 11, 53, 79, 80, 86
 real, 53
 W-Soul, 70
 'of thoughts alone', 54, 81, 88–9, 138
Worship, 43, 164, 171, 180
 of ancestors, 148